REINVENTING RACISM

REINVENTING RACISM

Why "White Fragility" Is the Wrong Way to Think about Racial Inequality

Jonathan D. Church

ROWMAN & LITTLEFIELD
Lanham • Boulder • New York • London

Published by Rowman & Littlefield
An imprint of The Rowman & Littlefield Publishing Group, Inc.
4501 Forbes Boulevard, Suite 200, Lanham, Maryland 20706
www.rowman.com

6 Tinworth Street, London SE11 5AL, United Kingdom

British Library Cataloguing in Publication Information Available

Library of Congress Cataloging-in-Publication Data

Names: Church, Jonathan D., 1978- author.
Title: Reinventing racism : why "white fragility" is the wrong way to think about racial inequality / Jonathan Church.
Description: Lanham : Rowman & Littlefield, [2020] | Includes bibliographical references . | Summary: "The theory of white fragility is one of the most influential ideas to emerge in recent years on the topics of race, racism, and racial inequality. White fragility is defined as an unwillingness on the part of white people to engage in the difficult conversations necessary to address racial inequality. This 'fragility' allegedly undermines the fight against racial inequality. Despite its wide acclaim and rapid acceptance, the theory of white fragility has received no serious and sustained scrutiny. This book argues that the theory is flawed on numerous fronts. The theory functions as a divisive rhetorical device to shut down debate. It relies on the flawed premise of implicit bias. It posits a faulty way of understanding racism. It has serious methodological problems. It conflates objectivity and neutrality. It exploits narrative at the expense of facts. It distorts many of the ideas upon which the theory relies. This book also offers a more constructive way to think about Whiteness, white privilege, and 'white fragility,' pointing us to a more promising vision for addressing racial inequality"— Provided by publisher.
Identifiers: LCCN 2020035500 (print) | LCCN 2020035501 (ebook) | ISBN 9781475858174 (hardcover) | ISBN 9781475858181 (paperback) | ISBN 9781475858198 (ebook)
Subjects: LCSH: Whites—Attitudes. | Whites—Psychology. | Discrimination. | Racism.
Classification: LCC HT1575 .C58 2020 (print) | LCC HT1575 (ebook) | DDC 305.809—dc23
LC record available at https://lccn.loc.gov/2020035500
LC ebook record available at https://lccn.loc.gov/2020035501

∞ ™ The paper used in this publication meets the minimum requirements of American National Standard for Information Sciences Permanence of Paper for Printed Library Materials, ANSI/NISO Z39.48-1992.

Dedicated to David Randall Church, Linda Carroll Church, and Lincoln Lee Simmons-Church

CONTENTS

ACKNOWLEDGMENTS

I begin with an expression of sincere gratitude to the editors of *Areo*, *Quillette*, *Arc Digital*, *The Agonist Journal*, and *Merion West*. In particular, I thank Claire Lehmann and Jamie Palmer for publishing my first article on white fragility, as well as Christopher DeGroot, Berny Belvedere, and Erich Prince for publishing subsequent articles. I reserve special gratitude to *Areo* editors Helen Pluckrose and Iona Italia, who published several essays that established a systematic critique of the *theory* of white fragility. These articles all laid the foundation for a more extensive, thorough, and comprehensive critique of white fragility theory, which the reader will find in this book.

Peter Boghossian deserves my genuine thanks for his support and encouragement. I also am indebted to James Lindsay and Helen Pluckrose for the insights I gleaned from their sustained critique of "critical social justice" orthodoxy. Wilhelm Cortez deserves credit for giving me the opportunity to publish several articles on social justice at *The Good Men Project* when I began thinking about the controversies in social justice activism that have emerged in the 2010s.

I am grateful to Philadelphia public school teacher Christopher Paslay for his review of the manuscript for this book. I would be exceedingly remiss not to thank Donald Weise for his thorough review of the manuscript, and for his insights over the years on how to be a better writer. Lee Jussim and Gregory Mitchell deserve recognition for their thorough reviews of my chapter on the implicit bias paradigm. I also appreciate review and encouragement from Philip Tetlock and Aaron Kindsvatter. Jeffrey Badger has my thanks for helping to envisage the book's cover design.

Finally, I would like to thank Curtis Bowman, who taught many of the philosophy courses I took as an undergraduate student at the University of Pennsylvania. Dr. Bowman, a popular professor in the Penn philosophy department during the late 1990s and early 2000s, was an engaging teacher who helped me understand many of the ideas that underlie "continental" philosophy and that have become relevant to a critique of white fragility theory as well as controversies surrounding "social justice" scholarship and activism in the first decades of this century.

INTRODUCTION

If you keep up with progressive lexicons on racism, you have probably heard of the term *white fragility*. The brainchild of sociologist and social justice activist Robin DiAngelo, "white fragility" has gained much attention in academic and progressive circles in recent years as a concept that goes a long way in ostensibly explaining why it's supposedly so hard to talk to white people about racism.

According to DiAngelo, white people have been "[s]ocialized" to live with "a deeply internalized sense of superiority and entitlement" but they are not consciously aware of it. As a result, they experience "race-based stress" when faced with a challenge to their "racial worldview" because they perceive it to be an affront to their "identities as good, moral people"—an "unfair moral offense," as well as an attack on their "rightful place in the hierarchy." This makes it hard to talk to white people about how their attitudes and beliefs make them complicit in the perpetuation of "institutional racism."[1]

This "racialized" consciousness has become so entrenched that, as DiAngelo puts it, "even a minimum amount of racial stress becomes intolerable, triggering a range of defensive moves." "These moves include the outward display of emotions such as anger, fear, and guilt, and behaviors such as argumentation, silence, and leaving the stress-inducing situation."[2] As a rule, white people are simply not interested in the interrogation of Whiteness and white privilege. As a result, they are ill-equipped to tackle "systemic" racism. When confronted with challenges to interrogate Whiteness and white privilege, they feel blindsided and become defensive. This "white fragility" gets in the way of the pursuit of racial justice and keeps white supremacy in place.

Robin DiAngelo, a white woman with a PhD in multicultural education, proposed this concept in a 2011 paper in the *International Journal of Critical Pedagogy*.[3] The basic ideas in the paper show up repeatedly in her published work, including two books titled *What Does It Mean to Be White? Developing White Racial Literacy* and *Is Everyone Really Equal? An Introduction to Key Concepts in Social Justice Education.* They were repackaged and summarized in her 2018 bestselling book *White Fragility: Why It's So Hard to Talk to White People about Racism.*[4]

DiAngelo proposed the concept of "white fragility" as "one aspect of Whiteness."[5] But it is really a theory about Whiteness, white privilege, and the perpetuation of racism in America. In this book, I argue that the theory is unhelpful, and even undermines the effort to reduce racial inequality. In chapter 3, we explore the meaning of Whiteness and how it relates, or does not relate, to racism. In the final chapter, we explore a better way to think about Whiteness and white privilege. The remainder of the book explains the conceptual, empirical, and logical flaws in the theory of white fragility.

The theory of "white fragility" has gained much traction. It has also encountered a lot of resistance from white people who unsurprisingly do not like being called racists. DiAngelo wants to convince white people to let down their guard and open up their minds to the possibility that they misunderstand the nature of racism. Racism, she claims, is not so much about conscious beliefs that white people hold about people of color, but about implicit—or unconscious—biases. These biases, she claims, are what contemporary racism is all about. If they are not addressed, racial inequality will persist.[6] Implicit bias is at the root of racism in America.

The controversy generated by "white fragility" is perhaps as it should be. The theory is derived from scholarship in sociology, postmodern and poststructuralist philosophy, critical race theory, and an increasingly influential field called Whiteness studies. Presumably, most people are not up to date on the cutting-edge research of specialized academic niches.

On one level, then, the backlash DiAngelo has received in her career as a diversity trainer is to be expected no matter how sound and well-evidenced her theories are. The theory of white fragility makes strong claims based on a body of scholarship that can run up against long-held preconceptions about the problem of racism and how to counter it. This will naturally produce a degree of cognitive dissonance that makes it hard to be receptive to new ideas and insights, especially about sensitive topics like race and racism.

While a general audience might stubbornly adhere to old beliefs and refuse to consider new ideas, it is not entirely a one-way street. Scholars can also become so enamored of their theories that they dismiss any objections that might point out flaws in their work, especially if the objections come from a general audience rather than specialists in the field. In fact, DiAngelo and her followers have become so convinced they are right that they simply refuse to believe that any reasonable objections can be raised. The theory of white fragility has become a doctrine of faith. If you do not join the crusade, your inaction makes you complicit in the preservation of racism.

For white people, it exposes their "white fragility."

Despite its wide acclaim and rapid embrace, the theory of white fragility has received little scrutiny beyond the knee-jerk animosity of white people who don't like being told that everything they say and do is racist and makes them complicit in the perpetuation of white supremacy and institutional racism. This book fills this void by articulating a comprehensive and rigorous critique.

Why is this needed? One reason is the theory is severely flawed. The other is that the theory has been so widely promoted and accepted despite being so severely flawed. Indeed, according to an article in the *New Yorker*, DiAngelo has become "perhaps the country's most visible expert in anti-bias training."[7]

In February 2019, Beacon Broadside celebrated her book's status as a *New York Times* bestseller for more than six months.[8] A Google search of "DiAngelo white fragility" yields information about workshops,[9] book reviews,[10] book talks,[11] news articles,[12] interviews,[13] public talks,[14] and articles authored by Robin DiAngelo.[15] Luminaries like Michael Eric Dyson and Claudia Rankine laud her work. In the wake of the tragic and horrific killing of George Floyd, her book became a bestseller once again, rocketing to the top of the Amazon and New York Times bestseller lists.[16]

"White fragility" theory also shows up in the classroom. For example, in one law school seminar on race and the law, a professor declared, "We talk about white fragility. . . . What is the purpose of white fragility? What does it mean to live in a white culture, with white norms and a white power structure? What does it mean that we are in a culture dominated by white folks?"[17] In April 2019, the Friends Select School in Philadelphia organized an event at the Race Street Meetinghouse in Philadelphia in which Robin DiAngelo was invited to discuss her book *White Fragility*.[18] Philadelphia public school teacher Christopher Paslay has written a book on the theory's divisive impact in America's classrooms.[19]

The basic tenets are incorporated into diversity trainings. The National Education Association (NEA) passed a directive to adopt the concept of white fragility into NEA trainings/staff development, literature, and other existing communications on social justice.[20] On February 28, 2020, DiAngelo delivered the keynote speech at the annual meeting of the American Association of Colleges for Teacher Education in Atlanta, Georgia.[21] It is no understatement to say that the theory has gained, and will continue to gain, widespread traction.

Unfortunately, this widespread attention is undeserving on the merits. As the rest of this book will argue, the theory of white fragility:

1. Is a Kafka trap.
2. Relies on the dubious premise of implicit bias.
3. Relies on a faulty way of understanding racism.
4. Has serious methodological problems.

5. Exploits narratives at the expense of facts.
6. Distorts the Enlightenment and the Frankfurt School's conception of critical theory.
7. Runs afoul of reason and logic.
8. Replaces scholarship with sermonizing.
9. Is a rhetorical weapon for activist bullies.
10. Imposes a substantial "transaction cost" that impedes the pursuit of racial justice.

In sum, white fragility theory is based on flawed methodology, factual errors, logical fallacies, and conceptual incoherence. In treating the lecture circuit as a political campaign, it survives as an article of faith rather than as a robust intellectual framework for the study of racial inequality.

I

"WHITE FRAGILITY" IS A TRAP

I first came across the notion of "white fragility" when I began gently raising concerns about what I took to be some of the ideological excesses of social justice activism. In 2016, I began writing a weekly column for *The Good Men Project*, a progressive media outlet passionately committed to the cause of social justice activism. In many articles over the ensuing two years, I expressed support for social justice imperatives and initiatives. For example, I wrote about sexist language,[1] the importance of male introspection in the wake of #MeToo,[2] changing tables in men's restrooms,[3] the tragedy at Charlottesville,[4] how *The Adventures of Huckleberry Finn* promotes the cause of Black Lives Matter,[5] and the persistence of discriminatory job advertisements.[6]

However, I also expressed concerns that social justice activism sometimes goes astray. I questioned whether microaggressions really are a thing.[7] I pointed out problems in the concept of white privilege.[8] I discussed ambiguities in the notion of Whiteness.[9] I questioned whether "confirmation bias" affects the judgment of social justice activists—in other words, whether there is an excessive tendency to see power and privilege in every social interaction.[10]

I sent this last article about confirmation bias to someone who is professionally active in social justice circles. The responses: Why are you so uptight? Why do you get defensive about white privilege? Why are you so fragile? I was then directed to the work of Robin DiAngelo on white fragility.

No matter what I said, the response (and mocking tone) was the same: I was being fragile. This came across as a classic Kafka trap, whereby any attempt to defend one's position is viewed as evidence of one's guilt. This was a frustrating bind to find myself in. There was a clear absence of good faith commitment to working out a difference of opinion. I was expected to agree. If I disagreed, I was accused of being fragile. In chapter 9, we will see how this attitude of intolerance shows that the theory of white fragility is a perfect weapon for activists who seek to bully people into joining their crusade.

It simply was not true that my motivation was to protect "white" feelings. If our first allegiance is to the truth, however elusive truth may be, everything should be fair game. Indeed, one should have no problem pointing out that racial inequities prevail in our society. One might highlight the progress we have made, but the data on social and economic outcomes across racial groups are clear. White people, on average, by a number of measures, fare better than many ethnic and racial minorities.[11]

While the racial divide is clear, it is not clear how it works and what is the best way to remedy it. Hence, the policy debates that drive news cycles, motivate social science research, and galvanize the tirades rampant on social media. This is to be expected from a complex issue in a large and diverse society.

What is regrettable is that, even if critics concede that proponents of white fragility theory raise important concerns and make some good points, proponents are so convinced they have it all figured out that they are unwilling to tolerate any skepticism. All objections are dismissed as "white fragility." This is highly unfortunate since there are many reasons to be skeptical. In the next chapter, for example, we examine the premise of implicit bias. We will see that we do not have good reason to believe that implicit bias is a root cause of ongoing racial inequality. In other chapters, we examine a number of conceptual, empirical, and logical flaws in the theory.

TRANSFORMING EDUCATION INTO INDOCTRINATION

DiAngelo wants to disrupt the comfort that white people have allegedly come to expect in their daily lives as people steeped in the privilege of being members of the dominant social group. After years of experience studying race and confronting white people about the nature of racism, DiAngelo has encountered many emotional reactions running diversity-training workshops. For example, she writes, "In this position, I have observed countless enactments of white fragility. One of the most common is outrage: 'How dare you suggest that I could have said or done something racist!'"[12]

We should not simply discard what DiAngelo is trying to say. She has undoubtedly observed common forms of resistance and reaction among the white people she has attempted to educate on racism over the years. We can acknowledge that these patterns of resistance and reaction can also function as a kind of Kafka trap. The resistance white people have apparently exhibited toward her ideas about racism may reveal an inflexibility that treats any suggestion of a "teachable moment" (DiAngelo's term for opportunities to teach white people about racism[13]) as "evidence" of her hostile disposition. In effect, white people can be as close-minded as DiAngelo has become.

The key is to strike a balance between encouraging openness to new ideas and permitting a healthy skepticism. It may be that many white people have exhibited a hostility to DiAngelo's ideas over the years that is unwarranted to the extent it stems from an unwillingness to engage in self-reflection or to grapple with new ideas. But, as this book argues, the same has become true for proponents of white fragility theory.

As DiAngelo emphasizes, implicit bias is the where the fault line erupts.[14] In the next chapter, we will see that the implicit bias paradigm is deeply flawed. Psychologists do not know exactly what it is or how to define it. Implicit bias is not a measure of unconscious prejudice. It has deep psychometric flaws. It does not reliably predict behavior. It does not seem to explain much about racial inequality. One psychology professor described it to me as a "scientific Rorschach test."

For DiAngelo, none of this matters. Although she has moderated her tone according to one report,[15] DiAngelo remains determined to demonstrate to "red-faced" white people that they have been "socialized" to have an implicitly racist worldview. Every objection they raise is evidence of white fragility because it shows that they are unwilling to interrogate their unconscious biases.

In her persistence, DiAngelo slyly turns psychological defense mechanisms, which are common in human nature, into a sleight of hand employed by white people, however unwittingly and innocuously, to maintain white dominance and racial inequality. There is, however, a supreme arrogance in presuming to have unlocked the secrets of what white people think, or do not think, about race.

If arrogance were the end of it, we could be content to ignore the pious divinity of DiAngelo's approach to social justice activism. But there is something more insidious at work. DiAngelo wants to confront white people with their complicity in the perpetuation of racism. She insists that "systemic and institutional control allows those of us who are white in North America to live in a social environment that protects and insulates us from race-based stress." In a bullet point list of examples, DiAngelo's first example of a challenge "that trigger(s) racial stress for white people" is the suggestion "that a white person's viewpoint comes from a racialized frame of reference," which is interpreted as a "challenge to objectivity."[16]

One is right to be skeptical when presented with the suggestion that one's viewpoint comes from a "racialized frame of reference." It is not about believing oneself to be omniscient. It is about objective inquiry. The suggestion that a viewpoint comes from a "racialized frame of reference" is, in fact, an expression of doubt about the ability to engage in impartial inquiry and analysis.

Of course, objectivity demands that we question any claim of objectivity. Indeed, objectivity necessarily requires humility. We will see in chapter 4 why DiAngelo is wrong to insist that objectivity is impossible, but in principle, she is not wrong in imploring white people to be humble about what they think they know. In keeping with objectivity and the scientific method, however, introspection should lead to testable hypotheses about whether one's thoughts stem from a subjective or objective point of view. None of this means that one is neutral, which is not the same as being objective.

The available research does not currently provide incontrovertible support for the implicit bias paradigm. DiAngelo should reevaluate her assumptions about the nature of racism, as well as her claims about the role of white fragility in perpetuating "institutional" racism. She does not, however, appear keen to do so. For anyone who cares about the scientific method, this inflexibility is both unfortunate and indicative of a willingness to subordinate facts and data to ideology.

This kind of thinking also transforms education into indoctrination. When the scientific method is subordinated to political orthodoxy, we cease to learn about the hows and whys of social and economic disparities across racial groups and instead become immersed in a crusade that propagates ideas lacking support from social science research. At this point, it becomes difficult to dismiss concerns that DiAngelo's scholarship is not built upon sound research that can help advance the cause of social justice, but on a political agenda, intolerance of dissent, and an activist drive for conformity.

2

BEHIND THE CURVE ON IMPLICIT BIAS

Racism, in the words of Robin DiAngelo, is not only about "simple, isolated, and extreme acts of prejudice."[1] This "good/bad" binary is misleading. The "dominant paradigm of racism as discrete, individual, intentional, and malicious acts makes it unlikely that whites will acknowledge any of our actions as racism."[2] It "obscures the structural nature of racism and makes it difficult for us to see or understand."[3]

The tendency to believe in the "good/bad binary" manifests when white people insist that they are "color-blind" or that they actively promote diversity.[4] This insistence "rests on a definition of racism as *conscious intolerance*." But this is a superficial definition. As DiAngelo writes, "Someone who claims to have been taught to treat everyone the same is simply telling me that he or she doesn't understand socialization." Why? "We can be told, and often are told, to treat everyone the same, but we cannot successfully be taught to do so because human beings are not objective."[5]

We cannot rely on objectivity because, as DiAngelo writes, "Once we understand the power of implicit bias . . . we know that we must deepen rather than close off further reflection."[6] Indeed, "The good/bad binary," she writes, "is the fundamental misunderstanding driving white defensiveness about being connected to racism. We simply do not understand how socialization and implicit bias work."[7] In other words, white fragility theory relies crucially on the idea that implicit bias is a root cause of "systemic" racism.

Being raised in a particular society and culture undoubtedly exerts a powerful impact on how people think about social, political, and economic issues. But it does not make it impossible to step away from social norms and tradition to think critically and objectively about issues. To believe otherwise is to categorize any objections as manifestations of "white fragility." In other words, "white fragility" becomes a rhetorical device to wipe out any resistance to dogma, or in this case, any attempt to point out that the research on implicit bias is not nearly as conclusive as DiAngelo presumes. In this chapter, we see that a second generation of research has raised serious doubts about the implicit bias paradigm.

THE IMPLICIT BIAS PARADIGM

In 1998, three psychologists published a paper about the Implicit Association Test (IAT), a test designed to measure "individual differences in implicit cognition." The test measured "differential association of 2 target concepts with an attribute" as a way of capturing information about our unconscious biases.[8]

The test was developed by psychologists Anthony Greenwald, Mahzarin Banaji, and Brian Nosek in the mid-1990s. According to the Association for Psychological Science (APS), "the IAT asks participants to categorize words or images that appear onscreen by pressing specific keys on a keyboard. The time it takes for participants to respond to different combinations of stimuli is thought to shed light on the mental associations they make, even when they aren't aware of them." In the ensuing years, "millions of people have used an online test to probe attitudes they didn't know they had."[9]

Test takers, writes journalist Jesse Singal, "may not feel racist, but in fact, the test shows that in a variety of intergroup settings, they will act racist."[10] In the *Chronicle of Higher Education*, Tom Bartlett writes, "[a]bout 70 percent of people who take the race version of the Implicit

Association Test show the same tendency—that is, they prefer faces with typically European-American features over those with African-American features."[11]

The IAT, the APS claims, "has led to the examination of unconscious and automatic thought processes among people in different contexts, including employers, police officers, jurors, and voters." As a result, "the IAT has allowed people to discover potential prejudices that lurk beneath their awareness—and that researchers therefore wouldn't find through participant self-reports."[12]

Psychologists Hart Blanton and James Jaccard note that "dozens of implicit attitude measures [have been] advanced to measure racial biases." The IAT, however, has emerged as "by far the most popular and empirically assessed of the new instruments."[13] The IAT has since given great heft to the idea that "implicit bias" is a root cause of "systemic" racism. After all, Blanton and Jaccard write, "The term implicit attitudes refers to attitudes that cannot be directly perceived and must therefore be measured indirectly."[14] It is not hard to see how implicit attitudes could be writ large in society.

If we cannot perceive our biases, we presumably cannot control how they will affect our actions and decisions. The collective impact can only exacerbate racial inequality, though Blanton and Jaccard warn against conflating "the concept of control with the concept of consciousness."[15] (Alcoholics and gambling addicts are probably quite aware of the actions they cannot adequately control.)

Implicit bias has since become a wildly popular idea, even inspiring *TED Talks* that anyone can view on YouTube by Melanie Funchess, director of community engagement at the Mental Health Association of Rochester, New York, and Dushaw Hockett, founder and executive director of Safe Places for the Advancement of Community and Equity.[16] Unsurprisingly, proponents of white fragility theory have run with the idea, equating implicit bias with unconscious prejudice as a way of advancing the narrative that contemporary society is systemically organized around the subliminal ideologies of white supremacy.

This idea would carry greater weight, however, if there was clear consensus in the psychology profession about what implicit bias is and how it relates to socioeconomic outcomes. Contrary to popular opinion, the implicit bias paradigm has come up against serious skepticism in the psychology profession, especially in recent years. It turns out that the implicit bias paradigm got ahead of the science.

Why does it persist in the wider culture? According to a primer on implicit bias by law professor Gregory Mitchell, whose research includes a focus on psychology and implicit bias, "many popularizations of the implicit bias concept, both in law reviews and mainstream media, rely on statements made during the first generation of implicit bias research, when there was great optimism about the power of measures of implicit bias to identify persons who are more and less likely to engage in acts of discrimination—but little data at that time to support such optimism."

However, he continues, "[t]he second generation of implicit bias research has produced decidedly less optimistic views about the predictive and explanatory power of implicit bias measures. This second generation of research has also complicated our understanding of the nature of implicit bias and how it may relate to explicit bias."[17] Indeed, several studies suggest that a definitive consensus on what implicit bias is, and how it relates to behavioral outcomes, remains somewhat, if not wholly, elusive.[18]

In short, the psychology profession and the culture at large got ahead of itself in promoting the concept of implicit bias. This is perhaps not unexpected given the increasingly serious attention given to the idea that racism is a systemic and persistent plague upon society. Unfortunately, the initial excitement led to a great deal of overconfidence and misinformation about what exactly implicit bias is, what it measures, and what it says about how people will behave.

IT IS NOT CLEAR WHAT IMPLICIT BIAS IS

In one paper, psychologists Hart Blanton and James Jaccard present three definitions of implicit bias that revolve around the idea that there are limits to introspection. Implicit bias could mean:

1. Being unaware of the effects of one's biased actions on other people.
2. Being unaware of the causes of one's biased actions on other people.
3. Being unaware of the presence and content of one's biases.

Blanton and Jaccard discuss why these different ways of defining implicit bias are unsatisfactory, and why there is no consensus about which definition is best.[19] For example, on (1), it is not news to say that "ignorance can lead to unintended consequences." Moreover, research on the nature of unconscious bias inevitably introduces a political dimension whereby researchers end up having to justify why one set of values (e.g., to emphasize equality) is better than another (e.g., those that emphasize individualism). Politics distracts attention from the science.[20]

The most important point from the analysis by Blanton and Jaccard is that "there is little evidence to support the more provocative claim: that people possess unconscious racist attitudes."[21] In his primer on implicit bias, Professor Mitchell explains why we can no longer equate implicit bias with unconscious bias:

1. Recent research reveals that many people can predict how they will respond on implicit bias tests. If so, people are aware of an apparent bias even if they are unaware of where the apparent bias comes from. But "[u]nconscious bias . . . assumes a lack of awareness of the bias itself."
2. People can learn how to fake their patterns of response on implicit bias tests, even without instruction on how to do so.

3. The empirical data currently "do not allow researchers to declare whether implicit bias and explicit bias are truly distinct."[22]

If implicit bias is not unconscious prejudice, then what is it? Mitchell discusses two ways of thinking about it:

1. It may mean that, if we observe that many NBA players are black, we will tend to associate black people with athleticism (the *association* model).
2. It may refer to how we respond to stimuli after being exposed to propositions like "Whites are privileged" or "Blacks have suffered" (the *proposition* model).

On (1), context often matters. Mitchell notes that "when researchers portrayed the faces in the racial attitudes IAT as churchgoers, the usual observed bias toward Blacks was no longer observed and respondents showed no measured bias for Blacks or Whites." Further, "[a] particular response pattern may signify *negative associations* about one group or *sympathetic propositions* about that group."[23]

In a comprehensive review of the literature for a chapter in an upcoming book on implicit bias research, Lee Jussim, Akeela Careem, Zach Goldberg, Nathan Honeycutt, and Sean T. Stevens summarize various conceptions of implicit bias that only minimally overlap with each other. Implicit bias can be defined as:

1. "mental associations based on race, gender, and other social categories that may lead to discrimination without intent, or possibly even awareness" (Payne et al., 2017).
2. Behavior that results from implicit messages and cues one internalizes as a member of a social group (de Houwer, 2019, p. 836).
3. "unintended biases in decision-making" (Chapman, Kaatz, & Carnes, 2013, p. 1504).

Unfortunately, they write, mental associations (first definition), behavior (second) and decision-making (third) are entirely different models for thinking about implicit bias. Moreover, "[t]hese definitions are also packed with claims and assumptions that are dubious at best." For example, the "mere existence" of cultural stereotypes does not necessarily mean such stereotypes influence anything (such causal claims require sufficient empirical evidence). Finally, "[d]efining associations of concepts in memory as 'bias' imports a subterranean assumption that there is something wrong with those associations in the absence of empirical evidence demonstrating wrongness."[24]

Yet another definition of implicit bias comes from Anthony Greenwald, "one of the IAT's creators and foremost proponents." Greenwald defines implicit bias as follows: "Introspectively unidentified (or inaccurately identified) effects of past experience that mediate discriminatory behavior." But if this is the definition, it is not clear that the IAT measures implicit bias. Here's why:

1. The IAT "is a reaction time measure that assesses the difference in time it takes to do two different yet related categorization tasks. Difference in reaction times is not discrimination."
2. "Implicit bias" is only one variable, which may or may not explain discrimination relative to other variables.
3. People can accurately predict their IAT scores.[25]

This is only a sample of the many complications that arise when trying to define implicit bias. But at least one thing is clear. As Mitchell writes, "the extent to which people are consciously aware of and able to control their implicit biases remains an open question."[26] It comes as little surprise, then, that a February 2020 paper, which "provides a comprehensive review of divergent conceptualizations of the 'implicit' construct that have emerged in attitude research over the past two decades," recommends "discontinuing the usage of the 'implicit' terminology."[27]

IT IS NOT CLEAR WHAT THE IMPLICIT ASSOCIATION TEST MEASURES

In a 2008 paper, Gregory Mitchell and Philip Tetlock highlight flaws in the research underlying "the elusive construct of unconscious prejudice." They write, "Unconscious-prejudice researchers report startling discoveries that . . . roughly 75% of the million-plus whites who have taken the IAT score as unconsciously prejudiced against African Americans—and that the IAT predicts propensity to discriminate against target groups in a variety of ways and settings."[28]

They write that such "[s]trong claims . . . require strong evidence, and proponents have yet to provide compelling evidence for their assertions about the pervasiveness of unconscious bias and its behavioral consequences in early twenty-first century America."[29] They then run through "three domains of ignorance" about the validity of the IAT, the now-infamous test that its inventors claimed can detect a test-taker's bias at the subconscious level.[30] These include the following issues:

1. Test results for any individual vary a lot from one test to another, and depend on many factors such as age, experience, and cognitive ability. This means the IAT may measure a situational state of mind rather than a durable characteristic.
2. Test results do not reliably predict discriminatory behavior and may simply reflect underlying "base rates" (discussed later in this chapter).
3. Test results that may show discriminatory behavior in a lab setting may not show discriminatory behavior in real-world settings where people are accountable to equal-opportunity laws.

In a chapter titled "Popularity as a Poor Proxy for Utility," Mitchell and Tetlock cast further doubt on the IAT. They summarize the research on the IAT as follows:

> On issue after issue, there is little evidence of positive impacts from IAT research: theories and understandings of prejudice have not

> converged as a result of the IAT research; bold claims about the superior predictive validity of the IAT over explicit measures have been falsified; IAT scores have been found to add practically no explanatory power in studies of discriminatory behavior; and IAT research has not led to new practical solutions to discrimination.[31]

In their comprehensive overview of the literature on "IAT Scores, Racial Gaps, and Scientific Gaps," Jussim and colleagues conclude:

> There are many scientific gaps in understanding the IAT: it has dubious construct validity and low test-retest reliability; it is subject to various other psychometric oddities; its bias effect has often been computed in a way that appears to exaggerate its size; it has been almost universally misinterpreted and misrepresented as measuring "implicit bias" when, by Greenwald's own definition, it does not do so. Its predictive validity has often been found to be modest and is, at best, controversial. Even if we ignore all that, its ability to account for inequality in the present is likely to be limited.[32]

Despite all this, the concept of implicit bias has taken hold in the culture as if it were a well-established fact. Jussim and colleagues speculate "that much of this probably reflects not the strength of research based on the IAT, but rather that large portions of the public are hungry for ideas that can explain continuing racial disparities in the absence of draconian systems such as Jim Crow." Nonetheless, "a great wave of scholarship" has emerged "acknowledging a slew of problems, limitations, reinterpretations, revisions, and uncertainty about almost everything involving the IAT and implicit bias."[33]

While there are many shortcomings, one major crack in the edifice is the consistent finding of low "test-retest" correlations. This means that people who take successive IAT tests do not consistently generate the same scores. This variability lends support to the cautionary note by Mitchell and Tetlock that the IAT may measure a situational state of mind rather than a durable characteristic.[34]

According to Jesse Singal, "[t]here's a serious dearth of published information on test-retest reliability of the race IAT specifically." Nonetheless, "[t]he individual results that have been published . . . suggest the race IAT's test-retest reliability is far too low for it to be safe to use in real-world settings." After running through a litany of studies, he summarizes the state of research as follows:

> What all these numbers mean is that there doesn't appear to be any published evidence that the race IAT has test-retest reliability that is close to acceptable for real-world evaluation. If you take the test today, and then take it again tomorrow—or even in just a few hours—there's a solid chance you'll get a very different result.[35]

The best that can be said is that the reasons for this variability are not well understood, which indicates the importance of conducting more research before we draw definitive conclusions about what the IAT actually measures.

IAT RESULTS MAY REFLECT BASE RATES RATHER THAN BIAS

It seems the IAT neither improves our understanding of racism nor provides definitive solutions to it. The IAT is a reaction-time test. As such, test-takers may respond more quickly to stimuli because they are more familiar with the underlying "base rates." For example, if you see a photo of a burly man with a tattoo, arms folded, and a serious disposition, you might not be inclined to associate his characteristics with that of a rarefied, impeccably groomed Harvard professor. You may be wrong about this particular man, but you may be right that it is less likely that, in the overall population, Harvard professors look like tall, burly, tattoo-wearing men with an aggressive-seeming demeanor.

Indeed, one study that explored "base rate effects on the IAT" found that "the stimulus context moderates the magnitude of the IAT effect." Such a finding highlights "the need to explore the extent to which implicit measures reflect properties of the task or the environment rather than attributes of test-takers."[36] Another study that explored base rates found that, "[d]espite learning individuating facts about a particular male and female that rendered base rates inapplicable, implicit beliefs still relied on base rates."[37]

This latter finding by Dr. Mahazarin Banaji indicates that there may be value in the IAT as a self-learning tool. The Project Implicit website states, "At this stage in its development, it is preferable to use the IAT mainly as an educational tool to develop awareness of implicit preferences and stereotypes."[38] Nonetheless, it is not clear what lessons we are to draw when we learn about our "biases." It could mean that we hold internal biases that do not reflect the realities around us. Alternatively, it could mean that our "biases" simply reflect accurate perceptions of our environment.

IMPLICIT BIAS DOES NOT RELIABLY PREDICT BEHAVIOR

Psychologists are also not convinced that implicit bias affects behavior or social outcomes. As Jesse Singal writes:

1. "[W]hen you use meta-analyses to examine the question of whether IAT scores predict discriminatory behavior accurately enough for the test to be useful in real-world settings, the answer is: No. Race IAT scores are weak predictors of discriminatory behavior."[39]
2. "[T]he key experts involved in IAT research no longer claim that the IAT can be used to predict individual behavior. In this sense, the IAT has simply failed to deliver on a promise it has been making since its inception—that it can reveal otherwise hidden propensities to commit acts of racial bias. There's no evidence it can."[40]

According to Mitchell, "[t]he empirical evidence now establishes that indirect measures of bias such as the IAT should not be interpreted as measures of an individual's propensity to discriminate."[41] Indeed, he writes, "with respect to individual-level behavior, the accumulated research findings reveal that it is scientifically inappropriate to use any individual's score on an implicit bias measure as a measure of how likely it is that the individual will have engaged in acts of discrimination in the past or will do so in the future."[42]

In September 2019, seven psychologists published a paper on implicit bias that "synthesized evidence from 492 studies (87,418 participants) to investigate the effectiveness of procedures in changing implicit measures" and "evaluated these procedures' effects on explicit and behavioral measures." Their "findings suggest that changes in implicit measures are possible, but *those changes do not necessarily translate into changes in explicit measures or behavior*."[43] In a tweet, one of the authors, Patrick S. Forscher:

1. Explained that he has "started to doubt that implicit bias is an important driver of behavior in the first place."
2. Suggests that implicit bias is the "scar tissue" of past explicit biases.[44]

Another author of this aggregate study, Brian A. Nosek, is one of the original architects of the IAT and is also a member of the Project Implicit Executive Committee.[45] Anthony Greenwald, another original architect of the IAT, has publicly expressed the view that "taking the IAT to discover one's own implicit biases does nothing to remove or reduce those implicit biases."[46]

Yet another, though earlier, analysis of aggregated data examined "the predictive validity of the [IAT] and explicit measures of bias for a wide range of criterion measures of discrimination." This study by multiple scholars also found that "IATs were poor predictors of [almost] every criterion category . . . and the IATs performed no better than simple explicit measures."[47]

With respect to specific outcomes, one paper provides a reanalysis of an influential study on implicit bias and finds "a pattern of behavior consistent with a pro-Black behavioral bias, rather than the anti-Black bias suggested in the original study."[48] Another study "tested 80 police patrol officers by applying [a] leading edge method" that involves examining "racial bias in police decisions by pressing 'shoot' or 'don't-shoot' buttons in response to pictures of armed and unarmed suspects."

The latter study "found that, despite clear evidence of implicit bias against Black suspects, officers were slower to shoot armed Black suspects than armed White suspects, and they were less likely to shoot unarmed Black suspects than unarmed White suspects," calling into question "[t]he assumption that implicit racial bias affects police behavior in deadly encounters with Black suspects."[49]

This finding should not be shocking. To reiterate Mitchell's warning, "[w]ith respect to individual-level behavior, the accumulated research findings reveal that it is scientifically inappropriate to use any individual's score on an implicit bias measure as a measure of how likely it is that the individual will have engaged in acts of discrimination in the past or will do so in the future." In fact, "[a]n individual who supposedly shows high implicit bias on the IAT is no more likely to discriminate in any given situation than an individual who supposedly shows low implicit bias on the IAT. Indeed, in a number of studies 'high bias' persons behave *more positively* toward minorities than 'low bias' persons."[50]

Mitchell further notes that, "[b]ecause the IAT is cognitively demanding, the age and general cognitive processing speed of the respondents have been found to affect the pattern of results observed. Likewise, because the IAT becomes easier with practice, the pattern of responding observed on IATs tends to look less biased with practice."[51] In other words, the IAT may simply reflect cognitive abilities rather than cognitive biases.

The research currently points to one conclusion: the IAT has not proven to be a reliable predictor of behavior.[52]

IMPLICIT BIAS TRAINING HAS NOT BEEN SHOWN TO WORK

Given the many weaknesses uncovered in the implicit bias paradigm, it should not be surprising that there is also much reason to doubt whether implicit bias training works. As only one example, one paper "conducted a systematic review . . . [of] peer-reviewed studies conducted on adults between May 2005 and April 2015, testing interventions designed to reduce implicit bias, with results measured using the [IAT] or sufficiently similar methods."

After a review of thirty articles, the results indicate that "[s]ome techniques, such as engaging with others' perspective, appear unfruitful, at least in short term implicit bias reduction, while other techniques, such as exposure to counter-stereotypical exemplars, are more promising. Robust data is lacking for many of these interventions." In sum, the paper advises caution "when it comes to programs aiming at reducing biases."[53]

Additional studies, though not all studies, have also given us reason to doubt whether implicit bias training reduces overall bias in society.[54] Mitchell summarizes in his primer on implicit bias:

> [V]ery few studies have examined the long-term effects of such interventions by monitoring changes in implicit bias measurements at multiple points in time following the interventions. Most notably, the interventions have been found to have little or no effect on behavior (i.e., have not been shown to change how people behave toward members of other groups). This fact may reflect the tenuous relationship between implicit bias and behavior just as much as the ineffectiveness of the interventions.[55]

IMPLICIT BIAS DOES NOT CURRENTLY TELL US MUCH ABOUT RACISM

Rutgers University social psychologist Lee Jussim writes, "[a]lmost everything about implicit bias is controversial in scientific circles. It is not clear, for instance, what most implicit bias methods actually measure; their ability to predict discrimination is modest at best; their reliability is low; early claims about their power and immutability have proven unjustified."[56] In a review of the literature, Jussim and colleagues write that, while "several meta-analyses have shown that IAT scores predict discrimination to at least a modest extent," there are alternative explanations for racial gaps that suggest "that IAT scores offer only one of many possible such explanations."[57]

As a result, "IAT scores can only explain what is left over, after accounting for other explanations of gaps," and "IAT scores explain only a modest portion of those gaps." In other words, "even if the IAT fully captures implicit biases, and those implicit biases were completely eliminated, the extent to which racial gaps would be reduced is minimal." Jussim and colleagues recommend that "the IAT should not be abandoned, but that, even after 20 years, much more research is needed to fully understand what the IAT measures and explains."[58] Jussim notes that a prominent advocate for the implicit bias concept, Dr. Mahazarin Banaji, recommends against mandatory implicit bias trainings.[59]

If the science on implicit bias is, at best, inconclusive, then there is something amiss in Robin DiAngelo's inflexible insistence that the implicit biases of white people are a central force in perpetuating systemic inequities in the distribution of societal resources—what many people call "institutional racism." In the next chapter, we examine how the theory of white fragility relies on a particular way of understanding racism that presumes implicit bias is the root cause of ongoing racial inequality.

3

REINVENTING RACISM

The theory of "white fragility" is heavily motivated by Whiteness studies. As such, it relies on a unique way of understanding racism. Racism, it says, is rooted in the reign of Whiteness.

Whiteness studies is devoted to the study of Whiteness as a central pillar of society. What is Whiteness? It is hard to say, but the basic idea that motivates the study of Whiteness is that all the institutions of society are "white"—made by white people, ruled by white people, and kept in place by white people to make sure that white people continue to benefit from them while people of color do not.

As a result, white supremacy survives and thrives. We will have more to say about this throughout the chapter. For now, the takeaway is that racism is to be seen as a "system" that perpetuates racial inequality. It takes some effort, however, to figure out what the nature of this "system" is. Whatever it is, Whiteness sits at the center of it. It supports, defines, and affects all features of the system.

Because society is anchored on Whiteness, racial inequality is unavoidably a result of Whiteness. The only way to solve racial inequality is to *de-center* Whiteness. Ian Haney Lopez, a law professor at the University of California–Berkeley who has written on the development of Whiteness in American legal history, explains that the pursuit of racial equity depends crucially on "the development of a White race-consciousness predicated on rejecting Whiteness," and insists that "there is no other way."[1]

In practice, this means analyzing, exposing, and fighting all the ways that language and behavior continually institutionalize habits, norms, and mores that reinforce white supremacy. Political correctness, in the guise of anti-Whiteness, is not primarily an attack on free speech. Its purpose is to enforce a strict dismantling of "white" norms of speech that underlie "racialized" institutions.

The central problem with this framework is that "Whiteness" appears to be a term that scholars and activists cooked up for their own explanatory and political purposes. It is not, however, something real that we can easily point out in reality. More technically, scholars and activists see Whiteness as reified in society. Reification involves treating an abstraction—Whiteness—as if it had a material existence that embodies social relations. For example, it involves seeing library collections as embodiments of Whiteness.[2]

Books by white authors like William Shakespeare or Jane Austen embody the ideology of Whiteness. They are "physically taking up space" in libraries.[3] We must learn to see white people as talking in certain ways, engaging in certain kinds of social activities, and interacting with nonwhites in ways that are harmful. These "white" habits relentlessly institutionalize social mores that reinforce white supremacy.

For example, in an essay about reading Jane Austen's novel *Mansfield Park* for a class, one graduate student writes, "Unmarked, and universal, whiteness structures this classroom, this university, this world. It structures the topics they bring up, how they engage with one another, the ability for them to get along so well, and why I am on the outside of it all."

It is not that this student has no desire to read Austen. He wants "to read as many dead white writers as I can." But he "must read them from this body." At one point, "[a]fter finding myself fatigued towards the end of the semester by all the British domestic drama of Austen's oeuvre, I zone out during a class period and think, 'These novels are some big-time white people problems.' I want to say this out loud in good fun, but then I take a good look around me. Everyone is white besides me."[4]

As a result, racial inequality persists.

Why? Because white people are oblivious to Whiteness. White people stand at the center, and at the top, of society. As such, they can take their habits for granted. They do not have to put in work to figure out how to fit in. They already fit in. The result is that Whiteness survives through their everyday thoughts and actions.

If only they could see that this position in society is a position of privilege they don't deserve, white people would be persuaded to eschew their defensiveness, their "fragility," and embrace responsibility for undoing the ongoing "reification" of Whiteness in society. Ending racism depends on learning to read Jane Austen's novel as a "white" novel. It depends on white people opening their eyes to Whiteness.

This reification argument, however, is a logical fallacy. Ideas are not people. Abstractions do not walk side by side with us on the sidewalk and whisper in our ears. Of course, ideas and abstractions often influence how we think and what we say. But as we can imagine, the nature of that influence is hard to pin down. That's why the reification fallacy can be so insidious. "Whiteness" is rife with ambiguity and speculation. If we assume that something like Whiteness is at the center of everything, that it is the root of all evil, we start imagining that "Whiteness" is here, there, and everywhere, when, in many if not most cases, it is not.

We see Whiteness as a kind of serpentine ghost always lurking around, whispering in the ears of white people, telling them to think, talk, and act in ways that reinforce a prevailing hierarchy, without white people realizing it. If we are made to believe in the nefarious ghost of Whiteness, we make ourselves susceptible to confirmation bias. That is, we start to see everything as examples of Whiteness in action. We believe what we want to believe. We see what we want to see.

It is by no means certain, however, that Whiteness is invisible to white people. For example, one of the few empirical studies of Whiteness—conducted by sociologists Douglas Hartmann, Joseph Gerteis, and Paul R. Croll—provides evidence that white Americans do not universally abide by "ideologies" of color-blindness and individualism, and that white racial identity is not as invisible to white people as is often assumed. Nor is it the case that nonwhite people repudiate the idea of individualism.[5] These findings challenge a core claim of Whiteness studies that Whiteness is invisible to white Americans because of their steadfast belief that they are "color-blind."

In subsequent chapters, we will see that confirmation bias is indicative of deep methodological problems in the theory of white fragility. The theory does not encourage inquiry. Instead, it seeks interrogation, guided by activist orthodoxy that permits no questions about whether a claim holds up under evidence and scrutiny.[6]

The fallacy of reification[7] effectively becomes a fallacy of ambiguity. Whiteness can mean anything. We are given little beyond speculation and "theory" to test whether one meaning is better than another. As a result, "reified" Whiteness becomes an unclear term used in the premise of every argument that says racial disparity is the result of Whiteness. Inferences drawn about racial inequality are invariably drawn from a presumed understanding of racism as a system grounded in a vague abstraction called Whiteness.

THE "REIFICATION" OF WHITENESS

In an article for the *Paris Review*, "White People Must Save Themselves from Whiteness," Venita Blackburn, assistant professor of creative writing at California State University–Fresno, contends that "America was born in cardiac arrest" and that "[t]he cognitive dissonance necessary to profit off of gruesome human suffering and yet remain happy is too great." She ponders whether "all civilization works this way, in a state of eternal adjustment," but laments, "when every attempt at a correction is met with deviation and denial, implosion is very much a possibility."[8]

She concludes that "[w]hite people must save themselves from whiteness . . . [and] must meet every test of whiteness with more than silence or a plea for civility." Perhaps unwittingly, however, Blackburn concludes her article with a line that exposes the fallacious idea of reification that underlies the theory of white fragility: "[t]o do so is to awake fully into one's body for the first time."[9] That is, white people must learn to see themselves as the embodiment of Whiteness.

The theory of white fragility sees racism and racial inequality as the same thing. Because society is anchored on Whiteness, evidence of racial inequality is direct evidence of the ongoing reign of Whiteness. Since all the institutions of society are "white," they continue to benefit white people but not people of color. This is racism and must be met with antiracism. If not, white people are not actively working to undo Whiteness. In effect, they are working to keep racism in place.

Suppose, however, that a white person reads a 2018 *Quillette* article by the writer Coleman Hughes. Mr. Hughes describes what he calls the *disparity fallacy*.[10] According to Hughes, "The disparity fallacy holds that unequal outcomes between two groups must be caused primarily by discrimination, whether overt or systemic." This belief is puzzling, Hughes argues, because it is applied too *narrowly* rather than too *broadly*.

In other words, "[a]ny instance of whites outperforming blacks is adduced as evidence of discrimination." Hughes then cites research showing that "black women have higher college attendance rates than white men, and higher incomes than white women, conditional on parental income." In such cases, "discrimination is never invoked as a causal factor."

Reading this article, a white person might agree that this is a good point. If so, this white person exhibits white fragility and contributes to the ongoing reification of Whiteness. He acts as a white supremacist because he has allowed himself to be distracted from the essential point that racism can only go one way in a society anchored on Whiteness.

To think otherwise is to fail to understand that racism is about "structural" inequality. What is "structural" inequality? It is racial inequality in a "white" society in which white people consistently enjoy better outcomes than nonwhite people. Any inequalities that run the other way in a "white" society do not dispel the reality that racism is based on Whiteness. To think otherwise is to be guilty of *aversive racism*, or "enact[ing] racism while maintaining a positive self-image."[11] Robin DiAngelo invokes examples such as "[a]ttributing inequality between whites and people of color to causes other than racism" [12] (which, for DiAngelo, only refers to inequality that benefits whites).

Another example is the suggestion that Hughes is right about the disparity fallacy. To do so is to avert attention from the meaning of racism. It is to distract us from the truth that inequality in a "white" society is racist only when it benefits white people. Inequality that runs the other way is not racist because our society is fundamentally built on Whiteness. That is, we might observe inequalities that run the other way, but by and large, white people rule. Even if inequalities that run the other way *are* a result of some form of prejudice, we can only see this prejudice, at worst, as a form of bigotry, and bigotry is not racism. Why? Because at the level of institutions, white people rule.

So, where does all this come from?

Whiteness, according to pioneering scholar Ruth Frankenberg, is (1) "a location of structural advantage, of race privilege"; (2) a standpoint, a place from which white people look at themselves, at others, and at society; and (3) "a set of cultural practices that are usually unmarked and unnamed."[13] According to DiAngelo:

> Whiteness is thus conceptualized as a constellation of processes and practices rather than as a discrete entity (i.e., skin color). Whiteness is dynamic, relational, and operating at all times and on myriad levels. These processes and practices include basic rights, values, beliefs, perspectives and experiences purported to be commonly shared by all but which are actually only consistently afforded to white people. Whiteness Studies begin with the premise that racism and white privilege exist in both traditional and modern forms, and rather than work to prove its existence, work to reveal it.[14]

In other words, Whiteness is reified in society. To be white is to have the mystical force of Whiteness *position* you as "white" in social relations. While Blackburn states that "a white person is not whiteness itself,"[15] she implies that to awake "fully into one's body for the first time"[16] as a white person is to eschew fragility and begin the work of undoing Whiteness. It is to recognize the vital importance of plumbing the depths of one's unconscious mind to root out the biases that have been piling up since birth.

In the words of Frankenberg, "To speak of the 'social construction of whiteness' asserts that there are locations, discourses, and material relations to which the term 'whiteness' applies." Whiteness thus "refers to a set of locations that are historically, socially, politically, and culturally produced and, moreover, are intrinsically linked to unfolding relations of domination," and "[n]aming 'whiteness' displaces it from the unmarked, unnamed status that is itself an effect of its dominance." This is imperative because one of "the effects on white people both of race privilege and of the dominance of whiteness are their seeming normativity, their structured invisibility."[17]

Thus, "[t]o look at the social construction of whiteness . . . is to look head-on at a site of dominance . . . [and] [t]o speak of whiteness is . . . to assign everyone a place in the relations of racism." Racism, she emphasizes, "is not merely an option for white people." It "shapes [their] lives and identities in a way that is inseparable from other facets of daily life."[18] It follows that "[e]xamining the co-construction of whiteness and other racial identities is useful because it may help lead white activists (and also . . . activists of color) away from the incorporation of 'old' discursive elements into 'new' strategies."[19]

For example, Frankenberg argues "that we need to displace the colonial construction of whiteness as an 'empty' cultural space, in part by refiguring it as constructed and dominant rather than as norm." If culture is not thus reconceptualized, "we run the risk of reifying and dehistoricizing all cultural practices, valorizing or romanticizing some while discounting others as not cultural at all."[20]

White people must be convinced to reject fragility and embrace responsibility for the ongoing reification of Whiteness in society. In other words, white people must awake fully into their bodies for the first time.[21] They must awaken to the stark reality that they *are* Whiteness, at least in the ways they think, talk, and act. They must see that silence and pleas for civility are failures to acknowledge the power of Whiteness. They must be motivated to check their privilege. They must become "woke." Otherwise, they remain complicit in the survival of Whiteness.

To be white is not simply to have white skin. It is to be a racist. It is not simply that white people have racial bias (all people have racial bias, DiAngelo asserts in one paper[22]), but that they benefit from the advantages of a society characterized by white supremacy (i.e., racial inequality). The only escape from racism is to undergo a lifelong struggle session. White people must renounce Whiteness.

They must also resist fragility because it impedes the dissection and decoding of all the implicit biases one inherits as a white person enriched by "unearned assets [one] can count on cashing in each day"[23] in a culture denominated in the currency of white supremacy. As Professor Ian Haney Lopez writes, "If the racial systems of meaning that tie Whites and non-Whites together into hierarchies of social worth are to be brought down, it *will only be through choice and struggle.*"[24]

In one lecture, University of Michigan School of Social Work graduate and therapist Andy Horning talked about "White Fragility: The New Racism, and More Effective Steps to Undoing Racism."[25] Horning claims that "fragility is everywhere . . . when you run from that, you're never free."

He doesn't clarify what you're supposed to be free of—it can't be racial injustice since DiAngelo (and co-author Özlem Sensoy) write in one paper that a "basic premise of antiracist education is that it is lifelong work; the process of identifying and challenging patterns of racism is always evolving and never finished."[26] He advises the audience that the "antidote to fragility" is to "[g]o toward struggle, not away." We can only locate racism in the language and behaviors of Whiteness, and thus we have no choice but to fight racism by fighting the language and behaviors of Whiteness.

This fight never ends. Frankenberg writes that "Whiteness changes over time and space and is in no way a transhistorical essence."[27] DiAngelo writes in her seminal paper that "[w]hiteness is thus conceptualized as a constellation of processes and practices rather than as a discrete entity (i.e., skin color alone)."[28] In the *Paris Review*, Blackburn states that "whiteness is not personal"—in other words, "a white person is not whiteness itself" because "whiteness is institutional."[29]

Nonetheless, Frankenberg writes that "the range of possible ways of living whiteness, for an individual white woman in a particular time and place, is delimited by the relations of racism at that moment and in that place."[30] As philosophy professors Bettina Bergo and Tracey Nicholls write, "Whiteness is a mythological category—denoting sameness, purity, and an internally changing yet fixed 'transcendental'—even before it is ethnic or demographic."[31] The white, or dominant, perspective centers every aspect of society around itself. Because society historically has been built on Whiteness, white people cannot escape the all-powerful force of the white perspective that filters everything through the lens of its own implicit bias. Whiteness may be perpetually evolving, but only in ways that keep it in place at the center of society.

At first glance, this all seems to make sense. There are wide discrepancies between whites and blacks in terms of unemployment rates; earnings; and other measures such as wealth, poverty, educational attainment, and homeownership.[32] Moreover, white men largely hold sway in terms of leadership and influence in politics, Silicon Valley, business, university faculties, and the media.[33]

When the odds appear so heavily slanted in favor of white people, and white men in particular, it seems Whiteness has been unquestionably reified. White people need to stop pretending reverse racism is real[34]—or as DiAngelo and Sensoy write in one paper, "racism is not fluid and cannot be wielded by individuals regardless of their racial positions; thus, reverse racism does not exist."[35]

For centuries, white America believed that white and black were distinct biological types that could not be reconciled. "White" was superior. "Black" was inferior. This dichotomy rationalized slavery and Jim Crow. This history has led to a system of racial inequality that can only be undone by rooting out the unconscious prejudice that incessantly puts nonwhite people on the margins of society.[36]

Implicit bias thus incriminates society as a racist system, which continues to foster white supremacy and white complicity. But, while this may seem like a bracing idea, it does not, in fact, necessarily follow that racial disparity is the mirror image of implicit bias and socialization. In the previous chapter, we saw that implicit bias may not be as powerful a cause of ongoing racial inequality. It might be the "scar tissue" of a history of racial discrimination rather than the cause of present and future racial inequality.

In this chapter, we see why there is reason to doubt the existence of a dominant ideology called Whiteness to which all white people helplessly and implicitly subscribe, and that serves, as James Baldwin apparently believed, as the price of a ticket for entry into America.[37] The main reason for doubt is that it is based on the fallacy of reification. This means treating an abstraction (Whiteness) as a real thing. If this were true, then we have to see Whiteness as an insidious life force working its way like a thread through every institution, norm, and way of life that defines American society.

Here is how writer Samuel Kronen describes it in *Areo* magazine:

> British journalist Reni Eddo-Lodge defines whiteness as a "political ideology that is concerned with maintaining power through domination and exclusion." Ta-Nehisi Coates describes whiteness as the "organizing principle" used to justify historical and ongoing oppression: even claiming that the need to be white may be responsible for the impending destruction of the natural environment. American novelist Danzy Senna thinks of whiteness as a disease, a "condition" that might be "contagious."[38]

In short, Whiteness is reified, in the sense used by György Lukács in *History and Class Consciousness*, as "a relation between people [that] takes on the character of a thing and thus acquires a 'phantom objectivity,' an autonomy that seems so strictly rational and all-embracing as to conceal every trace of its fundamental nature: the relation between people."[39]

White fragility is a kind of complacency that keeps the wheels of reified Whiteness churning in full gear. The fight against racism, then, involves a fight against "white fragility." We must unmask the fragility and correct the beliefs of people with white skin. Otherwise, white people will keep racial inequality in place.

This may work as metaphor, but it does not work as logic. Ideas have consequences, but they are not, as *New York Times* journalist and *1619 Project* director Nikole Hannah-Jones says about slavery and antiblack racism, like self-regenerating DNA built into society.[40] This view leads to what historian James Oakes calls "political paralysis" whereby the possibility of progress is made to be logically impossible.[41]

Indeed, Whiteness scholars schooled in the critical race theory of Derrick Bell and his disciples tend to see racism as a permanent state of affairs but encourage activism anyway.[42] They reject the idea that activism is pointless if racism is permanent because resistance is inherently worthwhile. Resistance is its own reward. Even if this point of view were granted, it is still the case that equating racism with DNA "makes nihilism," as Hughes writes, "the only logical option."[43]

REINVENTING RACISM

Blackburn's metaphor of an America born in cardiac arrest vividly illustrates the undeniable crucible of contradictions inherent in a society whose original political leaders enshrined the rights to life, liberty, and the pursuit of happiness in the Declaration of Independence, while simultaneously denying the right to life, liberty, and the pursuit of happiness to a significant share of its population on the basis of skin color. Yet the claim that "every attempt at a correction is met with deviation and denial"[44] is an odd and curious assessment of America.

America is a country that was already trying to end slavery at its conception.[45] It fought a devastating Civil War when contradictions in the "peculiar institution" of slavery became too great to bear.[46] It struck down a century of Jim Crow with transformative civil rights legislation. Over the last half-century, it has undergone a massive shift in attitudes on race relations and issues such as miscegenation, legal protections for minority groups, and the importance of diversity and inclusion.

Undoubtedly, the legacy of racism, slavery, and Jim Crow has marred the legacy of a country that boasts impressive accomplishments. Moreover, deep racial inequalities persist. This history has played a big part in structural problems like inner-city blight and racial segregation. It has fostered gulfs between racial communities that militate against a more harmonious blend of our diverse society.

Yet, as Coleman Hughes argues in his essay on what he calls the *racism treadmill*, "the data take a clear side in [the] debate" about whether there has been significant progress in the fight against racism.[47] Indeed, America has elected a black president. The N word is regarded as hate speech. The law is on the side of antidiscrimination. Twitter mobs erupt at any hint of racial insensitivity by a person of influence. Racist remarks can disrupt, if not destroy, careers.[48] (Remember Don Imus being fired for saying that Rutgers women's basketball players looked like "nappy-headed hoes"?[49])

In spite of all this, "[t]he prevailing view among progressives today," Hughes observes, "is that America hasn't made much progress on racism."[50] Hughes suggests, following Harvard psychology professor Steven Pinker, that *availability bias* (the tendency, for example, to believe that headline news events are more common than they are) and *negativity bias* (when you think negative influences or events have more impact than positive influences or events) help to explain this "progressophobia."[51]

He declares that "our denialism about racial progress calls for a deeper explanation—an explanation in terms of widely held beliefs about race and inequality."[52] For Whiteness scholars, the deeper explanation is "systemic" racism. As Ibram X. Kendi says, "when I see racial disparities, I see racism."[53] The nature of "systemic" racism lies in what we have been calling Whiteness.

If so, however, systemic disparities should always work in one direction. Hughes explains how this belief succumbs to the "disparity fallacy," or assuming that inequality "must be caused primarily by discrimination, whether overt or systemic." The problem is, it doesn't have to be, and in many cases, is not. We need only consider, as Kronen recounts, the experience of other minorities:

> If the success of minorities were contingent on the extent to which racism is persistent in society, we would expect to see a clear socioeconomic dividing line between whites and groups who have been historically marginalized. Yet in terms of household income, both Indians and East Asians outperform whites by a significant margin, and no one would argue that their success is a result of having experienced less racism than whites. South African Americans earn almost double the national average; Native Americans from the Chickasaw Nation make twice as much as Apache, but there is no reason to think that racism plays any role in these outcomes.[54]

Indeed, according to the US Census Bureau, the real median household income of whites in 2018 was $63,293. As expected, this exceeds the income of $41,899 for blacks and $51,450 for Hispanics but is less than the income of $86,815 for Asians (alone or in combination) and $76,256 for Asian and Pacific Islander.[55]

In addition, Census Bureau data analyzed by Vincent Harinam and Rob Henderson, who are PhD students at the University of Cambridge, show that "the median household income of non-Hispanic whites in 2017 was $68,145," which is "considerably lower than the incomes of several ethnic groups. Indian Americans, Pakistani Americans, Filipino Americans, and Taiwanese Americans each out-earned whites in 2017, boasting median household incomes of $110,716, $83,956, $83,256, and $81,903, respectively. Lebanese Americans ($76,805), Sri Lankan Americans ($73,856), Chinese Americans ($72,927), and Iranian Americans ($72,733) also out-earned whites."[56]

Legal discrimination has ended. There has been a dramatic decline in explicit bias among white people. White guilt among progressives helps explain why "white liberals in Iowa and New Hampshire [were] less inclined to support" Joe Biden for president even as Biden held "a commanding lead in national polls with nonwhite Democrats." Moreover, as Harinam and Henderson point out in their article, "white progressives insist on spreading the gospel of white privilege."[57]

As sociologist Eduardo Bonilla-Silva observes, "whereas the majority of whites supported segregated neighborhoods, schools, transportation, jobs, and public accommodations in the 1940s, less than a quarter indicated they did in the 1970s. Similarly . . . [a]lthough the number is still high (ranging from 20 percent to 50 percent, depending on the stereotype), the proportion of whites who state in surveys that blacks are lazy, stupid, irresponsible, and violent has declined since the 1940s."[58]

Hughes delves into "black culture" as a meaningful factor to consider in attempting to explain racial inequality. To illustrate, Hughes notes that most NBA basketball players are black, which is not the case in baseball. Progressives try to explain black underrepresentation in baseball by turning to usual suspects, such as mass incarceration or the desire of fans for baseball to "stay white." Progressives act "like detectives to the scene of an unsolved murder, determined to consider every possible explanation except for the 'lazy' one: that in black culture, basketball is more popular than baseball."

Hughes's ultimate point is that "[t]he disparity fallacy and the denial of cultural factors conspire to create a dynamic that I call the Racism Treadmill: as long as cultural differences continue to cause disparities between racial groups, and as long as progressives imagine that systemic racism lies behind every disparity, then no amount of progress in reducing systemic racism, however large or concrete, will ever look like progress to progressives." We are left with "a Sisyphean politics; an agitated march to nowhere in particular."[59]

The implication, Hughes submits, is that "[t]here's no reason to think that the definition of racism will stop expanding any time soon."[60] Indeed, as DiAngelo and her co-author Özlem Sensoy put it, "racial justice learning is ongoing and our learning is never finished."[61]

In addition, Hughes surmises, "there's no reason to think that progressives will ever stop demanding institutional reforms to fix racism—up to and including attempts to reform our subconscious minds with such things as mandatory implicit bias trainings."[62] He then cites the acclaimed poet Benjamin Zephaniah, who writes, "laws can control people's actions, but they can't control people's thoughts. As racism becomes more subtle, we need to keep pressuring our institutions to change."[63]

Implicit bias is, in fact, the central premise of the theory of white fragility and its underlying worldview that racism is a "system" defined by the structure of Whiteness. We saw in chapter 2 why this is a flawed premise. We should acknowledge that the absence of evidence does not imply evidence of absence, but to the extent that implicit bias does exert influence, cognitive missteps can lead one to overweight the effect of implicit bias on specific real-world outcomes.

Examples of cognitive biases:

1. Confirmation bias: the tendency to believe what you want to believe, ignoring contradictory evidence.
2. Availability bias: the tendency to believe that events which come to mind quickly, such as trending news stories, happen more often than they do.
3. Omitted-variable bias: the tendency to ignore additional factors that might explain events.
4. Base-rate neglect: the tendency, for example, to overestimate (underestimate) the probability of being abused by the police given that one is black (white) because one does not take into account the "base rate" probability of people being abused by the police—say, in a large metropolitan area versus a small metropolitan area, or in a poverty-stricken area versus an area not stricken by poverty.

It is also conceivable that Whiteness scholars have their own biases when they examine race issues. For example, in his review of the literature on microaggressions, psychologist Scott Lilienfeld wrote that "the decision about which behaviors to include under the vast microaggression umbrella has in some cases been influenced substantially by embedded political values that have not been adequately explicated."[64]

The upshot is that Whiteness studies has helped precipitate a dramatic transformation in the definition of racism. It has, in effect, *reinvented racism.* In 1991, the US Senate took up the nomination of African American Clarence Thomas to replace Thurgood Marshall as Supreme Court Justice. Thomas's nomination was controversial because many doubted his qualifications, a concern heightened by his notably conservative views. The nomination process exploded, however, when Anita Hill, Thomas's former colleague at the US Equal Employment Opportunity Commission, accused Thomas of sexual harassment while under his supervision.

Many people might see the nomination of one African American justice to replace another African American justice on the Supreme Court as a sign that racism was declining in America. At the time, in fact, Harvard sociologist Orlando Patterson wrote that "the sociological truths are that America . . . is now the least racist white-majority society in the world" because "it has a better record of legal protection of minorities than any other society, white or black; offers more opportunities to a greater number of black persons than any other society, including all those of Africa; and has gone through a dramatic change in its attitude toward miscegenation over the past 25 years."[65]

Whiteness scholars, however, would disagree.

Whiteness studies has transformed the definition of racism so profoundly that emphasizing evidence of progress is seen as a shrewd, self-congratulatory sleight of hand. In chapter 5 of *White Fragility*, DiAngelo writes that the "most effective adaptation of racism in recent history" is "the good/bad binary."[66] In the wake of successes of the Civil Rights movement, and the marked improvement in race relations, "racism first needed to be reduced to simple, isolated, and extreme acts of prejudice" which are "intentional, malicious, and based on conscious dislike of someone because of race."[67] DiAngelo asserts that this "adaptation" of racism disguises the "true" nature of racism.

For DiAngelo, attitudes about miscegenation or legal protections for minorities are positive developments, but they do not mean America is less racist. Racism is not simply the belief in pernicious stereotypes, as if the only thing that makes you a racist is to have bigoted views that cause you to treat minorities badly. To hold this belief is to conflate racism with bigotry. It is to obscure the "systemic," or "structural," nature of racism. In fact, suggesting that black "cultural factors" may have explanatory relevance, as Hughes does, is an example of "aversive racism."[68]

As DiAngelo writes, "The critical element that differentiates *racism* from individual racial prejudice and racial discrimination is the historical accumulation and ongoing use of institutional power and authority to support the prejudice and to enforce discriminatory behaviors in systemic ways with far-reaching effects." She then notes that people can hold prejudice against whites or other people of color, but this is different from people of color holding institutional power as a group. A person of color "may refuse to wait on me if I enter her shop, but people of color cannot pass legislation that prohibits me from buying a home in a certain neighborhood."[69] DiAngelo quotes Omowale Akintunde (an African American scholar and filmmaker):

> Racism is a systemic, societal, institutional, omnipresent, and epistemologically embedded phenomenon that pervades every vestige of our reality. For most whites, however, racism is like murder: the concept exists, but someone has to commit it in order for it to happen. This limited view of such a multilayered syndrome cultivates the sinister nature of racism and, in fact, perpetuates racist phenomena rather than eradicates them.[70]

Given this view of racism, we might believe there is a supreme irony in the confirmation of the nomination and confirmation of Justice Thomas to replace Justice Marshall. The confirmation of Justice Thomas meant that a black person would continue to sit as a justice on the highest court in the land, influencing the outcome of legal controversies that will affect people for generations.

According to Whiteness scholars, however, this belief would be a mistake. As DiAngelo writes:

> Although rare individual people of color may be inside the circles of power—Colin Powell, Clarence Thomas, Marco Rubio, Barack Obama—they support the status quo and do not challenge racism in any way significant enough to be threatening. Their positions of power do not mean these public figures don't experience racism . . . but the status remains intact.[71]

For DiAngelo and Whiteness scholars, Patterson's 1991 opinion on racism in America was an example of invoking the good/bad binary. His opinion overlooks that racism is a "system." It overlooked the central role of Whiteness as the structural scaffold of racism in American society. It reinforced the "tokenism" that was evident in the nomination hearings for Justice Thomas. Patterson should have known better since, according to Barbara Applebaum, "scholars of color . . . [such as] Ralph Ellison, James Baldwin, and Franz Fanon have [long] maintained that whiteness lies at the center of the problem of racism."[72]

Perhaps Whiteness scholars can forgive Patterson since "[i]t is only relatively recently that the critical study of whiteness has become an academic field, committed to disrupting racism by problematizing whiteness as a corrective to the traditional exclusive focus on the racialized 'other.'"[73] Indeed, Patterson's op-ed was written approximately two years before Ruth Frankenberg published her book, White Women, Race Matters: The Social Construction of Whiteness,[74] which one paper by John T. Warren describes as "one of the most influential works in whiteness research."[75] DiAngelo repeatedly quotes and references Frankenberg in her own academic publications.[76]

Based on interviews with only thirty white women,[77] Frankenberg delineates, according to Warren's paper, "four ways that these women went about 'thinking about race' in their everyday lives," and in so doing, "advance[d] a compelling discussion of how race and racial oppression are enacted and constituted through social interaction," while "claiming that those who can understand their implication in oppressive racial systems of power and work to enact antiracist agendas are leading the way toward a better social world."[78]

Ever since, according to Warren's paper, Whiteness scholars have examined Whiteness "through the institutional location of the classroom," as well as in literature, cinema, and scholarship.[79] This direction focuses on "rhetorical location," with one paper explaining that the research attempts to link the ways "individuals and groups construct identity, administer power, and make sense of their everyday lives." The goal "is not to claim an essentialized white subject," but to examine "what power is embedded within the rhetorical location of whiteness."[80]

For example, Toni Morrison "examines the way 'virtually all of American fiction [has] positioned [the reader] as white.'"[81] This has major implications for multicultural education: "Rather than making the center bigger, including more voices and more cultures, whiteness studies demands a critical examination of the center in the hope that the center will fall apart."[82] Warren writes, "Multicultural education will be more than glances outward and will also include critical and focused attention inward toward the powerful center of racial privilege. This examination will shed light on the invisible power behind the center, which will work toward dismantling the system of racial inequality at the core."[83]

One example of this center is the white gaze, a notion one finds in work by David Roediger,[84] as well as in work by Michael E. Staub on "how whiteness was represented in the Clarence Thomas and Anita Hill hearings," in which "Congress specifically represented whiteness as a complete ignorance of black culture, which then allowed Thomas to serve 'as the expert on anything relating to blackness' . . . [a] framing of Thomas . . . [that] allowed his lack of qualifications for the Supreme Court to go unchallenged by the Congress."[85] One of the qualifications he presumably lacked was an understanding of the what the "real work" of antiracism entails.

In other words, Congress treated Thomas as a token black man who could speak for blackness. This patronizing approach was racist, not antiracist. The idea might have seemed reasonable: widening the circle of inclusion by welcoming another African American justice to the Supreme Court. Instead, it undermined the work of antiracism by reinforcing the status quo of Whiteness.

How did it do this? By "othering" Blackness from the standpoint of Whiteness. The notion of othering, examined in the work of scholars like UC–Berkeley law professor John Powell,[86] refers to the process of reinforcing differences between empowered and disempowered groups, which then reinforce inequality. Antiblackness, then, is an essential feature of Whiteness. In this case, the "white gaze" of Congress looked outward from the center rather than inward at its perch of power. It kept Blackness outside the circles of power under the guise of allowing a token black man inside the center. Whiteness and Blackness went unexamined.

The notion of "othering" returns us to the idea of decentering Whiteness. The nomination and confirmation of Justice Thomas was not a landmark achievement in the fight against racism, but a quintessential example of the ongoing reification of Whiteness, and thus the continuation of racism.

THE FALLACY OF REINVENTING RACISM

Let's now be as clear as we can about why "reification" is a fallacy. As a conceptual matter, reification is a fallacy because an abstraction is not a concrete thing. Practically speaking, however, we can get a better understanding of the reification fallacy by thinking of it as a fallacy of ambiguity.

There is no such thing as "Whiteness" whispering racial biases into the ears of white people. But the problem with "reification" does not end there. It is also fallacious because we are given no robust and clear guide for identifying Whiteness in practice. In the next chapter, we will see how the theory of white fragility ignores the principle of falsification. In other words, it provides no robust way of evaluating whether a claim about Whiteness is or is not true. The result is rampant, "feelings-based" speculation at best and, at worst, an epidemic of confirmation bias. It also means that when we attribute ongoing racial inequality to the reification of Whiteness, we are attributing inequality to the reification of an ill-defined word, namely, Whiteness.

The galvanizing theme of Whiteness Studies is the structural nature of racism. What is this structure made of? It is made of Whiteness. In practice, the actual materials of Whiteness, and how they form a structure that forever keeps racial inequality in place, are exceedingly hard to identify. Whiteness scholars make it even harder to identify them by concentrating so single-mindedly on "critical theory" at the expense of the scientific method, which would allow us to test the core claims of Whiteness.

For example, a paper by sociologists Douglas Hartmann, Joseph Gerteis, and Paul R. Croll provides quantitative evidence that white Americans are more aware of white racial identity, privilege, and structural inequalities than Whiteness scholars seem to assume.[87] It found that nearly seventy-five percent of white Americans saw their racial identity as "very important" or "somewhat important." It also found that nearly two out of five whites agreed that laws and institutions are important factors contributing to African American disadvantage. Moreover, nearly half of whites agreed that laws and institutions are important factors contributing to white advantage.[88] These findings challenge a core claim of Whiteness studies that white Americans universally and blindly adhere to a "color-blind" ideology whereby race is held to be unimportant or meaningless.

As we will see more clearly in the next chapter, this contrast between empirical testing and abstract "theorizing" lies at the heart of white fragility theory's methodological failings. But Whiteness scholars are undeterred. They insist that racial inequality will remain systemic so long as the centripetal force of Whiteness continues to draw everything and everyone to its own center of cultural power, conferring privilege on anyone who is white, while "othering" anyone who is not white.

This seems to make sense because the legacy of racism in America has greatly contributed to racial inequality. UC–Berkeley professor John Powell has written thoughtfully and informatively on how cumulative patterns over time in housing policies (redlining, subprime mortgages) have been harmful to the African American community.[89] His point that we should not assume that racial neutrality in the design of policy necessarily leads to racial neutrality in the effects of policy is well taken (though the idea that policy intent and policy effects can diverge is certainly not unique to race policy).[90]

Moreover, as one can see from reading literary classics like Mark Twain's *Adventures of Huckleberry Finn*, vicious racism was a pillar of American society in the nineteenth century. We cannot understand the racism of today without understanding the racism of yesterday. The long arc of racism, from the nineteenth century through the twentieth century and into the twenty-first century, helps motivate the discussion around topics like white privilege, institutional racism, and the ongoing disempowerment of minority communities in America.[91]

For Whiteness scholars, however, legacy not only matters more than progress. Legacy *is* racism. Hughes writes that "as long as progressives imagine that systemic racism lies behind every disparity, then no amount of progress in reducing systemic racism, however large or concrete, will ever look like progress to progressives."[92] In a paper on interrogating white racial privilege and how it contributes to the "othering" of marginalized groups, Powell argues that "[t]he recently popular but subsequently disfavored term 'underprivileged' functions problematically as a linguistic companion to privilege; it reifies the notion of privilege as normal and unquestionable."[93]

In other words, being aware that many people lack privilege is not a sign of progress in one's understanding of disempowerment and disenfranchisement in society. It is instead a further reification of privilege and Whiteness. It is not progressives who are problematic because they refuse to see progress. It is whites who are problematic because they exhibit white fragility if they dare to wonder why the term "underprivileged" is problematic.

Given this backdrop, it should not come as a surprise that a central theme in progressive discourse and scholarship on racism is that one cannot be racist toward white people. Racism is not about bigotry. It is about "white" beliefs in such "ideologies" as individualism which keep intergroup power structures in place, elevating whites at the expense of people of color. Never mind any contrary evidence that may arise, such as a finding by Hartmann, Gerteis, and Croll that "[w]hites and minorities show a nearly identical enthusiasm for individual freedoms and a preference for conformity" and "also show similar skepticism of claims to group-based differences."[94]

In that paper, survey data are presented showing that nearly one hundred percent of both whites and nonwhites consider the "[i]mportance of Individual Freedoms in making America what it is" to be "very important" or "somewhat important." Moreover, a solid majority of both whites and nonwhites "strongly agree" or "somewhat agree" that "[i]t's a problem if people think of themselves mostly as members of groups rather than as individuals."[95] For social justice activists such as DiAngelo, it doesn't matter. Systemic racial inequality is synonymous with racism. As the progressive lexicon would have it, racism is structural —institutionalized, or reified, by social norms that inexorably recenter Whiteness and the white privilege to which it gives rise. If nonwhites assert a belief in individualism, it is a sign of internalized oppression that further reifies Whiteness.

The refrain admittedly seems intuitive when one considers the raw data showing deep and persistent inequalities between whites and people of color. Moreover, as a metaphor, the idea that Whiteness is the reason for ongoing racial inequality provides us with a vivid and compelling blueprint for how to frame and interpret purportedly oppressive social relations between white people and people of color.

However, as explained succinctly in one article, "reification is really just the use of metaphor," and "[t]hese metaphors become fallacies when they are taken too far and conclusions are formed on the basis of the metaphor." Of course, "[i]t can be very useful to employ metaphors and abstractions in what we write, but they carry a danger in that we can begin to believe, without realizing it, that our abstract entities have the concrete attributes we metaphorically ascribe to them."[96] In other words, we might find it useful to see institutions as "white" to the extent that white people historically have shaped and ruled over them, but we take it too far when we see these institutions themselves as living, breathing personifications of so-called Whiteness.

People may be repositories of ideology, but they are not stand-ins for ideology. Their lived experiences are complex and contingent, not one-dimensionally or even primarily shaped by notions of "racialization" conceived in the ivory tower. For example, Peggy McIntosh claims that one example of white privilege is that "[w]hen I am told about our national heritage or about 'civilization', I am shown that people of my color made it what it is."[97]

Putting aside questions about what exactly it means to say that people of a certain color made a national heritage, suppose a white male student in a history class argued that Howard Zinn's *People's History of the United States* should not be on the curriculum because it is bad history.[98]

A teacher might have a knee-jerk inclination to try to convince him that his objection is a symptom of white fragility. In other words, the objection to Zinn's retelling of American history stems from a "privileged" expectation that an account of history should reflect a narrative written by white oppressors rather than a narrative written from the perspective of the historically disenfranchised.[99] But maybe the classroom provocateur simply believes that Zinn's *People's History* is not good history.

He has no objection to books written from different perspectives as long as they are well-researched, rigorous, not prone to polemical agendas, and do not, as historian Michael Kazin writes, reduce the past to a Manichean fable.[100] In other words, he is open to different perspectives as long as they are objective, which, as Princeton historian Sean Wilentz notes, is not the same as neutral.[101]

The white male student may derive little or no comfort from the mere fact that white people "made" his national heritage or civilization. He is not "whitesplaining." He is simply saying that "white privilege" is a red herring when it comes to explaining why Zinn's *People's History* is bad history.

In another example, students at the University of Pennsylvania removed a large Shakespeare portrait from a staircase that students and faculty members in the English department walk by every day. They then "put up a photograph of Audre Lorde, the black feminist poet who died in 1992." The students "said the action reflects their interest in reading a more diverse range of voices than has been the case in the past, and sending a message that study of literature isn't just about the traditionally revered authors."[102]

Maybe the point was not to call into question the legitimacy of the literary canon, but the influence of Whiteness studies was apparent. Decentering the canon means decentering Whiteness. It's not about inclusion, but about reframing the narrative of Great Books as ideological universalism, which reflects how color-blind ideology reifies Whiteness as a literary norm.

This is unfortunate. One should be encouraged to read Audre Lorde. But it is not a display of white fragility or Whiteness to emphasize that "[t]raditionally revered authors" are revered because their works have stood the test of time, rather than merely having served the nefarious interests of European colonialism. Shakespeare's portrait on the wall does not center Whiteness. It simply represents his status as a great playwright.

Removing the portrait as a political act brings to mind DiAngelo's chilling admission that she denies "equal time to all narratives in our classrooms" in order "to correct the existing power imbalances by turning down the volume on dominant narratives."[103] DiAngelo (and her co-author Sensoy) thus "believe that restricting dominant narratives is actually more equalizing."[104] In short, the point of education is not to examine whether "dominant" narratives are right or wrong, but to resist "dominant" narratives as such because to do so facilitates the work of undoing inequality.

Of course, DiAngelo's unstated assumption is that she can singlehandedly identify when a narrative is dominant. In one paper, she challenges the idea of "respecting differences" in the context of "challenging the common guidelines of social justice education."[105] Unfortunately, this challenge itself cannot be challenged, even to point out how it ironically sabotages the elevation of alternative voices, including some that DiAngelo's followers would probably champion.

For example, what if we read the writings of Frederick Douglass or Toni Morrison as a political act of decentering Whiteness? *The Narrative of the Life of Frederick Douglass* may be about Douglass's ascendance from slavery to freedom, but Douglass's autobiography is not merely a polemical diary or political narrative. It is a work of literary genius that masterfully guides us through the intellectual maturation of a former slave in spite of the nearly insurmountable challenges of being a black man in a profoundly racist society.

Reading literature with the primary intent of decentering Whiteness relegates one's study of the human condition, and the brilliance of a mind like Douglass's that would shed light on it, to the domain of political polemics, a mere attempt to illuminate what is ultimately a logical fallacy—the reification of Whiteness.[106]

Similarly, to read Toni Morrison's novel Song of Solomon as a mere counternarrative in literary history is to diminish its aesthetic glory as a complex intra- and intergenerational family drama about an ambivalent character named Macon Dead III, who seeks to unravel the mysterious history of the fissures between members of his family, from whom he feels estranged. This all takes place in interplay with Jim Crow America rather than as a mere instrument to illustrate the injustices of Jim Crow America.[107]

The goal of inclusion should be deepening our understanding of the human condition, not fighting a contrived "reified" ideology of Whiteness. Universalism is not always and everywhere a reification of Whiteness. For modern progressives inspired by Whiteness studies, however, one can only arrive at the truth about white moral responsibility in our society by understanding Whiteness. When it comes to racism, nuances in the perspectives and experiences of individual white people can be understood primarily, or at least significantly, in terms of Whiteness.

But this turns the fallacy of reification into a fallacy of ambiguity. As the labor historian Eric Arsenen writes, "whiteness has become a blank screen onto which those who claim to analyze it can project their own meanings."[108] In other words, the situational intricacies of white people's lived experience, or reasonable objections one might raise after a critical reading of Howard Zinn's *People's History of the United States*, get sucked into the vacuum of an abstraction conceived in the ivory tower of progressive ideology.

In closing, we should ask: are we making too big a deal of all this? Why worry about unproven generalizations about white people when white people largely sit atop the institutional pillars of society?

Consider an article by Andrew Sullivan about the controversy that erupted over virulent antiwhite tweets by journalist Sarah Jeong, who claimed she posted them in response to "torrents of online hate."[109] Sullivan writes, "If you want to respond to trolls by trolling them, you respond to them directly. You don't post slurs about an entire race of people (the overwhelming majority of whom are not trolls) on an open-forum website like Twitter."[110] To do so assumes that all white people are complicit in the actions of the trolls who apparently provoked Jeong's slurs when they posted hateful comments on her Twitter profile. Indeed, most white people would recognize these comments as repugnant, immoral, and intolerable.

Progressives may dismiss the example of Jeong's tweets as extreme or unrepresentative. But we should keep them in mind when progressives generalize about white people, which they often do in the most absurd ways. For example, we can envisage students of Whiteness insinuating that a white person describing vicious trolling as repugnant is self-serving because it allows him to register moral integrity in a way that further reifies the taboo against any open discussion of the subliminal biases and habits that, in a world of Whiteness, make such explicit trolling possible and sustain white domination.[111]

CONFLATING RACISM WITH THE LEGACY OF RACISM

Whiteness scholars assert that we should not confuse racism with bigotry.[112] But this transformation in how we are supposed to understand racism illustrates one of the serious pitfalls of positing the reification of Whiteness. Instead of serving to alleviate racial tensions, the focus on reified Whiteness, and the diversity trainings motivated by this paradigm, may actually make things worse.[113]

Grievance studies[114] are an inevitable consequence of such tribalistic ramifications. In an essay on "[t]he Influence of Anti-Racist Scholarship-Activism on Evergreen College," Helen Pluckrose and James Lindsay note, "While surveys show a rapid decrease in racist attitudes throughout white populations in the US over the last few decades, diversity training, which seeks to make people more aware of racial issues, actually seems to make them worse."[115] Diversity trainings can instigate an "us versus them" mentality deeply rooted in our innate tribal instincts as human beings. Mandatory trainings exacerbate the divisiveness because people do not respond well to being told what to do.[116]

It may also be the case that training that highlights *racial* diversity makes things worse. Research by New York University neuroscientist Jay Van Bavel suggests that mixed-race team building reduces the importance of race for team members. People on the same teams tend to perceive each other as members of the same "in-group."[117] As neuroscience and leadership expert David Rock writes in *Psychology Today*, "Inclusion programs can make a start by creating teams whose members matter to one another because they're part of the same in-group, pursuing the same interests."[118]

This makes sense. DiAngelo states at the very beginning of her book that her work is unapologetically rooted in identity politics.[119] The study of race thus comes down to the study of tribal conflicts that arise from intersectional classifications,[120] obscuring the nuances and situational intricacies of lived experience in favor of a puritanical focus on the intersection of group-based characteristics of both white people and people of color. Racial group affiliation is the essential feature of one's existence whenever "social justice" activism turns its attention to racial oppression and marginalization.

For white people, identity politics means being challenged for invariably sharing in the privileges of dominance that Whiteness confers upon them. This is in spite of ambiguities inherent in the notion of white privilege that even proponents of white privilege analysis, such as philosopher Lawrence Blum, have conceded, and which we will explore in the final chapter of this book.

For people of color, identity politics means challenging a society in which they are perpetually unable to escape the nefarious pull of Whiteness. As Blackburn colorfully describes it, they "watch [their] bodies wrecked for the economic and sadistic benefit of whiteness [while their] screams are silenced through disbelief."[121] Unless Whiteness is decimated with the full and willing participation of white people themselves, racism will be with us until kingdom come, unless, of course, progressives find another way to reinvent and redefine racism, which, given all we have discussed, is not unlikely.

Power and privilege as a function of past racism matter.[122] But while power and privilege may be evidence of racism in the past, they are not necessarily evidence of racism in the present. We must distinguish between racism and the legacy of racism, and then focus on undoing the legacy of racism.

4

FLAWED METHODOLOGY

The theory of white fragility makes a lot of strong claims about racism and white complicity. Is there a strong and robust methodology by which it arrives at these claims? The answer is no.

To understand where the theory goes wrong, you first have to understand that proponents do not trust the standards we will use to judge the validity of its claims. These standards involve things like logic, hypothesis testing, and the principle of falsification. In short, the scientific method. This distrust of positivism and the scientific method helps explain the theory's dismissal of objectivity as an ideology, its heavy reliance on impressionistic observation and "discourse" analysis, and its neglect of the principle of falsification.

It is not that proponents completely dismiss the scientific method. Rather, they believe the scientific method is limited in its reach. It must, at the very least, be supplemented by things like "deconstruction," "discourse" analysis, and "critical theory."[1] The scientific method is not equipped to eradicate racism. To rely on science alone is to fall into complacency and reinforce white supremacy.

We will see, however, that in urging us to supplement the scientific method with the deconstructive, discursive, and critical approaches of social justice activism, proponents of white fragility theory undermine the theory's claims by not adhering to the robust standards of the scientific method. In urging us to supplement the scientific method, they end up having to ignore it because applying the scientific method reveals flaws in the theory that cannot be ignored.

CONFLATING OBJECTIVITY AND NEUTRALITY

The theory of white fragility is "unapologetically rooted in identity politics."[2] It also seeks the "decolonization" of modern universities. It rejects the "presumed neutrality" of the Western Enlightenment's ideas about knowledge, which privileges "particular forms of knowledge over others"—"written over oral, history over memory, rationalism over wisdom"—to the detriment of anyone who is not white.[3]

In short, the theory does not trust objective measurement. As Robin DiAngelo says in one interview, "[T]here is no objective, neutral reality."[4] But this view conflates objectivity and neutrality. Regardless of what one thinks about the possibility of neutrality, objectivity is something different. To insist on objectivity is to insist on the gathering of facts, data, and other evidence to support an argument, which can be tested in accordance with rigorous standards of measurement. If objectivity is impossible, so are measurement, debate, and consensus. That, in fact, seems to be the point.

The theory of white fragility contends that the "racialized" position of white people in American society rests on social, political, economic, and cultural dominance. Ensconced in privilege, white people exhibit white fragility when aroused by any challenge to their privilege. In white fragility, there is the root of implicit bias. Because of implicit bias, white people cannot possibly be objective.[5] To dismantle racism, it is necessary to dismantle the ideological foundations of society itself.

As we saw in chapter 2, the research on implicit bias gives us reason to doubt whether implicit bias is as fundamental to the preservation of racism as white fragility theory assumes. But for DiAngelo and her acolytes, implicit bias and its connection to "systemic" racism is a first principle. You cannot question it without being deemed racist. There is only one takeaway: you must commit to a tenacious and ongoing effort to dissect the implicit biases of people who hold the keys to power. Namely, white people.

In practice, white fragility theory is devoted to exposing endless examples of implicit bias and explaining how these implicit biases underlie and perpetuate the institutional construct of racism.

Putting all this aside for a moment, we can acknowledge that DiAngelo has extracted her thesis from a voluminous reading of the scholarship in her profession. She also bases her work on many years of clinical experience with intergroup and intragroup dialogues on racism in formal settings—focus groups, case studies, workshops, seminars, and talks. In these settings, she has served as a mediator, facilitator, or speaker.

In these settings, she has frequently encountered resistance and defensiveness from white people after confronting them on their racial biases. In her seminal paper, she describes this resistance as white fragility, a condition in which "even a minimum amount of racial stress becomes intolerable, triggering a range of defensive moves" such as an "outward display of emotions such as anger, fear, and guilt, and behaviors such as argumentation, silence, and leaving the stress-inducing situation."[6]

DiAngelo believes that white fragility stems from a misunderstanding of what racism is and how it works. Racism, according to DiAngelo, is inextricably tied to the powerful grip that white people have on the levers of institutional control. Their grip will remain ironclad until they learn to let go of their biases and allow proponents of white fragility theory to explain how everything they say and do is racist. White people must learn how Whiteness is a scaffold of socialization on which white supremacy survives, against the gravitational pull of social justice activists who seek to bring about its collapse.

At first glance, it all seems to make sense given the premise of implicit bias as well as data showing that racial inequality persists. It seems straightforward that conditioned prejudices reinforce social outcomes that benefit white people at the expense of people of color. Ending racism is not about eradicating overt prejudice, but about dismantling the unconscious biases of white people, who hold the cards and thus necessarily retard progress in the eradication of racial inequality. Relying on objective analysis is unhelpful because objectivity is not possible because of implicit bias.

WHY IS OBJECTIVITY DISTRUSTED?

Clear as the data are on socioeconomic outcomes, the hows and whys have long remained a contentious source of debate.[7] While proponents of white fragility theory may be inclined to attribute this contentiousness to white fragility or Whiteness, eminent black scholars such as Thomas Sowell, John McWhorter, Jason Riley, and Glenn Loury do not invariably toe the party line on the structural nature of racism.[8]

Moreover, the scholarship on racial inequalities is so vast as to make one skeptical that a consensus on cause and effect has ever been reached. In chapter 7, we will review a single paper by economists Steve Levitt and Roland G. Fryer Jr. that carefully examines a conspicuous uptrend in parents giving distinctively "black" names to black children since the Black Power movement of the late 1960s.[9]

We will see the restraint Levitt and Fryer show in interpreting their results, explaining caveats that limit their conclusions and avoiding sweeping generalizations about the role of "black" names in socioeconomic outcomes. In reviewing this paper, we see scholars conveying results that are insightful and suggestive, while indicating that more work must be done. In short, we will see scholars engaging in objective analysis: gathering facts, data, and other evidence in pursuit of an analysis, and then testing hypotheses about the data in accordance with rigorous standards of measurement.

In contrast, DiAngelo is sure that she has the answers, and is not shy about telling us what she believes has caused these outcomes and keeps them in place. She does call attention to alleged aspects of white racial illiteracy that may be worthy of study, but with an aura of ideological rectitude that converts her concerns not into hypotheses to be examined and tested, but into doctrines that must be inculcated.

In one paper, she describes a morning session in an "antiracist" work group as having "gone well" because the white trainer "finished an in-depth presentation on white privilege" and "the group listened attentively and no challenges were raised." Then a white woman raises objections to a black trainer's presentation on the impact of racism on people of color. The woman argues that an example the black trainer used to illustrate her point shortchanged the complexity of the topic.

The white trainer intervenes to point out why the white woman is being "racially problematic." When a black man comes to the defense of the white woman, a black woman in class accuses him of "acting on his internalized racial oppression by 'rescuing' the white woman."[10]

The class session spirals out of control.

Thus, when debate erupts, the session becomes "problematic," a view that stands in stark contrast to the usual presumption in talks and seminars that debate is a healthy indicator of interest in a topic. This is not unusual. DiAngelo's papers have consistently exposed her tendency for indoctrination over debate, arguing, for example, that:

- Relying on individual experience is a "move of whiteness" that protects white privilege.[11]
- Expressing a dissenting opinion "functions as a specific legitimization of existing relations of power."[12]
- "White silence" often "functions to maintain white power and privilege" if "it is not strategically enacted from an antiracist framework."[13]

This overall tendency reflects a distrust of objectivity that stems from the influence of philosophers such as Michel Foucault and Jacques Derrida.[14] While this is not the place for a deep dive into philosophy, the basic idea for DiAngelo is that knowledge is compromised by power. Power and knowledge are so connected that it is virtually, if not entirely, impossible to make an objective claim about what we know, because knowledge is never neutral. As noted previously, this view conflates objectivity and neutrality. It is also wrong. A basic overview of the philosophy will help illustrate.

In her book *Is Everyone Really Equal?*, DiAngelo invokes Foucault's panopticon to illustrate how "[p]ower in the context of understanding social justice refers to the ideological, technical, and discursive elements by which those in authority impose their ideas and interests on everyone." For example, she writes about how "[s]chools train students to conform to a set of self-disciplining measures by structuring students' time and handing out rewards and punishments such as grades, honors, tracked placements, detentions, and expulsions." The punch line: "While this seems normal to us, the organization of the school is *not neutral* [emphasis mine]." She runs through a litany of ways that the school regiments and monitors all aspects of student activity in ways that reflect the prevailing interests of the people in authority.[15]

The control that school authorities exert over students and their families—via what is studied, how students are evaluated, how students spend their day, parental involvement, and so on—affects "the degree to which families are included or marginalized within the system and the extent to which children can remain connected to their families and still succeed in conforming to the norms and requirements of the school."[16]

There is also the way "that power circulates . . . through the mechanisms of knowledge and how knowledge is constructed, validated, and taught."[17] According to DiAngelo, there are two kinds of knowledge that matter:

1. Knowledge about how the system works, which is necessary to have if families are to "help their children navigate the system, or to challenge it when it has treated their children unfairly"
2. Knowledge about how learning is regimented and how students are categorized, which "translates into [students'] sense of place in society; for example, as either those who *manage* others or those who are *managed* by others"

The upshot is "that school knowledge is not neutral."[18] Indeed, DiAngelo repeatedly emphasizes in her work that knowledge is not neutral. Unfortunately, she uses neutrality and objectivity interchangeably, conflating a basic difference that obscures the vital importance of objective inquiry. She does so to such an extent that school authority is made to appear almost arbitrary, as if the only point of education is to impose a ruling ideology on students and families, rather than to educate via the dissemination of knowledge and the cultivation of objective inquiry.

This mix up reflects a misreading of Foucault. Though Foucault wrote many works, one of his central concerns is the relationship between knowledge and power. In particular, he is concerned with "discourses" of power, or how language reflects and reinforces societal rules, assumptions, and ways of acquiring and disseminating knowledge, all of which flow chiefly from the dominant interests that employ the discourse. He is also concerned with the social, historical, and cultural conditions that make possible the kinds of claims we make about what we know. As he writes in *The Order of Things*, Foucault seeks "to reveal a positive unconscious of knowledge."[19]

In his works, he examines how these "discourses" historically have served the purposes of oppression and marginalization in areas such as law, medicine, and psychology.[20] In this sense, Foucault agrees with DiAngelo and social justice activists that knowledge is not neutral, and that the ways knowledge is deployed, if examined closely, usually reveals something about the interests of the people in authority who deploy them.

It is a misreading, however, to infer that Foucault argues knowledge is never objective. Foucault simply directs our attention to how power influences what is accepted as true, *whether or not it is actually true*. In other words, Foucault's concern is with how power influences what counts as standard methods for discovering truth.

He is concerned not so much with the truth of theories, but how theories come into being and how they oppress or marginalize. He seeks to reveal a "positive unconscious of knowledge: a level that eludes the consciousness of the scientist and yet is part of the scientific discourse, *instead of disputing its validity and seeking to diminish its scientific nature*."[21] His concern is with the social, political, and historical circumstances in which knowledge is pursued, not with making knowledge and morality relative. Practically and morally, he devotes much study to how these accepted methods create "discourses" of power.

It should not be controversial to say that knowledge can be exploited by dominant vested interests. But to say that knowledge is not neutral is not to say that it is not objective. Neutrality and objectivity are not the same thing.

Now to Derrida's "deconstruction." The basic idea is that meaning is elusive because the language we use to talk about the world is not centered on a body of absolute knowledge that can be apprehended with the "right" words that correspond to things in the world. When we talk about institutions of learning, we treat these institutions as centers of learning in which a fixed body of knowledge is accessible to anyone who wants to learn it. Deconstruction calls this into question by claiming that the meaning of words we use to talk about knowledge is constructed from how words differ from other words. But you can never fully grasp their meaning by simply reading a dictionary.

If you look up a word in a dictionary, you cannot learn the meaning of the word without making use of other words used to define the word. Every word always has a "trace" of another word. For example, you cannot think of *white* without having implicitly referred to *black*. Similarly, you cannot refer to *black* without implicitly referring to *white*. The political implication is that knowledge is always rooted in a perspective that can be traced to the ways that words are related to each other and furthermore, they are usually arranged in hierarchical relation to each other.

To say that someone is "underprivileged" is to also say that someone else is "privileged."[22] The interpretation of meaning is never-ending. In a political context, interpretation must always have an eye to the ways that language reinforces social hierarchies. Since language constantly reinforces hierarchies, and language is what is used to convey meaning whether in the form of an argument or otherwise, the use of language is always a matter of hierarchical, or biased, perspective.

In one paper, DiAngelo and her co-author David Allen write, "[c]ategories such as woman or African American are power and knowledge classifications that are already caught up in the practices being opposed by the radical traditions. Hence, *deconstructionists argue*, they cannot be used without reproducing at least some of the politics that produced them in the first place."[23] This is the political project of deconstruction: to penetrate hierarchies by picking apart the hierarchy, precisely in order to put the pieces together again as a way of uncovering their meaning, which is nonetheless always eluding our grasp because we must use words to articulate meaning, and words never stop depending on the "traces" of other words. The project of deconstruction never ends.

This passage invokes deconstruction, but it brings us back to Foucault in identifying "knowledge classifications" as "power classifications." Racial inequality stays in place because linguistic classifications reinforce relationships of domination and marginalization. DiAngelo thus argues that language is key to understanding the connection between Whiteness and racism. "Discourse" keeps "performing" in ways that "reify" Whiteness. In DiAngelo's study, people in class were *encouraged* to rely on experience "as a critical practice designed to undermine elite expertise," yet "in this study the discourse of personal experience functioned to protect . . . privileged whites."[24]

At least as far back as her PhD dissertation, DiAngelo has identified individualism and universalism as "two master discourses of Whiteness in practice."[25] Whiteness operates via the language used, however unwittingly, to internalize supremacy among whites and internalize coercion among people of color. Language that reinforces the "discourses" of individualism and universalism thereby underlies the norms and practices that define a society characterized by Whiteness—in other words, racism.

The patterns of racism are to be found in language, either by "deconstructing" the meaning of the words we use, or by investigating how linguistic norms and classifications are deployed in the service of dominant interests. We must be fanatics, never ceasing the interrogation of language (especially with *leading* questions that do not permit critique of the orthodox antiracist premises from which pedagogical investigations about social justice begin[26]). This is the key to undoing racial inequality.

It is a mistake, however, to believe that objectivity is impossible.

THE VITAL IMPORTANCE OF OBJECTIVITY

The claims of white fragility theory are extraordinary not simply because they are so sensational, but because they are so all-encompassing. They are rooted in a comprehensive rethinking of how we are supposed to understand not only the nature of racism and its connection to social outcomes, but the entirety of American society. But if we are to take these claims seriously, then natural questions to ask include:

1. What is the methodology?
2. How do theorists state and present their hypotheses?
3. What tests do they run?
4. What data do they collect?
5. What criteria do they use to evaluate and interpret their results?

In the previous section, we discussed discourse and deconstruction. But in the social sciences, the answer to these questions often involves the use of data and statistical analysis. Statistics provides techniques suited to the rigorous examination of data on a scale applicable to questions about systematic trends and patterns in society. Quantitative data analysis easily can be misleading if not done right, but it is usually unavoidable when trying to measure the accuracy and precision of general claims about patterns in the social, economic, political, and cultural dimensions of society.

Let's be clear that data do not give us definite answers. Data give us something to investigate. There are few more organized ways of examining data in a way that facilitates measurable inferences than statistics, which provides tools to develop quantitative measures of trends and patterns in social life.

DiAngelo makes sweeping generalizations about cultural and other dimensions of society without ever making use of sophisticated statistical analysis. She has published three books and several papers in peer-reviewed journals.[27] She has participated in multiple talks.[28] She has written articles for *Medium* and *The Good Men Project*.[29] But in all her work, there is a complete absence of statistical analysis that quantitatively measures how white fragility contributes to institutional racism, or more generally, the many factors (aside from racism) that may cause racial inequality.

In fairness, in defining *racism* in chapter 7 of her book *What Does It Mean to Be White?* as a "form of oppression in which one racial group dominates others," she cites data on racial discrepancies in health care, wealth and representation in the criminal justice system.[30] In chapter 2 of her book *White Fragility*, she cites data on the demographic composition of Congress, governors, college professors and teachers. In defining racism as a social construct, she cites data on racial discrepancies to prove her point.[31]

Nowhere in her work, however, does one find a study in which she employs statistical techniques to examine a well-defined model of the relationship between disparities in outcomes and a specific measure of white fragility—or other factors—that can be tested for accuracy and precision. In fact, she implicitly dismisses statistical analysis altogether when discussing "aversive racism," an example of which she describes as "attributing inequality between whites and people of color to causes other than racism."[32]

In *What Does It Mean to Be White?*, DiAngelo does cite seemingly more rigorous studies to draw a correlation between "white flight" and white aversion to racial diversity in their neighborhoods. For example, she cites "attitude surveys" that purportedly show "most whites say they would prefer neighborhoods that are no more than 30% black." But as is typical, she treats studies that support her view as decisive. She writes that "[s]tudies of actual mobility patterns not only confirm these preferences, but show that whites downplay them," and concludes that "[w]hite flight is the primary reason that racial integration has not been achieved; the majority of whites, in both the expression of their beliefs and the practice of their lives, do not want to integrate with blacks."[33]

Should we take DiAngelo at her word? Not necessarily. Correlation is not causation, as we will see in chapter 7. More importantly, there may be other factors at work besides white aversion to racial diversity in their neighborhoods. For example, DiAngelo cites a paper by Northwestern University sociologist Lincoln Quillian to support her claim about white flight.[34] This paper does indeed "suggest that White avoidance of predominately Black and racially mixed neighborhoods is a very important process upholding segregation."[35] Note, however, that it says white avoidance "is a very important process," which is not the same thing as saying it is *the only, or primary, process* that explains racial segregation.

Indeed, another study notes that "[t]he causes of persistent patterns of racial residential segregation have been hotly debated for decades, with the focus traditionally on three factors: economics, preferences, and discrimination."[36] More recently, a careful quantitative study by Princeton economist Leah Boustan establishes a link between black migration and white flight, finding that each black arrival during the black migration of mid-twentieth-century America was associated with 2.7 white people leaving for the suburbs. While the paper quantifies "the relationship between black arrivals and white departures from postwar cities," it is more cautious in drawing inferences "about the mechanisms by which racial diversity affected the demand for urban residence."[37]

One the one hand, "[s]ome white residents were undoubtedly concerned about the changing racial and socio-economic composition of their immediate neighborhoods." On the other hand, "many others [who left] lived in all-white enclaves far from burgeoning black ghettos. These residents may have been motivated by changes in local policy accompanying a shift in the racial and socioeconomic composition of the urban electorate." Boustan writes that public school desegregation "in the 1960s and 1970s provided another reason to leave the city," but goes only so far as to say that "[e]xploring these mechanisms offers a promising direction for future research."[38]

Summing up her research in an article for the *New York Times* in 2017, Boustan writes that white flight was motivated by both racial and economic considerations:

> For the third of white households near a black enclave in 1940, concerns about new black neighbors was indeed a primary motivation. And those households moved out of the city at a higher rate than others, contributing more than a third to the white exodus. But for the remainder of urban whites, most of whom never interacted with a black family, leaving for the resource-rich suburbs was an economic calculus, one that was accelerated by the steady stream of poor migrants, both white and black, into central cities.[39]

In contrast, DiAngelo simply infers systemic oppression from data on racial disparities. That is the end of the story. No more questions asked. As she states in *What Does It Mean to Be White?*, "In the United States the dominant group is white, therefore racism is white racial and cultural prejudice and discrimination, supported intentionally or unintentionally by institutional power and authority, and used to the advantage of whites and the disadvantage of people of color."[40] But as students of the implicit bias paradigm have come to learn (see chapter 2), saying there is a link is not the same as proving it. To put it terms of statistical "discourse," DiAngelo seems unmindful of the notion of "spurious correlation"—in other words, that correlation often does not mean causation.

For anyone interested in sustained, rigorous, statistical hypothesis testing, her structuralist leaps are not obvious. They are hypotheses, not foregone conclusions. Unfortunately, one finds not one example in her work of rigorous, statistical hypothesis testing that might stand the test of time. In fact, as one can glean from a reading of her PhD dissertation (a rich source of insight into her future research), her central focus on "discourse analysis" pushes aside falsification as a criterion for judging the validity of results. Instead, her analytical approach emphasizes intricate interpretations of the social, institutional, and political dimensions of language that confirm all the basic tenets of the Whiteness paradigm.[41] We saw examples in the previous section.

The absence of statistical analysis in DiAngelo's work is also astonishing considering how she responds to an objection she frequently encounters in interactions with white people: that she is prone to generalization. She argues that this objection reflects the pervasive ideology of individualism in America. This belief is an obstacle to understanding racism because it cultivates the perception that the contingencies and vicissitudes of experience for each individual are sufficiently unique to make one immune to racialized conditioning. Given their belief in the singularity of experience, white people refuse to believe that they can be pigeon-holed as racists who reinforce white supremacy because they are complacent about a status quo characterized by racial privilege.

She relegates this objection to ideology and explains it away as white fragility. But in her book, *White Fragility*, she writes: "As a sociologist, I am quite comfortable generalizing; social life is patterned and predictable in measurable ways."[42] There is, of course, a jarring insouciance in this claim, given that social scientists are typically not "comfortable" with generalizations. Social life has observable patterns that can be detected using techniques conducive to measurable predictions. These patterns, however, are hard to capture and must be interpreted with great care.

In her PhD dissertation, DiAngelo seems to acknowledge this difficulty when she writes, "Campbell and Stanley (1963) recognize that generalizability is never completely answerable and accept the truism that generalization is never fully justified logically." But her focus is on "discourse analysis," whereby confirmation of the Whiteness paradigm, rather than falsification of testable claims about Whiteness, is the fundamental criterion for judging the validity of general claims about racial inequality.

Indeed, in her dissertation she "supported the generalizability of [her] study by using the considerable literature on what constitutes White privilege across a range of settings." To her credit, she "used that literature to develop a set of coding criteria" and "had others review these criteria" while remaining "open to emergent strategies that [she] had not included in [her] coding."[43]

Nonetheless, "starting with the Whiteness literature, and moving into a discourse analysis of a specific example, [she] tied the results of [her] study to the larger body of research on how Whiteness functions discursively." DiAngelo faithfully adheres to the idea that "Whiteness is a discourse that is structurally, not individually, produced." Indeed, her "primary measure of generalizability was [her] ability to tie the discourses documented in this study to the larger body of research in the Whiteness literature."[44]

There are merits to this approach. Unfortunately, DiAngelo has made poor use of them in the development of her theory about white people. For the theory of white fragility, a general claim about Whiteness or white fragility is valid only when it confirms and reinforces the Whiteness framework for understanding and explaining racial inequality. As she writes in her seminal paper on white fragility: "Whiteness Studies begin with the premise that racism and white privilege exist in both traditional and modern forms, and rather than work to prove its existence, work to reveal it."[45]

DiAngelo has spent her career collecting innumerable anecdotes that supposedly reveal privilege and fragility. If a white person "objects" that any given anecdote demonstrates what she claims it demonstrates, she dismisses the person as exhibiting white fragility. No need to test a hypothesis, because it's about revelation, not proof. If pressed, she would say that "generalizability functions differently within discourse analysis than in research methodologies that assume correspondence with an external reality as the primary standard."[46] As she writes in her dissertation:

> Generalizability is not constituted in discourse analysis by arguing that an analysis reflects reality and therefore can be generalized. Discourse analysts recognize that humans construct their social reality, although this construction interacts with and is constrained by physical reality. Discourse analysts also recognize that language is

> related to the situations that provide it with meaning. Similarly, discourse analysis is about the exploration of the interaction of "language-plus-situation." These points about language and meaning do not imply that discourse analysis is subjective or simply a function of opinion. Generalizability is important in discourse analysis. However, generalizability functions differently within discourse analysis than in research methodologies that assume correspondence with an external reality as the primary standard.[47]

Note the use of the word "constituted" as well as the phrase "humans construct their social reality." These are code words for a tradition of postmodern (and poststructuralist) ideas that express a radical skepticism about the possibility of objective truth.[48] For the original postmodern thinkers, as well as their twenty-first century descendants who apply "critical theory" to various academic disciplines closely tied to "social justice" activism, knowledge is inseparable from, and inevitably compromised by, power relations between dominant and marginalized groups.

For Whiteness scholars and proponents of white fragility theory, who are heavily invested in the postmodern and poststructuralist ideas we briefly reviewed in the previous section, racial inequality stays in place because linguistic practices reinforce relationships of domination and marginalization. Ironically, however, white fragility theory has given rise to the same kind of power relations between "social justice" crusaders who seek to indoctrinate people with the principles of white fragility theory and anyone who argues that the principles are flawed.

In other words, "knowledge classifications" about Whiteness, privilege, fragility, and racial inequality have become "power classifications." Foucault's "positive unconscious of knowledge" consists of the premises of Whiteness studies that cannot be questioned and are taken wholly for granted by proponents of white fragility theory, many if not most of whom are in positions of power in the academic, media, political, corporate, and other institutions that seek to instill principles of "social justice" activism. DiAngelo ironically undermines her application of Foucault's ideas about power and knowledge classifications by implicitly insisting on the general and universal applicability of the Whiteness paradigm, unwittingly proving Foucault's point at her own expense.

We can now see why objective analysis is crucial. Given the biases of researchers who seek to confirm how the discourse paradigm of Whiteness studies explains racial inequality, it is imperative that we have objective standards by which claims about racial inequality can be tested. Moreover, given the organic and dynamic nature of social forces, these forces can rarely be measured or predicted with great accuracy and precision. Measurement is a delicate matter in scientific research. It gives rise to much disagreement. What questions should be asked? How should results be interpreted?

If one is inclined to generalize about social patterns, especially when dealing with issues as broad, complex, and controversial as racism and structural inequalities, the effort usually requires an extraordinary effort at data collection and analysis. Otherwise, it is nearly impossible to decipher whether one hypothesis or interpretation about societal patterns is more or less correct, unless one is content to defer to the knowledge (power) classifications of Whiteness studies and white fragility theory.

WHAT IS OBJECTIVE MEASUREMENT?

As someone who has spent decades in the field of multicultural education, DiAngelo calls for humility in our thinking about race and racism. She does not excuse herself from the ignorance that all white people have on matters of race and racism. She also claims in many of her talks that if you haven't spent many years studying and struggling with the problems of race and racism, then your opinions are necessarily very limited and uninformed.[49] In her book *White Fragility*, she reiterates the same point: "We must be willing to consider that unless we have devoted intentional and ongoing study, our opinions (on racism) are necessarily uninformed, even ignorant."[50]

This statement is obvious, but fair enough. It does, however, ignore the possibility that one can come to the wrong conclusions even after devoting many years of one's life to the study of a topic. DiAngelo's statement also draws attention to a fundamental concern about how she claims to know what she claims to know. If there is a starting point for social science research, it is an appeal for caution about the inferences one can draw about whole populations. In short, one should be wary of generalization. That does not mean we should consider ourselves impossibly handicapped by the depth, breadth, and complexity of a topic. But it does mean that methodological rigor, coupled with caution, is imperative.

Social science methodology can be divided into qualitative and quantitative techniques. On the quantitative side, statistics is widely used to measure central tendency and dispersion in a sample population. Given samples of data for variables such as income, demographics, educational attainment and homeownership, statistical analysis involves the formulation of hypotheses about relationships between variables and provides a set of tools to rigorously measure the relationship between a dependent variable and an independent variable or set of independent variables. Finally, statistics provides a set of criteria by which to test the significance of these relationships.

These criteria are not a highway to truth. Instead, they provide a framework for data analysis that allows us to go beyond the realm of impressions and intuition derived from direct experience. This is of utmost importance when studying the prevalence of racism and alleged "white fragility" in the entire white population of the United States. Regardless, without statistics, DiAngelo claims to have observed consistent, frequent, and general patterns in her work. She draws on these patterns to develop a litany of examples, which allegedly demonstrate the racialized experience of white people; its relevance to racial inequality; and how it instills, influences, and sustains white supremacy.

In failing to make use of quantitative techniques that are customized for generalizing about populations, DiAngelo falls short of her claim to humility by failing to formulate her claims as testable, falsifiable hypotheses. When Karl Popper identified the concept of falsification as a foundational pillar of sound scientific inquiry, he was demarcating science from pseudoscience. As explained in the *Stanford Encyclopedia of Philosophy*:

> The dominance of the critical spirit in Einstein, and its total absence in Marx, Freud and Adler, struck Popper as being of fundamental importance: the pioneers of psychoanalysis, he came to think, couched their theories in terms which made them amenable only to confirmation, while Einstein's theory, crucially, had testable implications which, if false, would have falsified the theory itself.[51]

Similarly, the theory of white fragility is couched entirely in terms amenable to its confirmation rather than its falsifiability. This is reflected most starkly in the discovery that there is not one example in her research of rigorous hypothesis testing using statistical techniques. It also comes across blatantly in its practical application because, as DiAngelo writes, and as is repeatedly evidenced in her work, "Whiteness Studies begin with the premise that racism and white privilege exist in both traditional and modern forms, and rather than work to prove its existence, work to reveal it."[52]

White fragility theory is about revelation, not proof—confirmation, not falsification. The claims of white fragility theory are based exclusively on qualitative assessments of the linguistic practices of white people interacting with people of color in group settings. Objections are invariably explained away as examples of white fragility. Analyses and interpretations are treated as nonfalsifiable, subject to "critique" only in relation to how well they confirm the basic tenets of Whiteness studies.

It is not that qualitative research is necessarily always inferior, or that there is something wholly wrong with DiAngelo relying on intuition from her years of experience in multicultural education. Moreover, qualitative research techniques are regularly employed in social science research. But it is hard to take seriously any research that consistently and frequently makes comprehensive claims about patterns in social life, without ever once having made competent use of hypothesis testing to conduct an analysis of data that are relevant to a claim about patterns in social life.

One main concern is that qualitative research is usually limited to small sample sizes. Results are necessarily and unavoidably related to the context in which the study is undertaken, while interpretation of results is often unduly influenced by political and other biases that the researcher brings to the table. While researchers can glean useful insights from the variety of perspectives offered by participants in focus groups, workshops, and intragroup dialogues, it is rare if not impossible for researchers to draw inferences about systemic patterns in society from small sample studies that are inherently susceptible to sampling bias, self-selection bias and the Hawthorne effect (i.e., the bias that results from participants in a study being aware that they are being observed).[53]

Brainstorming is one thing. Systematic data collection and hypothesis testing is quite another.

DiAngelo does not formulate her claims into hypotheses that can be tested using statistical techniques. DiAngelo's theory of white fragility is presented as nonfalsifiable. As such, it cannot be distinguished from pseudoscience. DiAngelo offers us no way of evaluating whether she commits a type 1 or type 2 error when she makes one of her innumerable assertions about how the reactions of white people, when confronted with their alleged racialization and privilege, exhibit white fragility.

A type 1 error is a *false positive*. For example, let's say DiAngelo observes a white person drawing on personal experience in intergroup dialogues on racism. She then claims that the white person thereby invalidates the views of people of color about the damaging effects of racism.

Is she right? Maybe in this case, but maybe not in other cases. The question then becomes, is she right on average? In order to answer, we form two hypotheses:

1. The "null" hypothesis: on average, a white person drawing on personal experience *does not* invalidate the views of people of color about the effects of racism.

2. DiAngelo's hypothesis: on average, a white person drawing on personal experience invalidates the views of people of color about the effects of racism.

The statistical, systematic approach is to then develop a model that attempts to predict whether a white person bringing personal experience into the conversation invalidates the views of people of color about the effects of racism.

This would involve a careful effort to figure out a way to measure "invalidation." Then one could develop a "dummy variable" that captures whether a white person does or does not draw on personal experience. Then one could develop another "dummy variable" that captures whether or not "invalidation" occurs, perhaps by administering a survey with appropriately worded questions (note the emphasis on language) about whether a person of color feels that her views about the effects of racism are invalidated when a white person invokes personal experience. The data could then be used to test a model that formalizes the hypothesis about whether white people relying on personal experience invalidate the views of people of color when it comes to the effects of racism.

Without getting into further details, if a study like this could be conducted (and it would be difficult), we could get some idea about whether DiAngelo is right on average. Let's say she is not. Then her claim that a white person invalidates the person of color's views in a given situation, and that this situation is common, is a *false positive* (type 1 error). That is, even if she is right in one case, she is not right on average. On the other side of the coin, a type 2 error is a false negative, claiming that white people do *not* invalidate the views of people of color when, in fact, they do.

In one interview, DiAngelo states, "[h]uman objectivity is not actually possible, but as long as we construct the world as if it is, and then ascribe it only to ourselves, we keep White experience and people centered and people of color in the margins."[54] Unfortunately, DiAngelo confuses objectivity with neutrality. But if objectivity is impossible, so is measurement. One cannot measure social outcomes in a way that achieves consensus. Truth becomes relative. Battles over ideas become battles over power.

DiAngelo might agree that truth comes down to power, but if so, her theory collapses. If objectivity is impossible, she cannot measure social patterns in a way that can achieve consensus. She writes in her seminal paper on white fragility, "Whiteness Studies begin with the premise that racism and white privilege exist in both traditional and modern forms, and rather than work to prove its existence, work to reveal it."[55] She thus goes about collecting innumerable anecdotes that supposedly reveal privilege and fragility. If a white person "objects" to any of it, she accuses the person of white fragility. No need to test a hypothesis, because it's all about revelation, not proof.

5

EXPLOITING NARRATIVES AT THE EXPENSE OF FACTS

The last chapter addressed the methodological flaws that plague the theory of white fragility. In this chapter, we examine three examples used by Robin DiAngelo to illustrate alleged white racial illiteracy. In doing so, we observe practically how the theory of white fragility goes awry as a result of flawed methodology. In general, the theory adapts facts to its narratives rather its narratives to facts.

WHAT CAN A *JEOPARDY!* EPISODE TELL US ABOUT WHITE RACIAL ILLITERACY?

In a public talk broadcast on C-SPAN on June 30, 2018, DiAngelo presented a snapshot of a *Jeopardy!* episode. The snapshot shows a board with all questions answered except for questions under the category "African-American History." DiAngelo sighs while the audience laughs. We are supposed to be disheartened, if not shocked, that three contestants in a College Championship tournament answered every question on the board before answering any questions about "African-American History."

These questions, DiAngelo asserts, were "clearly the hardest and nobody wanted to lose." Saying she cannot "do justice to the profundity of that disconnect," she concludes, "If we do not know our history, and we cannot trace it into the present, we are left confronted with the most problematic explanations for current conditions."

"There's a lot that's going on with that category," she adds, "because the first thing is you know what's behind the category, right? Civil War and Civil Rights, because that's their [DiAngelo's emphasis] history." She then corrects this answer, saying: "No, that's the history of this country. That's the foundation." The punch line: "You cannot understand US history and separate that out. It didn't happen in a vacuum."[1]

DiAngelo assumes these are the hardest questions on the board and concludes that white people do not know their history.

Is she right?

She provides us with no way of knowing. She does not indicate if she has consulted experts on the ranking of *Jeopardy!* questions in terms of difficulty. More fundamentally, her conclusion is based on one observation, and we are to accept it as such. No questions asked. This is a recipe for what psychologists call *confirmation bias*. According to an article in *Psychology Today*, Dr. Shahram Heshmat defines *confirmation bias* as the tendency to believe what you want to believe. Before accepting a claim, he writes, we should look for "evidence that contradicts our beliefs."[2] Otherwise, we might unwittingly accept a claim as true when it is not, a result that statisticians call a "false positive."

Statistics provides us with a disciplined way to search for contradictory evidence. As explained in the previous chapter, statistics is crucial *not because it is a Holy Grail of truth*, but because it provides techniques that allow us to test whether an observation is likely a "false positive" (belief that something is true when it is false) or "false negative" (belief that something is false when it is true).

This is not to deny that statistical analysis is fraught with perils. But the use of quantitative techniques is not about giving us certainty. It's about *forcing us to be wary of being certain*. Statistical tools are a disciplined way to measure the accuracy and precision of broad generalizations about society. They give us a way to study data in a way that facilitates clear and measurable inferences. We are forced to be clear about what we say, and to say it in a way that allows others to question whether it is correct or not correct according to robust standards. Statistics is, or at least should be, about being humble.

Take DiAngelo's inference about white racial illiteracy. On the basis of one observation, she makes a sweeping generalization about white racial illiteracy. As we will see in chapter 8, this is all in keeping with her broad focus on proselytization rather than scholarship. Like evangelicals engaged in sermonizing, DiAngelo is more interested in her rhetorical message than the precise accuracy of her factual claims. In sum, she adapts facts to her narrative rather than her narrative to the facts.

DiAngelo does not consider whether repeated samples of three college contestants appearing on multiple episodes would show the same result. She does not develop a model that attempts to predict whether white students in multiple College Championship tournaments would consistently fail to answer questions on African American history. But for the sake of argument, let's say we would observe the same result.

She then concludes: *If we do not know our history, and cannot trace it into the present, we are left with the most problematic explanations for current conditions.*

This statement could imply several things. Here are three:

1. The failure of three students, in one *Jeopardy!* episode, to take questions on African American history until the end means that *all white people* are ignorant about African American history.
2. The failure of three students in a College Championship episode to take questions on African American history until the end means that all *elite college students* do not know about African American history.
3. The students decided to prioritize other categories not because they do not know African American history, but because they were not interested in it.

On (3), maybe *these particular* students knew more about the other topics on the board *that day*. Assuming DiAngelo is referring to the 2014 contest, these topics included International Cinema Showcase,

Weather Verbs, and Kiwi Fauna.[3] DiAngelo does not ask what would happen if there were other categories on the board, or if *other* contestants would have waited until the end to answer questions on African American history. In short, she does not consider whether this was an unusual outcome.

On (1) and (2), DiAngelo invokes this one episode as an example of white ignorance of history. Statistically speaking, she has:

1. Posed a question: do "we" know our history?
2. Drawn a sample: three contestants on one *Jeopardy!* episode.
3. Observed a result: the contestants cleared the board before answering questions on African American history.
4. Drawn a conclusion: "we" do not know our history.

What's wrong with this reasoning?

First, the question is not well-stated. What does it mean to "know our history"? What areas of African American history? What facts? What narratives and interpretations? Who? What events?

Second, DiAngelo seems sure the questions will be about "Civil War and Civil Rights, because that's their history." How does she know this? If we are talking about the *Jeopardy!* board in her presentation, she does not. The episode occurred in 2014, which had clues on Martin Luther King Jr., the Apollo Theater, and Phillis Wheatley, which the contestants answered correctly, and the Scottsboro Boys and the 1st Rhode Island Regiment, which the contestants answered incorrectly.[4] That's only one question on "Civil War and Civil Rights" (Martin Luther King, Jr.). Third, the contestants got three out of five of the questions *right*. Clearly, it is *not* the case that they didn't know their history.

Fourth, DiAngelo does not consider whether the contestants assumed the questions would not be about the Civil War and Civil Rights. For example, it may have occurred to them that questions about the Civil War and Civil Rights were too obvious because they would be too easy. If so, they would have been right. Only one of the questions refers directly to either the Civil War or Civil Rights.

One question was on Phillis Wheatley, a famous eighteenth-century African American poet widely praised by her contemporaries[5]; another was on the Apollo Theater, which opened in 1914 and "has played a major role in the emergence of jazz, swing, bebop, R&B, gospel, blues, and soul"[6]; another was on the Scottsboro Boys, nine black teenagers falsely accused of raping two white women near Scottsboro, Alabama, in 1931[7]; and a fourth was the 1st Rhode Island Regiment, "a Continental Army regiment during the American Revolutionary War" that "became known as the 'Black Regiment' due to its allowing the recruitment of African Americans in 1778."[8]

Let's focus on the fundamental problem. DiAngelo says "we" do not know our history based on one sample with three contestants. In any statistical study, it is not sufficient to draw general inferences from a sample of three observations. Moreover, it is not clear that the sample of three contestants is drawn randomly. Thus, the possibility of self-selection bias arises. It may be that only certain kinds of ambitious students are motivated to follow through on the process of applying to be a contestant, thus skewing results in favor of elite students who want to compete on *Jeopardy!*

Presumably, DiAngelo is interested in the *Jeopardy!* episode because only "our best and our brightest"[9] compete, and thus, if *they* do not know their African American history, then the rest of us surely do not. But this assumes the three contestants on this specific episode are representative of elite college students, which may or may not be true. Even if true, it does not necessarily follow that "nonelite" students are less informed about African American history. It could, in fact, be the opposite.

In the *Jeopardy!* example, DiAngelo has posed an ambiguous question—Do we know our history?—and given us an answer based on a sample of three elite students, who may not be representative of either elite college students or white people in general, and who may *not* have waited until the end to answer questions on African American history if the board had categories *other than* International Cinema Showcase, Weather Verbs, and Kiwi Fauna. But even if they were representative, and granting that they waited until the end, it remains the case that they got three out of five questions right.

In short, it is not at all clear what we can say about one outcome on a *Jeopardy!* episode at a specific date and time, with three specific contestants, with a specific set of questions in addition to the questions on African American history. It is, in fact, recklessly irresponsible to draw sweeping generalizations about institutional racism or white racial illiteracy based on the observation of one outcome on one *Jeopardy!* episode.

The analysis I have presented might seem tedious. But it is necessary to show how and why the theory of white fragility suffers from the pitfalls of avoiding disciplined statistical analysis. The theory does not allow for falsification. If it did, her view that one *Jeopardy!* episode illustrates white racial illiteracy likely may well be falsified.

THE JACKIE ROBINSON STORY

In her C-SPAN talk, DiAngelo also uses the narrative that Jackie Robinson "broke the color line" to explain how we understand this narrative to mean that Jackie Robinson was exceptional. Robinson was an "exception to his group," she says. "Subtext," she continues, "his group is inferior." Her own subtext, which she proceeds to make explicit, is that all white people imbibe the following narrative when they hear this story: "Finally, one of them had what it took to break through and to play with us." As a result, she argues, white people infer that racism ended in sports on that day.[10]

Unfortunately, DiAngelo frames the Jackie Robinson narrative in way that disingenuously makes a general claim about white racial illiteracy by vastly oversimplifying history, ignoring crucial facts, and distorting our understanding of alleged white racial illiteracy. In her book *White Fragility*, she writes:

> The story of Jackie Robinson is a classic example of how whiteness obscures racism by rendering whites, white privilege, and racist insti-

> tutions invisible. Robinson is often celebrated as the first African American to break the color line and play in major-league baseball. While Robinson was certainly an amazing baseball player, this story line depicts him as racially special, a black man who broke the color line himself. The subtext is that Robinson finally had what it took to play with whites, as if no black athlete before him was strong enough to compete at that level. Imagine if instead, the story went something like this: "Jackie Robinson, the first black man whites allowed to play major league baseball." This version makes a critical distinction because no matter how fantastic a player Robinson was, he simply could not play in the major leagues if whites—who controlled the institution—did not allow it. Were he to walk onto the field before being granted permission by white owners and policy makers, the police would have removed him.[11]

She says exactly the same thing in her book *What Does It Mean to Be White?*[12] Unfortunately, DiAngelo's discussion of the Jackie Robinson story is all framing and no substance.

First, Robinson was not, in fact, the only exceptional black player at the time of his entry into the major leagues. DiAngelo argues that the subtext underlying the narrative that Jackie Robinson broke the color line in Major League Baseball is that "no black athlete before him was strong enough to compete at that level."[13] She ignores that Robinson was competing with Satchel Paige and Josh Gibson, whom many considered better than Robinson, to be the first black player to play Major League Baseball.[14]

She also neglects to mention that dozens of black players immediately followed Robinson. By 1952, only five years after Robinson entered the Major Leagues, there were 150 black players in the major leagues,[15] including such baseball greats as Roy Campanella and Willie Mays.

Second, Robinson was exceptional not simply because of his ball-playing ability, but because of his courageous adherence to an informal agreement with Brooklyn Dodgers owner Branch Rickey "not to fight back" when confronted with the barbarous cruelties expected to be encountered from racist crowds, umpires, and other ballplayers. Robinson biographer Arnold Ramperstead writes:

> Rickey made it clear that Jack's ability to run, throw, and hit was only one part of the challenge. Could he stand up to the physical, verbal, and psychological abuse that was bound to come? "I know you're a good ball player," Rickey barked. "What I don't know is whether you have the guts."
>
> Jack started to answer hotly, in defense of his manhood, when Rickey explained, "I'm looking for a ball player with the guts enough not to fight back."
>
> Caught up now in the drama, Rickey stripped off his coat and enacted out a variety of parts that portrayed examples of an offended Jim Crow. Now he was a white hotel clerk rudely refusing Jack accommodations; now a supercilious white waiter in a restaurant; now a brutish railroad conductor. He became a foul-mouthed opponent, Jack recalled, talking about "my race, my parents, in language that was almost unendurable." Now he was a vengeful base runner, vindictive spikes flashing in the sun, sliding into Jack's black flesh—"How do you like that, n***** boy?" At one point, he swung his pudgy fist at Jack's head. Above all, he insisted, Jack could not strike back. He could not explode in righteous indignation; only then would this experiment be likely to succeed, and other black men would follow in Robinson's footsteps to make a living reality of Rickey's unspoken promise to Charlie Thomas forty-one years before.[16]

The promise to Charlie Thomas was based on an incident Rickey had witnessed in South Bend, Indiana, in 1904. As coach of the Ohio Wesleyan baseball team playing a game against Notre Dame, he had vehemently protested a hotel manager's attempt to prevent the lone black team member, Charles Thomas, from staying at the team's hotel. Eventually, Thomas was allowed to stay in Rickey's room. When Rickey arrived at his room, he found Thomas "trying to peel the flesh from his hands," crying, "Damned skin . . . damned skin!" he muttered. "If I could only rub it off." Haunted by the scene, Rickey "vowed that I would always do whatever I could to see that other Americans did not have to face the bitter humiliation that was heaped upon Charles Thomas."[17]

Rickey could not do it on his own. He knew what he was up against. Almost a century after Abraham Lincoln led the nation to victory in the Civil War and the end of slavery, racism was still viciously endemic in American society, as illustrated by the saga of Charles Thomas. Rickey knew he needed not just a ballplayer, but a man who could endure the abuse that would surely be hurled at him by a society that had seen the end of slavery but had not, by any means, seen the end of racism.

As expected, despite the support of Montreal crowds (when Robinson was in the minor leagues), and black crowds elsewhere:

> Opposing pitchers threw repeatedly at his head; several base runners, according to Al Campanis and others, aimed their spikes at his flesh whenever they could. To the press, Jack offered hardly a murmur of complaint, but the Royals' general manager, Mel Jones, knew differently. "He came into the office more than once," Jones later revealed, "and he'd say, 'Nobody knows what I'm going through.'" At year's end one Montreal journalist looked back: "Because of his dark pigmentation Robbie could never protest. If there was a rhubarb on the field . . . he had to stay out of it. Otherwise there might have been a riot."[18]

When it came time for Robinson to be promoted to the major leagues and join the Dodgers, it did not get easier:

> Carefully, Jack followed Rickey's plan, as he told a reporter: "I guess Mr. Rickey wants to see if last season was just lucky for me, which I don't blame him." Rickey, if not Robinson, was aware of the deep opposition to Jack's promotion among the single most important group in baseball—*the team owners, who in a secret ballot had voted fifteen to one (with Rickey alone dissenting) against integration* [emphasis mine].[19]

To be fair, DiAngelo's broader aim is to reframe the narrative in order to emphasize that white people had to approve his entry in the first place. She certainly illuminates the valid, though obvious, point that white people were the gatekeepers of mainstream professional baseball. But she also conceals that "the team owners . . . in a secret ballot had voted fifteen to one (with Rickey alone dissenting) against integration."

She also conceals the appalling and relentless racial adversity Robinson overcame throughout his life in high school, college, the Army, and professional baseball. Branch Rickey, who recruited him, expected the worst from fans and opposing players, which is why he told Robinson that he was looking for a man who "had guts enough not to fight back." Robinson followed the advice "with remarkable restraint . . . [a]midst racial slurs, objects thrown at him from the crowd and even death threats."[20] The story did *not* go, as DiAngelo frames it, "something like this: 'Jackie Robinson, the first black man whites allowed to play major-league baseball.'"[21]

It is obviously true that "no matter how fantastic a player Robinson was, *he simply could not play in the major leagues if whites—who control all of the institutions—did not allow it*," because "[w]ere he to walk onto the field prior to being granted permission by white owners and policy makers, the police would have removed him."[22] DiAngelo, however, insists that "[t]he Jackie Robinson story is classic example of how whiteness renders racism invisible by rendering whites, white privilege, and racist institutions invisible."[23]

Unfortunately, her reframing of the story renders invisible the reality that whites largely did *not* allow Robinson to play major-league baseball, at least not with any sense of safety, security, or assurance that he would not be atrociously ill-treated and told in no uncertain terms that he was not welcome.

DiAngelo wants to counter the "[n]arratives of racial exceptionality [that] obscure the reality of ongoing institutional white control while reinforcing the ideologies of individualism and meritocracy."[24] She also wants to avoid doing "whites a disservice by obscuring the white allies behind the scenes who worked hard and long to open the field."[25] Unfortunately, she does a great disservice to Jackie Robinson by obscuring the harsh and sustained adversity Robinson endured throughout his career as a professional ball player.

Racism clearly did not end on the day Robinson played his first major league baseball game. Earl Lloyd had yet to become the first black person to play professional basketball in the NBA. America still awaited the *Brown v. Board of Education* decision. The Civil Rights Act had not been passed. Many whites may likely resent any implication that they are not perfectly well aware of this fact.

Equally frustrating is the blatant implication that America has not made any progress at all. Meanwhile, a fan in the twenty-first century was quickly given a lifetime ban from Fenway Park after hurling a racial epithet at Baltimore Orioles player Adam Jones, who then received a standing ovation from the Fenway crowd one night after being the target of the racial slur.[26] Clearly, we are not living in Jackie Robinson's world. In fact, we are quite far away from it. DiAngelo, like Whiteness scholars in general, certainly concede this point, but they are less interested in our progress than in the "lifelong work" of antiracist pedagogy and activism that are predicated on an understanding of racism that, as we saw in chapter 3, succumbs to the reification fallacy.[27]

US ECONOMIC HISTORY AND THE MEXICAN–AMERICAN WAR

In chapter 2 of her book *White Fragility*, DiAngelo writes that the US economy at the time of the nation's formation was based in part on the annexation of Mexican lands.[28] In fact, Texas had already won its independence from Mexico at the time of US annexation, in part because American settlers rose in revolt to what historians Allan Nevins and Henry Steele Commager describe as an "inefficient, corrupt, and tyrannical" Mexican government.[29]

Moreover, the California and New Mexico territories came into the possession of the United States after the Mexican–American War of the 1840s. They were part of a negotiated purchase following a war that started when Mexico fired the first shot.[30] Nevins and Commager further point out that the context in which these lands eventually came into the possession of the United States is more complicated than DiAngelo's simplistic narrative of land expropriation suggests:

> In 1845 California had a meager population of but eleven or twelve thousand people, clinging tightly to the coast. They had no money, no army, no political experience. They had more Spanish blood than the Mexican masses and regarded themselves as physically and intellectually superior and they were only nominally dependent upon Mexico. Indeed, they would have thrown off the Mexican authority altogether had it not been for their family jealousies and an old feud between northern and southern California. As it was, Mexico provided no courts, no police, no regular postal facilities, and no schools. Communication between California and Mexico City was rare and uncertain. So frankly did Mexico recognize that its sovereignty was a mere shadow that by the middle forties it showed a disposition to sell the region to Great Britain.[31]

History is about facts as much as it is about narrative. The facts detailed here are absolutely basic. But in white fragility theory, narrative takes precedence over facts. Of course, narrative is important and should not be discounted. It helps to put all the facts into perspective to form a coherent story about what happened in history. This is hard to do, which explains why multiple interpretations and narratives are possible when examining historical events. None of this means, however, that we should permit a blatant disregard for the most basic facts in the interest of trumpeting a narrative.

One reason is that we become susceptible to ignoring multiple dimensions of historical analysis. More basic is that we undermine learning, making education a matter of indoctrination that turns facts into political weapons rather than aspects of the world we seek to understand through narrative.

For example, according to the theory of white fragility, America is not a constitutional republic founded, as articulated in *The Federalist Papers*, on majoritarian constraints against the dangers of factionalism, with adequate protections for natural rights (imperfectly applied, of course).[32] America was instead founded on nothing more than "slavery, colonization, and genocide."[33]

This is in spite of debates among the founders that reveal complex divisions between slavery and antislavery advocates. In the end, a constitution emerged that provided no explicit sanction to "property in man."[34] For example, in his famous Cooper Union Address on February 27, 1860, former President Abraham Lincoln declared:

> An inspection of the Constitution will show that the right of property in a slave is not "*distinctly* and *expressly* affirmed" in it. Bear in mind, the Judges do not pledge their judicial opinion that such right is *impliedly* affirmed in the Constitution; but they pledge their veracity that it is "*distinctly* and *expressly*" affirmed there—"distinctly," that is, not mingled with anything else—"expressly," that is, in words meaning just that, without the aid of any inference, and susceptible of no other meaning.
>
> If they had only pledged their judicial opinion that such right is affirmed in the instrument by implication, it would be open to others to show that neither the word "slave" nor "slavery" is to be found in the Constitution, nor the word "property" even, in any connection with language alluding to the things slave, or slavery; and that wherever in that instrument the slave is alluded to, he is called a "person"—and wherever his master's legal right in relation to him is alluded to, it is spoken of as "service or labor which may be due"—as a debt payable in service or labor. Also, it would be open to show, by contemporaneous history, that this mode of alluding to slaves and slavery, instead of speaking of them, was employed on purpose to exclude from the Constitution the idea that there could be property in man.[35]

Moreover, Lincoln was not remiss in reminding his audience that President George Washington signed an act passed by Congress "enforcing the prohibition of slavery in the Northwestern Territory:

> Some of you delight to flaunt in our faces the warning against sectional parties given by Washington in his Farewell Address. Less than eight years before Washington gave that warning, he had, as

> President of the United States, approved and signed an act of Congress, enforcing the prohibition of slavery in the Northwestern Territory, which act embodied the policy of the Government upon that subject up to and at the very moment he penned that warning; and about one year after he penned it, he wrote LaFayette that he considered that prohibition a wise measure, expressing in the same connection his hope that we should at some time have a confederacy of free States.[36]

A final point is that the US was officially formed when the Constitution was signed on September 17, 1787.[37] Of course, from that point on, the territorial boundaries of the nation expanded, while ideas, laws, norms, and institutions evolved. One can acknowledge complexity about the exact date of the nation's official formation, as President Lincoln said in his first inaugural address:

> Descending from these general principles, we find the proposition that in legal contemplation the Union is perpetual confirmed by the history of the Union itself. The Union is much older than the Constitution. It was formed, in fact, by the Articles of Association in 1774. It was matured and continued by the Declaration of Independence in 1776. It was further matured, and the faith of all the then thirteen States expressly plighted and engaged that it should be perpetual, by the Articles of Confederation in 1778. And finally, in 1787, one of the declared objects for ordaining and establishing the Constitution was "to form a more perfect Union."[38]

Lincoln concedes that a narrative of Union formation can accommodate different dates of maturation, but his narrative remains grounded in documented facts. The theory of white fragility is not.

6

THE CRITIQUE OF REASON

In their book *Is Everyone Really Equal? An Introduction to Key Concepts in Social Justice Education*, Robin DiAngelo and Özlem Sensoy explain that "[c]ritical social justice recognizes inequality as deeply embedded in the fabric of society (i.e., structural), and actively seeks to change this."[1]

By this, DiAngelo and Sensoy mean inequality between social groups. They have in mind things like differences in income and wealth between white and black Americans or between men and women. This inequality is systemic in the sense that it is an inherent feature of society. It is unjust because it is direct evidence of dominant groups exploiting marginalized groups in society.

With this in mind, critical theory is key to the mission of social justice activism. DiAngelo and Sensoy write that "'Critical Theory' refers to a specific scholarly approach that explores the historical, cultural, and ideological lines of authority that underlie social conditions." It is "a complex theoretical perspective," which requires "ongoing study and practice" to master, though "a preliminary understanding of its principles can offer tools for thinking critically about how society works."[2]

To begin, DiAngelo and Sensoy distinguish between the "acquisition of new information" and the "meaning given to information." This distinction is murky, they argue, because we cannot neatly separate the "acquisition of new information" from the "the political investments" in the "meaning given to information." The key question that motivates social justice activism is "who benefits from that knowledge claim and whose lives are limited by it?"[3]

This question calls into question the integrity of the scientific method. The Critical Theory of Theodor Adorno, Max Horkheimer, Herbert Marcuse, and others "developed in part as a response to [the] presumed superiority and infallibility of scientific method, and raised questions about whose rationality and whose presumed objectivity underlies scientific methods."[4]

The work of "continental" philosophers who "were also grappling with similar questions," such as Jacques Derrida, Michel Foucault, and Jacques Lacan, then "merges in the North American context of the 1960s with antiwar, feminist, gay rights, Black power, Indigenous Peoples and other emerging social justice movements."[5]

CRITICAL THEORY AND THE CRITIQUE OF REASON

According to DiAngelo and Sensoy, "[t]hese movements initially advocated for a type of liberal humanism (individualism, freedom and peace) but quickly turned to a rejection of liberal humanism"[6]:

> [T]he ideal of individual autonomy that underlies liberal humanism (the idea that people are free to make independent rational decisions that determine their own fate) was viewed as a mechanism for keeping the marginalized in their place by obscuring larger structural systems of inequality. In other words, it fooled people into believing that they had more freedom and choice than societal structures actually allow.[7]

This is wrong. Adorno, Horkheimer, Marcuse, and even later-generation Critical Theorists associated with the Frankfurt School, such as Jürgen Habermas, did not directly criticize liberal humanism, which is not easy to define anyway.[8] Nor did they claim that reason and autonomy are sources of oppression. Instead, they supported and encouraged the Enlightenment project of promoting human autonomy. They did not criticize rationality. Instead, they examined how contemporary ideologies and other institutional impediments prevent us from exercising our rational faculties in the pursuit of autonomy.

They certainly had concerns about the mechanistic thinking that ostensibly characterizes modern science. They heavily criticized the logical positivism of the Vienna Circle. Logical positivism was a school of thought that insisted that statements are meaningful only if they can be logically or empirically verified. For the Frankfurt School, this limited conception of meaning cut off any attempt to evaluate the moral status of scientific claims about reality. The consequence, as Max Horkheimer writes in his book of essays titled *Critical Theory*, is the following:

> Thought relinquishes its claim to exercise criticism or to set tasks. Its purely recording and calculatory functions become detached from its spontaneity. Decision and praxis are held to be something opposed to thought—they are "value judgments," private caprices, and uncontrollable feelings. The intellect is declared to be connected only externally, if at all, with the conscious interest and course it may follow. . . . Thought and will, the parts of the mental process, are severed conceptually. . . . In view of the fact that the ruling economic powers use science as well as the whole of society for their special ends, this ideology, this identification of thought with the special sciences, must lead to the perpetuation of the status quo.[9]

This passage shows that the concern about rationality was not "whose rationality and whose presumed objectivity underlies scientific methods."[10] Instead, it focuses on the conception of rationality itself and how it might be misused, in the name of science, by dominant social interests. There is no presumption that the definition of rationality is simply a matter of perspective, or that truth is relative. Rationality is not the problem, nor is objective truth held to be an illusion. Instead, the concern is that rationality, if not properly cultivated, might be exploited by dominant social interests.

THE ECLIPSE OF REASON

As Horkheimer explains in *Eclipse of Reason*, reason has become *instrumentalized*, focused formulaically on calculating means to achieve ends, while attaching "little importance to the question whether the purposes as such are reasonable."[11] The concern was not about whose rationality and whose presumed objectivity underlies scientific methods. The concern was how reason had become a way of thinking only about how to pursue our goals, not about whether the goals are worth pursuing. Though Horkheimer's critique stems from concerns about the effects of "false consciousness" on marginalized groups, "instrumental reason" is as harmful to dominant groups as it is to marginalized groups because people in either group may be pursuing the "wrong" goals.

It does not occur to people that there might be better goals to pursue. As a result, thinking about whether society can be transformed for the better is seen as pointless. The crisis of reason is not its belief in objective truth, such as whether a society is just or not, but the *lack of* belief in objective truth.

> In Platonism, the Pythagorean theory of numbers, which originated in astral mythology, was transformed into the theory of ideas that attempts to define the supreme content of thinking as an absolute objectivity ultimately beyond, though related to, the faculty of thinking. *T he present crisis of reason consists fundamentally in the fact that at a certain point thinking either became incapable of conceiving such objectivity at all or began to negate it as a delusion* [emphasis mine].[12]

In *Dialectic of Enlightenment*, Max Horkheimer and Theodor Adorno argue that the Enlightenment, which philosopher Immanuel Kant defined as "man's emergence from his self-imposed immaturity,"[13] has failed to emancipate us from oppressive arrangements in society.[14] Enlightenment society put so much faith in technology, science, and material progress that people lost the capacity to think about the ways in which technology, science, and material progress might undermine human autonomy. Virtue and vice were seen as inextricably connected to the almighty dollar of industrial capitalism. The result was a uniformity in cultural life which crippled any potential for the kind of spontaneous creativity one might expect from genuine human autonomy.

How did this happen? The aim of the Enlightenment, in its commitment to scientific inquiry and the scientific method, was to explore, control, and dominate nature. Rationality was viewed as the supreme weapon for manipulating the world as it is, at the expense of using rationality as a guide to thinking about how the world should be.

Horkheimer and Adorno trace this development in part to the philosopher René Descartes, who sparked the development of modern philosophy by arguing that the thinking self is the starting point for making a claim about what people can know. Horkheimer and Adorno argue that, with the development of capitalism, the "rational" mind focused its attention only on learning what could be learned within the status quo of capitalism. When the rational mind does not consider whether the ends pursued within a given social order are worth pursuing, but focuses only on how to attain those ends, it effectively reproduces the social order, giving no thought to whether it should continue to do so.

Science and technology undoubtedly improve living standards, but better living standards do not eliminate the social tension between those who rule and those who are ruled. Enlightenment was supposed to free humanity from oppression, but it became oppressive when people arrived at a limited understanding of rationality as simply the calculation of means to achieve ends.

This limited conception of what rationality is and what it can achieve accommodated our minds to the ideology of a capitalist order, promising enhancements in material well-being in exchange for obedience to the efficiencies of mass production:

> [J]ust as the ruled have always taken the morality dispensed to them by the rulers more seriously than the rulers themselves, the defrauded masses today cling to the myth of success still more ardently

> than the successful. They, too, have their aspirations. They insist unwaveringly on the ideology by which they are enslaved.[15]

In the *Dialectic*, Horkheimer and Adorno emphasize their allegiance to the project of Enlightenment: "[H]erein lies our *petitio principii*—that freedom in society is inseparable from enlightenment thinking."[16] But the loss of *objective* reason has destroyed enlightened thinking: "[R]uthless toward itself, the Enlightenment has eradicated the last remnant of its own self-awareness."[17]

Influenced by Kant, they believed in rational autonomy. Influenced by Marx, they attempted to show how industrial capitalism undermined the rational mind's pursuit of human autonomy.

The concern was not reason, but the eclipse of reason.

CRITICAL THEORY SOUGHT TO RESCUE THE ENLIGHTENMENT, NOT ABANDON IT

The *Dialectic* conceives of enlightened thought as an escape from the kind of thinking that goes on in societies based on myth. Myth is an anthropomorphic interpretation of the world. Inanimate nature appears to people as being inhabited by animated beings: the sea is controlled by Poseidon; the rocks and trees are inhabited by spirits. Human societies based on mythical interpretations see their survival as dependent on the manipulation of these animate forces through sacrifice, prayer, and other rituals. This manipulation is carried out by persons in control of these societies.

In this way, the leaders of society are able to manipulate everyone else. This manipulation is possible because there is a widespread belief that deviation from mythical interpretation is destructive to survival. Thus a status quo emerges, defined by the relationship between the persons in authority, who oversee the practices that allow society to conform to the mythical interpretation, and the rest of the population, who take these mythical views to be true, and thus obey their leaders.[18]

The concern of the *Dialectic* is that enlightened society replaced myth-based society as another status quo characterized by the myths of capitalism, with its own power dynamics that dismantle autonomy: "[m]yth is already enlightenment; and enlightenment reverts to mythology."[19] Under capitalism, reason was made into a mechanical instrument of domination. The eclipse of *objective* reason sabotaged the Enlightenment project of thinking for oneself using one's inbred faculty of reason. At the level of society, we are distracted from a critique of society's moral compass.

In contrast to what DiAngelo and Sensoy say in their book on social justice education, rational autonomy was not viewed as a mechanism for keeping the marginalized in their place by obscuring structural systems of inequality. Rather, capitalist ideology instrumentalized reason and impeded the cultivation of autonomy.

The result was an eclipse of objective reason, fostering a kind of false consciousness, which makes people oblivious to the structural inequality associated with oppression and marginalization. Autonomy was not an obstacle to social justice. Social ideology and instrumental reason were obstacles that sat in the way of the cultivation of autonomy. The obstacle that sat in the way of a critique of social injustice was not autonomy, but the *lack* of autonomy.

CRITICAL THEORY PROMOTES RATIONAL AUTONOMY

One of the central aims of the Enlightenment was not simply to defend reason, but to figure out what it is.[20] Similarly, Frankfurt School philosophers were concerned with rescuing reason after it was corrupted by the ideologies of industrial capitalism. Even later critical theorists like Jürgen Habermas, and continental philosophers like Michel Foucault, did not reject reason outright, instead focusing on how reason fits within communicative discourse (in the case of Habermas) and how rational inquiry fits within the historical period in which investigation takes place (in the case of Foucault). They were not inherently anti-Enlightenment or antireason. They were committed to a critique of reason, in an attempt to improve our understanding of what reason is and what it can achieve.

In sum, contrary to what DiAngelo and Sensoy say in their book, Critical Theory did not originally promote a view that rationality is unreliable because it depends on one's position in the social hierarchy. It argued instead that social hierarchies and ideologies corrupt reason in ways that should not be ignored. Critical Theory sought to rescue reason from corruption by exposing hierarchies and ideologies. Rational autonomy was the goal of social justice, not an obstacle to social justice.

7

RUNNING AFOUL OF REASON AND LOGIC

The theory of white fragility, in its reliance on "social justice" ideology, is based on a misunderstanding of the Enlightenment and the critique of reason. It comes as little surprise, therefore, that it runs afoul of reason and logic. In this chapter, we look at examples of how the theory falls prey to faulty reasoning and logical fallacies. We complete our critique of the methodological shortcomings of the theory by illustrating where it goes wrong as a matter of logic, particularly with respect to prominent claims about Whiteness, white privilege, and white fragility.

CORRELATION AND CAUSATION

In chapter 1 of her book *White Fragility*, DiAngelo writes, "When I talk to white people about racism, their responses are so predictable I sometimes feel as though we are reciting lines from a shared script." "[O]n some level," she continues, "we are, because we are actors in a shared culture," in which "[a] significant aspect of the white script derives from our seeing ourselves as both objective and unique." She insists, however, that this script will lead us astray if we want to understand white fragility: "we have to begin to understand why we cannot fully be either; we must understand the forces of socialization."[1]

DiAngelo writes that "[w]e make sense of perceptions and experiences through our particular cultural lens," which is "neither universal nor objective, and without it, a person could not function in any human society. But exploring these cultural frameworks can be particularly challenging in Western culture precisely because of two key Western ideologies: individualism [which DiAngelo says is the belief that "we are each unique and stand apart from others, even those within our social groups"] and objectivity [which she describes as the belief that "it is possible to be free of all bias"]." These "ideologies" conspire to "make it very difficult for white people to explore the collective aspects of the white experience."[2]

The apparently ideological belief in individualism prevents us from appreciating how groups and group identity (e.g., rich and poor, able-bodied and disabled, heterosexual and gay) matter. Groups matter, however, because we are "socialized into these groups collectively"[3]: "watching and comparing ourselves to others,"[4] while receiving "the same messages about what these groups mean, why being in one group is a different experience from being in another,"[5] as filtered through "television, movies, news items, song lyrics, magazines, textbooks, schools, religion, literature, stories, jokes, traditions and practices, history, and so on."[6]

We are also taught to "know that it is 'better' to be in one of these groups than to be in its opposite—for example, to be young rather than old, able-bodied rather than have a disability, rich rather than poor."[7] In challenging individualism, DiAngelo wants to persuade us that "tackling group identity also challenges our belief in objectivity,"[8] because "[i]f group membership is relevant, then we don't see the world from the universal human perspective but from the perspective of a particular kind of human."[9]

This is "particularly challenging for many white people, because we are taught that to have a racial viewpoint is to be biased,"[10] which only serves to protect bias, "because denying that we have them ensures that we won't examine or change them."[11] It is not, however, that they "matter naturally, as we are often taught to believe."[12] Instead, "we are taught that they matter, and the social meaning ascribed to these groups creates a difference in lived experience."[13] Apparently, we are taught that groups matter naturally and socially, but we should only take the latter seriously.[14]

DiAngelo predicts that her reader will probably think "of all the ways that [he is] different from other white people"[15] in an attempt to argue that he is not racist—a "common reflex" she has witnessed "countless times in [her] work."[16] She concludes: "I can predict that many readers will make . . . claims of exception precisely because we are products of our culture, not separate from it " (emphasis mine).[17]

This is a generalization she is "quite comfortable" making because, as a sociologist, she understands that "social life is patterned and predictable in measurable ways" and, in spite of exceptions, "patterns are recognized as such precisely because they are recurring and predictable."[18]

DiAngelo's analysis conflates objectivity with neutrality. It is also incoherent because, in dismissing objectivity, she is making an objective statement. But we discussed these problems in chapter 4. That said, DiAngelo is probably right that her reader will think "of all the ways that [he is] different from other white people" in an attempt to argue that he is not racist.[19] But this should hardly be surprising.

First, psychological defense mechanisms are a universal aspect of human nature, regardless of race, gender, class, or other social classification. Second, one of the few empirical studies of Whiteness available, which we briefly reviewed in chapter 3, suggests that both white *and* nonwhite people insist that individual experience supersedes group experience if we are to understand lived experience.[20]

For example, the study by sociologists Douglas Hartmann, Joseph Gerteis, and Paul Croll finds that "[w]hites and minorities show a nearly identical enthusiasm for individual freedoms" as long as people follow the same rules. They "also show similar skepticism of claims to group-based differences." They generally agree that "it's a problem if people think of themselves as mostly members of groups rather than individuals" and that "focusing too much on people's different backgrounds divides people." DiAngelo may be wrong that white people are more likely than nonwhite people to adhere to individualism.[21] In other words, insistence on uniqueness is not problematic. It is another common feature of human nature.

There is, however, a more fundamental problem in her overall reasoning. The analysis conflates correlation and causation. DiAngelo claims the "common reflex" among white people to insist on their differences is a result of being socialized to believe in the "ideology" of individualism. When she insists that group identity matters, she challenges the individualist perspective of white people. This challenge instigates a "common reflex" in white people to insist on the uniqueness of their experiences. "Socialization" is the causal mechanism that connects the challenge to individualism to the "common reflex" to insist on uniqueness. Is she right?

Not according to the Enlightenment philosopher David Hume, who ironically gave us one of the greatest reasons to doubt the supposed "infallibility of the scientific method."[22] Hume's analysis of our understanding of causality was so incisive that it has stimulated debate among philosophers about the limits of knowledge ever since. It also provides us with reason to doubt that white people insisting that their experiences are unique is a necessary result of being "socialized" to believe in individualism.

DiAngelo observes a frequent connection between one event (saying groups matter) and another event (insistence on uniqueness). This frequent connection is what Hume called a "constant conjunction" of events. Hume's main point about causality is we cannot be certain that this "constant conjunction" occurs as a matter of necessity. In other words, we can never be sure that "socialization" causes white people to react as they do when DiAngelo asserts that groups matter.

Take two events, A and B. Event B frequently occurs after event A. People come to believe that event A causes event B. In *An Enquiry Concerning Human Understanding*,[23] Hume devotes attention to this idea that people infer causality from a "constant conjunction"[24] of events.[25] Hume claims that all one can say is that event B often follows event A. Event A and event B are constantly conjoined . The presumption that events A and B are causally connected is an *inductive inference*. It involves the formation of an idea about *how* events A and B are connected as a matter of necessity.

For example, consider the statement that groups matter, as well as the reaction of white people who say that individuals matter more than groups and assume that this reaction is frequently observed when DiAngelo says that groups matter. Does "socialization" explain this "constant conjunction" of two events? Does this "constant conjunction" occur as a result of being "socialized" by a collective "white" consciousness that trains white people to reflexively insist that individuals matter more than groups?

Hume writes in the *Enquiry*: "philosophers, who carry their scrutiny a little farther, immediately perceive, that, even in the most familiar events, the energy of the cause is as unintelligible as in the most unusual, and that we only learn by experience the frequent CONJUNCTION of objects, without being ever able to comprehend anything like CONNEXION between them.[26] All one can perceive is that "[o]ne event follows another; but we never can observe any tie between them."[27]

Hume continues:

> They seem conjoined, but never connected . And as we can have no idea of anything, which never appeared to our outward sense or inward sentiment, the necessary conclusion seems to be, that we have no idea of connexion or power at all, and that these words are absolutely without any meaning, when employed either in philosophical reasonings, or common life.[28]

Further:

> Our idea, therefore, of necessity and causation arises entirely from the uniformity, observable in the operations of nature; where similar objects are constantly conjoined together, and the mind is determined by custom to infer the one from the appearance of the other. These two circumstances form the whole of that necessity, which we ascribe to matter. Beyond the constant conjunction of similar ob-

> jects, and the consequent inference from one to the other, we have no notion of any necessity, or connexion.[29]

The basic idea is that people believe A *causes* B simply because they observe a "constant conjunction" between events A and B. But as summarized by the *Internet Encyclopedia of Philosophy*, "this is to say that (B) is grounded in (A)."[30] Hume argues that A by itself gives us no predictive power, and thus we have "merely pushed the question back one more step and must now ask with Hume, 'What is the foundation of all conclusions from experience?'"[31] This gives rise to the problem of induction.

The problem of induction refers to the difficulty of explaining *how* B is grounded in A. For example, *how* does "socialization" explain the "constant conjunction" between saying groups matter and white people saying that individuals matter more than groups? As the *Internet Encyclopedia of Philosophy* says, "What lets us reason from (A) to (B)?"[32]

One answer is known as the Principle of the Uniformity of Nature (PUN), "the doctrine that nature is always uniform, so unobserved instances of phenomena will resemble the observed."[33] But this is only an assumption because "we have not, as yet, established that we are justified in holding such a principle."[34] It is still something that can only be used to predict the course from A to B. We still do not directly observe this principle in action.

> This means that the PUN is an instance of (B), but we were invoking the PUN as the grounds for moving from beliefs of type (A) to beliefs of type (B), thus creating a vicious circle when attempting to justify type (B) matters of fact. We use knowledge of (B) as a justification for our knowledge of (B). The bottom line for Hume's problem of induction seems to be that there is no clear way to rationally justify any causal reasoning (and therefore no inductive inference) whatsoever. We have no ground that allows us to move from (A) to (B), to move beyond sensation and memory, so any matter of fact knowledge beyond these becomes suspect.[35]

DiAngelo's prediction that readers will react to her assertion that group identity matters (event A) by "thinking of all the ways that you are different from other white people"[36] (event B) may often turn out to be true. But she bases this prediction not only on the "constant conjunction" she observes between her challenge to individualism and the way white people react.

She bases her prediction also on the claim that "socialization" is the causal instrument by which A and B are constantly conjoined. This claim assumes that "socialization" is a uniformly observed societal force and that it works the same way for everyone. If she says that groups matter, white people will say that individuals matter more (though she does allow for the possibility of exceptions, i.e., that some white people will not react as such) because they have been socialized to react as such, not because they sincerely and correctly believe, as apparently many nonwhites do, that individuals matter more. Note that we have not even touched on the complicated matter of explaining what *socialization* means.

Hume's skepticism has long been a source of profound debate among philosophers. One can read more in the *Internet Encyclopedia of Philosophy* and many other sources about the complexity and details of Hume's skepticism and how it has been debated over the centuries,[37] but the basic point is that *correlation is not the same as causation.* DiAngelo's presumed omniscience about why white people react the way they do when she asserts that group identity matters should be met with the skepticism it deserves.

In fairness, DiAngelo suggests that she does not believe individualism is unimportant.[38] She simply wants to insist that individualism gets in the way of our attempt to understand that racism is a system. Thus, "[s]etting aside your sense of uniqueness is a critical skill that will allow you to see the big picture of the society in which we live."[39]

She exhorts readers to "try to let go of your individual narrative and grapple with the collective messages we all receive as members of a larger shared culture."[40] This is not bad advice. But it is also not the end of the story. If we cannot know for certain that "socialization" is the main reason why white people resist her claim that groups matter more than individuals, we might consider that they are right, rather than wrong, to resist. We might consider that they are not exhibiting white fragility, but rather making a solid point that individual experience does, in fact, matter as much as, if not more than, group experience. Identity politics may not be the best way to address racial inequality. If the study discussed earlier in this section is any indication, many nonwhites agree.

THE GENETIC FALLACY

We discussed the Kafka trap in chapter 1. To repeat, in relation to my argument, this trap refers to the insidious way in which the theory of white fragility frames the conversation around race so that it is impossible to raise doubts about the theory without being accused of fragility. Whiteness scholars hold that whiteness is so invisible to white people that they are simply not equipped to challenge white supremacy. This blindness precludes white people from having any meaningful insight into the nature of racism.

While frustrating, the Kafka trap is problematic not simply because it shuts down the possibility of debate. It also falters as a matter of logic. By dismissing all objections as *white fragility*, the theory effectively delegitimizes objections on the basis of the identity of the person raising objections. A white person who objects to the core tenets of Whiteness Studies, or otherwise disagrees about how Whiteness causes racial inequality, sees his viewpoint dismissed not on the merits but on the basis that he is a white person who has yet to come to grips with Whiteness and white privilege.

The Kafka trap thus falls prey to the genetic fallacy, which refers to a tendency to assume that the origin of an argument determines its quality.[41] This fallacy rears its head again and again. If you have ever been in a conversation with someone who responds to your point by saying, *that's according to you*, you are up against the genetic fallacy. The person is not explaining why your point is wrong. The person is dismissing your point out of hand simply because *you* are making the point.

Similarly, if critics dismiss what DiAngelo has to say simply because DiAngelo is saying it, critics also fall prey to the genetic fallacy. The point is to emphasize the importance of whether an argument is valid instead of focusing on *who* makes the argument.

The genetic fallacy takes us back to the previous chapter, in which we saw how Critical Theory, as conceived by the Frankfurt School, did not raise "questions about whose rationality and whose presumed objectivity underlies scientific methods."[42] Critical Theory was not suspicious of reason and logic. It was instead concerned that reason was not being used to its utmost potential. With the instrumentalization of reason in the age of industrial capitalism,[43] reason was not being used to cultivate human autonomy or to engage in transformative social critique.

This means that reason, the use of logic and factual analysis, has a central role in the critique of society. Thus, when proponents of white fragility theory dismiss any and all objections or disagreements from white people as examples of white fragility, ostensibly because the nature of racism remains invisible to white people, they are really saying that reason is not as central to the critique of society. They are also saying that they do not understand what Critical Theory, as originally conceived, is all about.

The genetic fallacy also creates a serious practical problem. If the truth of a claim really is just a matter of perspective, there is nothing to prevent a white person from responding the same exact way. The result is a vicious circle. A proponent of white fragility theory dismisses a counterargument by saying, *that's according to you*. The person making a counterargument might then defend his argument by responding to the critic of his argument in the same way. Any possibility of a productive conversation about how to address racial inequality falls apart, as we are left with a room of people dismissing ideas other than their own by saying, *that's according to you*.

The essential point is that logic matters. Without it, we deprive ourselves of the use of our reason to judge the validity of ideas about white fragility theory in particular, or about how to address racial inequality in general. The validity of an argument becomes a matter of mere opinion.

Skepticism of white fragility theory is certainly warranted, not only given the vicious circle described previously, but also given how much Whiteness scholars take for granted. For example, Hartmann and colleagues observe in their paper that "one of the most frequent and important criticisms [of the discipline] involves the empirical grounding upon which the claims of whiteness scholars are based."[44] "[M]any critical race scholars," they continue, "are fundamentally skeptical of (if not simply opposed to) quantitative data and techniques to begin with."[45] As we saw in chapter 5, this reluctance to make use of quantitative techniques can lead us to believe that one observation from a single *Jeopardy!* episode tells us all we need to know about white racial illiteracy.

The genetic fallacy should also make us wary of the problem of presentism,[46] which is the practice of judging history on the basis of societal standards that prevail in the present. Consider, for example an introductory warning[47] in a book titled *Kant's Critiques*.[48] The warning reads, "This book is a product of its time and does not reflect the same values as it would if it were written today." It adds that "[p]arents might wish to discuss with their children how views on race, gender, sexuality, ethnicity, and interpersonal relations have changed since this book was written before allowing them to read this classic work."[49] This is an example of presentism.

Kant's philosophy, like all philosophy, was certainly a product of its time. Kant undoubtedly held some views that many find unpalatable in today's world. But this has nothing to do with why we read Kant or why his work is important. Nor will identity politics help one bit in understanding the ideas that underlie Kant's arguments for the *synthetic a priori* or the categorical imperative.

Kant's philosophy was a reaction, in part, to the skepticism espoused by David Hume, notably regarding our understanding of causality. It also addressed the "crisis of the Enlightenment,"[50] trying to reconcile a mechanistic conception of reason with freedom and morality. One would be better prepared to delve into the intricacies of Kant's philosophy by reading up on Hume in particular, and Enlightenment thinkers in general, than by reflecting on modern identity politics. There is no reason to dismiss or reevaluate Kant on the grounds of presentism simply because he did not fully adhere to the moral standards that prevail in our own time.

The refrain, *that's according to you*, is supposed to call into question the supposed ideologies of individualism and objectivity. But individualism and objectivity are not tools of white supremacy. As philosopher Michael Ayers explained in a discussion with Bryan Magee on the philosophy of John Locke, an "individualistic view of knowledge" is simply the view "that nobody else can do my knowing for me. . . . I have to think things out for myself in order to have knowledge."[51]

Individuals are capable of reasoning through an argument objectively. They are capable of figuring out on their own the evils of racism. To dismiss individualism and objectivity, or to dismiss the speaker's objection on the basis of his group identity, is a surrender to the genetic fallacy.

If, however, individualism and objectivity render a white person incapable of understanding the evils of racism, it is reasonable to ask whether he is ever capable of apprehending those evils. Similarly, Whiteness scholars find themselves in a position of incoherence, making an inherently objective claim that objectivity is not possible. There is also the ironic result, as noted in chapter 4, that DiAngelo undermines her application of Foucault's ideas about power and knowledge classifications by implicitly insisting on the general and universal applicability of the Whiteness paradigm, unwittingly proving Foucault's point at her own expense.

Locke, Ayers reminds us, believed that in areas like ethics, "people ought to spend time, and ought to be given the time to spend, on thinking things out for themselves as far as possible, and if you have that, coupled with a very strong sense of how difficult this is, and how hard it is to get things right, then you've obviously got the recipe for a tolerant society."[52] We may take this perspective for granted today, but it was long in the making and far from being taken for granted in Locke's day.

In highlighting the genetic fallacy, we get a sense of the threat that white fragility theory poses to a tolerant society. It leaves us in the dark of Plato's cave, without the tools of reason and evidence to make our way out into the light. Only indoctrination, and its twin sister intolerance for dissent, are permitted. In this situation, we are also left with a perverted version of German philosopher Friedrich Neitzsche's "will to power," in which "victim" groups give themselves a license to impose their own will on their "oppressors."[53]

To get a sense of the grave consequences, consider the controversy that arose when, as reported by the *New York Post*, New York City Schools Chancellor Richard Carranza implemented mandatory bias trainings "targeting a 'white-supremacy culture' among school administrators . . . by disparaging ideas like 'individualism,' 'objectivity' and 'worship of the written word.'"[54]

"New York City's public-school educators," the *Post* reports, "have been told to focus on black children over white ones—and one Jewish superintendent who described her family's Holocaust tragedies was scolded and humiliated, according to firsthand accounts."[55] Even if well-intended, these trainings show how egregiously the Whiteness paradigm, and white fragility theory in particular, can instigate racial resentment without having truth on its side. Or rather, without having the means to test whether its claims are true.

The reactions of white people may reflect knee-jerk sensitivities rather than reasoned arguments that weigh and consider the premises and evidence. But they may also reflect a sound intuition that studying race and racism should not be about indoctrination but about dialogue, debate, and rigorous examination of competing ideas on how to address racial inequality. If Whiteness scholars believe strongly that Whiteness is the force that underlies ongoing racial inequality (a claim we examined in chapter 3), they should be able to defend their claim against critics with reasoned arguments. They should not resort to the rhetorical sophistry of a Kafka trap. In surrendering to the genetic fallacy, they do just that.

OTHER LOGICAL FALLACIES

The basic claim underlying the theory of white fragility is that all white people help keep a racist society alive. They can't help it because they have been socialized to have a "white racial frame."[56] If white people object to this claim, they reveal their *white fragility*.[57] This doesn't mean that all white people are bad, or that they consciously discriminate against minorities, or that they deny minorities the respect and dignity they deserve. Instead, it means that they benefit from a "system" that consistently benefits white people at the expense of minorities. Moreover, they perpetuate this system in their daily routines, habits, beliefs, and unwitting conformity to "white" social norms.

In the words of DiAngelo, white people have been "[s]ocialized" to live with "a deeply internalized sense of superiority and entitlement" without being aware of it.[58] As a claim about white people in general, however, this claim is vulnerable to the fallacy of division, which refers to the error of thinking what is true for the whole is also true for any part of the whole.[59] As an example, let's consider again the idea that one example of Whiteness is the belief in individualism.

We noted previously that DiAngelo predicts in chapter 1 of her book that a white reader will think "of all the ways that [he is] different from other white people" in an attempt to convince himself that he is not racist. This is a "common reflex" DiAngelo has seen "countless times in [her] work," leading her to "predict that many readers will make . . . claims of exception precisely because we are products of our culture, not separate from it."[60] We saw previously that the "common reflex" explanation mistakes correlation for causation. But like the genetic fallacy, it also illustrates the logical problems that arise from a theory that, in practice, operates as an insidious Kafka trap.

When white people object that their experiences are unique, white fragility theory dismisses the objection on the grounds that a white person is failing to come to terms with the ways he reinforces Whiteness. As DiAngelo writes in her seminal paper on white fragility, "Whiteness Studies begin with the premise that racism and white privilege exist in both traditional and modern forms, and rather than work to prove its existence, work to reveal it ."[61] This is circular reasoning: a basic presumption that all white people help keep a racist society alive, in all the ways that DiAngelo describes in her paper (universalism, individualism, racial comfort, racial arrogance, racial belonging, segregation, psychic freedom, constant messaging), *must* be acknowledged before we can proceed to show how all white people help keep a racist society alive.

It also gives rise to a fallacy of division. The "premise that racism and white privilege exist in both traditional and modern forms" means that all white people are endowed with white privilege. Unless they work to reveal privilege and undo Whiteness, they keep racism alive. In practice, white people have a hard time with this. They cannot help keeping a racist society alive because they have been socialized to have a "white racial frame." If white people object, they reveal their *white fragility*.[62]

In other words, disagreement is evidence of guilt. It indicates an unwillingness to combat racism. But this is not simply bad faith on the part of proponents of white fragility theory. It is also logically fallacious. If a white person insists that his own experiences are distinct from the experiences of another white person, or makes some other argument that goes against the grain of white fragility theory, he is seen as undermining the work of antiracist activists by refusing to come to terms with how his Whiteness keeps racism in place. The theory thus draws an inference about a *specific* white person, who may invoke his individual experiences to object to the theory, from a claim about collective identity that the theory makes about *all* white people. This is the fallacy of division.

This faulty reasoning can also be seen as fallacious by understanding "white privilege" in terms of probability. Thus, while every individual has a different experience and every experience is subject to varying interpretations, white privilege means that, *on average*, a black person can expect to encounter difficulties that a white person does not based on the color of his or her skin.[63] As suggested by Peggy McIntosh in her seminal essay on white privilege, the probability of seamlessly and affordably moving into a new neighborhood given that one is white is higher than the probability of seamlessly and affordably moving into a new neighborhood given that one is black.[64]

The point is that advantages that stem from being white are probabilistic in nature. On average, a white person is likely to benefit from privilege. But this does not mean that *every* white person *always* benefits from white privilege. To claim otherwise is to say that what may be true on average is true in every instance. In other words, it is to commit the fallacy of division.

It is perhaps even more precise to say that white fragility theory commits the ecological fallacy, which is the error of deducing something about individuals based on statistical inferences about groups.[65] It also may lead to the fallacy of composition, which is the error of thinking what is true for the part is also true for the whole.[66] Just because we find some, or many, white people engaging in (implicit) discriminatory behavior should not lead one to conclude that all white people do.

In her PhD dissertation, DiAngelo calls individualism one of "two master discourses of Whiteness in practice" (the other being "universalism").[67] Unfortunately, in dismissing individualism, DiAngelo hinges her theory so heavily on collective identity and experience that it dies on the sword of logical fallacies. It was with good sense that the Renaissance writer Niccolò Machiavelli declared, "Although men are apt to deceive themselves in general matters, yet they rarely do so in particulars."[68]

8

SERMONIZING, NOT SCHOLARSHIP

The theory of white fragility claims to know a lot about white racial illiteracy, the causes of racial disparities, and the nature of racism. What is striking, however, is the contrast between the theory's presumption of omniscience about racism and the zeal with which proponents implore white people to be humble when attempting to learn about racism. This is not the typical approach of theory in the natural or social sciences. It is, rather, the kind of sermonizing one gets from dogma.

DiAngelo insists that white fragility is the result of a misunderstanding of what racism is and how it works. Racism is about society, not about individuals. It is about institutions, not about whether you are a good or bad person. Racism is tied to the control white people have on the institutions through which society doles out benefits.

If those benefits are consistently doled out unequally, so that white people benefit more than nonwhite people, racism exists and will continue to exist until white people learn to let go of their biases and start learning how everything they say and do functions as a scaffold of socialization on which white supremacy survives, against the gravitational pull of social justice activists who seek to bring about its collapse.

The first thing one notices about white fragility theory is how certain its proponents are that they are right. This imperiousness gives us the Kafka trap that frustrates white people. There is an unwillingness to engage with anyone who objects to the fundamental starting point, as articulated by DiAngelo, "that racism and white privilege exist in both traditional and modern forms, and *rather than work to prove its existence,* [we must] *work to reveal it.*"[1] If you point out that this is circular reasoning, you would most likely encounter the accusation that you are being fragile.

This is not just the kind of rhetorical bullying tactic one gets from a Kafka trap. This is a standpoint of absolute certainty that one has figured it all out. In this view, the only thing that stands in the way of fighting racism is white people who won't get on board with the self-anointed antiracists who have duly read a vast corpus of Whiteness Studies literature and engaged with the "right" social justice circles. Unfortunately, proponents of the theory of white fragility too often exhibit no interest in good faith debate or constructive criticism of their views. The claims of white fragility theory constitute a doctrine to be instilled, rather than a set of hypotheses to be rigorously evaluated.

"THEORY"

In her work, Robin DiAngelo expresses skepticism about objectivity, the scientific method, and Enlightenment epistemology. She does, however, place a lot of weight on "theory." In *Is Everyone Really Equal? An Introduction to Key Concepts in Social Justice Education*, DiAngelo and Özlem Sensoy begin with a brief overview of Critical Theory, a "body of scholarship that examines how society works" and "a tradition that emerged in the early part of the 20th century from a group of scholars at the Institute for Social Research in Frankfurt, Germany."[2]

They explain that "theory can be conceptualized as the internal 'maps' we follow to 'navigate' and make sense of our lives and new things we encounter." In short, "[e]verything we do in the world (our actions) is guided by a worldview (our theory)."[3] Unfortunately, they irresponsibly mislead us about how theory works in the social sciences. When they invoke "Emile Durkheim's research questioning the infallibility of the scientific method,"[4] they do not appear to realize that scientists do not think of theoretical analysis and the scientific method as Holy Grails of truth.

The scientific method is about method, not content. Moreover, theory is all about humility. The humility arises from an understanding that theory must be able to withstand rigorous hypothesis testing. In the scientific literature, and in the academic seminars where working papers undergo scrutiny before they become published papers, one observes a serious atmosphere in which scientists, researchers, and scholars weigh and consider evidence that supports or undermines the theory.

Theory is a framework for guiding the pursuit of knowledge. In science, theory is typically conceived in the form of a quantitative model that attempts to identify the relevant explanatory factors as simply as possible. Mathematics is not a Rosetta Stone, but it does have the virtues of simplicity, clarity, and rigor. This does not always mean the model is easy to understand. But with a well-specified model in hand, one can go about evaluating how realistic and useful the model is in explaining something about the world. This is often done by testing the model, using data and statistical techniques.

In saying that "theory can be conceptualized as the internal 'maps' we follow to 'navigate' and make sense of our lives and new things we encounter,"[5] DiAngelo and Sensoy seem to confuse theory with a mental scheme of expectations about how the world works, which we absorb through cultural conditioning. While DiAngelo is correct that theory involves framing and conceptualizing our study of how the world works, she invariably presents theory as a rigid ideological lens, rather than a flexible conceptual framework. She seems to equate theory with dogma.

A CASE STUDY: THE SIGNIFICANCE OF "BLACK" NAMES

To illustrate a point about how socialization leads to cultural conformity, which then leads to systemic discrimination, DiAngelo cites research on résumé callbacks to argue that white recruiters in many industries will implicitly use "black" names as a way to identify and ignore supposedly unqualified candidates, which leads to socioeconomic outcomes that sustain racial inequality.

In *Is Everyone Really Equal?* DiAngelo and Sensoy cite this research and conclude that the human resource workers who screened these resumes "were likely not aware they were discriminating, and would probably have vigorously (and sincerely) denied any suggestion to the contrary."[6] If they deny this, they exhibit white fragility and thus maintain the status quo of racial inequality.

This is what theory is supposed to do: isolate the most pertinent explanatory factors. But is DiAngelo right about the implications of research on callbacks? Not necessarily. As we saw in chapter 2, the current state of research does not warrant a belief that "implicit bias" predicts behavior. As Professor Gregory Mitchell writes in a primer on implicit bias, "if we have two corporations identical in all respects except that one corporation has a higher percentage of persons with implicit bias than the other, we *cannot* validly predict that there will be many, if any, differences in the personnel decisions made within these two corporations and we *cannot* identify any particular persons more or less likely to discriminate from any measure of implicit bias."[7]

How could this be? Quite simple: there may be other factors at work, and DiAngelo does not consider them. Consider a 2004 paper published in the *Quarterly Journal of Economics* by Roland G. Fryer Jr. and Steve Levitt. Levitt and Fryer took note of a conspicuous increase in the number of black children receiving distinctively "black" names starting with the Black Power movement in the late 1960s.[8] They wanted to understand whether this had anything to do with social and economic outcomes.

They found that "black" names are strong predictors of socioeconomic status, a result that does not conflict with DiAngelo's claims. However, they also "find no compelling evidence of a negative relationship between Black names and a wide range of life outcomes after controlling for background characteristics." In other words, they concluded that black names do not necessarily have a *causal* impact on adult life outcomes, a result they are able to reconcile with résumé callback studies.[9]

They began with a dataset "drawn from the Birth Statistical Master File maintained by the Office of Vital Records in the California Department of Health Services." This dataset provides "information drawn from birth certificates for all children born in California over the period 1961–2000—over sixteen million births."[10]

After preliminary analyses, they find that it is more likely for black children to be given "black" names than white children to be given "white" names.[11] They also explore name-giving patterns in "black" and "white" hospitals, as well as whether there are different patterns in the giving of distinctively black names versus the giving of uniquely black names.[12] Next, they employ techniques to quantify the relationship between distinctively black names and an array of background, hospital, and county-level characteristics obtained from the birth certificates.

They arrive at three results:

1. The distinctiveness of black names has increased over time.[13]
2. Black names are linked to low socioeconomic status. This link becomes stronger over time.[14]
3. After 1989 (when a richer dataset becomes available), "Blacker names are associated with lower income zip codes, lower levels of parental education, not having private insurance, and having a mother who herself has a Blacker name."[15]

Explaining their results, they apply a model from identity economics, which says that "our conception of who we are and who we want to be may shape our economic lives more than any other factor."[16] Dismissing three alternative models as inconsistent with their results, they conclude that an identity model, in which black names are a means of defining what it means to be black, is most consistent with the patterns they observe. Their model is consistent with the Black Power movement in the 1960s, as well as cultural developments in the 1990s such as a rise in enrollment at historically black colleges and the emergence of politically motivated popular music.[17]

Finally, Levitt and Fryer examine the relationship between "black" names and adult life outcomes by linking "information from a woman's own birth certificate to her adult circumstances as reflected in the information on the birth certificates of her children at the time she gives birth."[18] Their analysis allows them to predict "adult life outcomes as a function of everything known about a woman and her parents at the time of her own birth, including her name."[19]

In contrast to proponents of white fragility theory like DiAngelo, Levitt and Fryer are cautious about what they can say. They emphasize that their "sample for testing the relationship between names and life outcomes is limited to females born in California who later give birth there before the age of 27."[20] They "do not observe individual wages or family economic circumstances, but rather, the median income of their zip code, years of education, etc., which are highly correlated with the relevant outcomes."[21] The key issue, however, is what statisticians call *omitted-variable bias*. This is exactly what it sounds like: bias that results from omitting other explanatory factors.

Levitt and Fryer are quite aware of this possibility and say explicitly that their results might be biased if they failed to account for other important factors. In fact, they worry that their study might *exaggerate* the impact of black names on adult life outcomes. This is because "Black names are associated with lower socioeconomic status."[22] Thus "one would expect that Black names are also likely to be positively correlated with omitted variables that predict worse life outcomes." If so, their estimates might "exaggerate the true relationship between a woman's name and her life outcomes."[23]

Surprisingly, in spite of concerns about omitted variable bias, they find the impact of a woman's name on her life outcomes is *limited "once we control for other factors that are present at the time of her birth."*[24] If they don't control for background characteristics, they find that Blacker names are associated with worse adult outcomes, an expected result given "the correlation between Black names, growing up in segregated neighborhoods, and more difficult home environments."[25] But despite concerns about finding "a spurious negative relationship between names and outcomes," they "conclude that there is little evidence that how Black one's name is negatively impacts life outcomes."[26]

Finally, there are "systematic differences in outcomes for Blacks and Whites with otherwise similar observable characteristics at birth," such as differences in birth weight, marital status, racial composition of mother's neighborhood, per capita income in their neighborhoods, and likelihood of having private insurance.[27]

They suggest that "[t]hese systematic racial differences may reflect either discrimination or unmeasured differences between Blacks and Whites; we have no power to distinguish between these competing hypotheses."[28] This last statement is the kind of Socratic admission one is unlikely to find in DiAngelo's writings.

Finally, Levitt and Fryer situate their paper within an emerging literature on how "black" culture relates to socioeconomic outcomes, without offering sweeping generalizations about the role of black culture in socioeconomic outcomes. Most impressively, they exhibit great care in the restraint with which they interpret their results, and in the use of rigorous techniques to analyze a vast dataset.

DON'T ASK QUESTIONS. LIBERATE YOURSELF!

Contrast the care with which Levitt and Fryer weigh and consider evidence with the approach DiAngelo takes when confronted with criticism of, or questions about, the theory of white fragility. In an overview of the theory of white fragility for the *Australian Financial Review*, journalist Matt Teffer recalls an interview with DiAngelo.[29]

"I think most people would agree that there is racial inequality," DiAngelo says. "An individualist-libertarian viewpoint would say 'Each individual is responsible for their condition.' But I'm coming from a framework that says society is structured in ways that some groups have more opportunities than others."

"This is where it gets hard," she goes on, "because they [her critics] don't start with the premise that their positions as white men have anything to do with it."[30] She does not appear willing to consider, or at least take seriously, the possibility that they do not start from that premise because they have good reasons not to (given all that we have examined so far in this book), whereas she presumes it to be true from the outset.

DiAngelo then makes a startling, and revealing, remark: "I'm just asking people to grapple with a different paradigm, try it on, and take it or leave it, really." Teffer asks, "And what happens if they do grapple, and still disagree?" DiAngelo responds that it is "less relevant to me whether we agree or disagree. . . . I don't really need everyone to agree with me," because "[Malcolm Gladwell's] tipping point theory says you just need 30 per cent to change culture."[31] In other words, DiAngelo is less concerned with proving she is right than she is with gaining adherents.

"'Get to work trying to figure out what racism looks like in your life, rather than defending, deflecting and denying,' she says. 'It's actually liberating.'"[32] This interview is typical of how DiAngelo handles debate and disagreement, as indicated in her academic papers, published books, and public talks.[33] Don't ask questions. Liberate yourself. In other words, she is a proselytizer, not a scholar.

9

A RHETORICAL WEAPON FOR ACTIVIST BULLIES

One goal of white fragility theory is to convince white people to shut up and listen. In an interview with *The Guardian*, Robin DiAngelo said, "The problem with white people . . . is that they just don't listen. In my experience, day in and day out, most white people are absolutely not receptive to finding out their impact on other people. There is a refusal to know or see, or to listen or hear, or to validate."[1]

There should be little doubt that listening is necessary if we are to learn from other people. But listening is only a necessary condition for understanding what other people have to say. It is not sufficient. Many people could listen to a three-hour lecture on nuclear physics, but there is little guarantee that they will understand it. Similarly, we should not expect white people to understand white fragility theory the first, or even the second or third or fourth, time they hear a lecture on it. Not if they are not permitted to ask questions to clear up disagreements or to pursue clarifications.

White fragility theory is attempting to address the important problem of racial inequality. But it has the wrong approach. It is thus not surprising that white people raise questions and objections. This is healthy skepticism. Asking questions and clearing up disagreements are key parts of any careful analysis. Proponents of white fragility theory, however, have little tolerance for questions and objections. They want white people only to shut up and listen. The point of white fragility theory, as we have already hinted in previous chapters, is to indoctrinate, not teach.

The theory of white fragility insists that a white person does not have much to say on racism, and what he does say is almost certain to be unhelpful. He is so mired in implicit biases that his intentions will invariably be at odds with the impact that his thoughts and actions have on people of color. He is simply not equipped to see how his privilege perpetuates a racist society. His "white racial frame"[2] is invisible to him. He does not see all the insidious ways that he keeps Whiteness in place. He cannot help viewing people of color from a perspective of white racial superiority.

This state of affairs gives rise to what DiAngelo calls "white fragility," a condition in which "even a minimum amount of racial stress becomes intolerable, triggering a range of defensive moves," such as an "outward display of emotions such as anger, fear, and guilt, and behaviors such as argumentation, silence, and leaving the stress-inducing situation."[3] Fragility is the status quo for white people. Naturally, any challenge to the status quo provokes and exposes it.

White people instinctively grow hostile when confronted with the suggestion that they support and maintain a racist society. They have not built the stamina to confront, and have not learned how to go about dismantling, their complicity in the perpetuation of racial inequality. This is why white fragility theory insists a white person's only option is to shut up and listen. In an interview with *Teaching Tolerance*, DiAngelo explained:

> I don't call myself a white ally. I'm involved in anti-racist work, but I don't call myself an anti-racist white. And that's because that is for people of color to decide, whether in any given moment I'm behaving in anti-racist ways. And notice that that keeps me accountable. It's for them to determine if in any given moment—it's not a fixed location—I haven't made it or arrived.[4]

Take a moment to think about what this means. Being accountable excludes any kind of due process. Shut up and listen. Take the feedback. Ask no questions. Ignore any tendency to wonder if the feedback might be wrong. Antiracist education is not about introspection, but indoctrination. The only active participation permitted is a zealous effort to internalize the feedback as part of an ongoing effort to root out all the implicit biases that support white privilege.[5]

A CASE STUDY: MICROAGGRESSIONS

DiAngelo's approach not only allows, but indeed encourages, discussion about "whether in any given moment I'm behaving in anti-racist ways" to be speculative rather than rigorous. Consider, for instance, Derald Wing Sue's seminal paper on "Racial Microaggressions in Everyday Life."[6]

Sue defines microaggressions as "brief and commonplace daily verbal, behavioral, or environmental indignities, whether intentional or unintentional, that communicate hostile, derogatory, or negative racial slights and insults toward people of color." The "[p]erpetrators of microaggressions are often unaware that they engage in such communications when they interact with racial/ethnic minorities."[7]

To illustrate, Sue describes a plane ride with an African American colleague from New York to Boston on "a small 'hopper' with a single row of seats on one side and double seats on the other." He writes that "we were told by the flight attendant (White) that we could sit anywhere, so we sat at the front, across the aisle from one another," a location that "made it easy for us to converse and provided a larger comfortable space on a small plane for both of us." Then, "[a]s the attendant was about to close the hatch, three White men in suits entered the plane, were informed they could sit anywhere, and promptly seated themselves in front of us."[8] Sue goes on:

> Just before take-off, the attendant proceeded to close all overhead compartments and seemed to scan the plane with her eyes. At that

> point she approached us, leaned over, interrupted our conversation, and asked if we would mind moving to the back of the plane. She indicated that she needed to distribute weight on the plane evenly [emphasis mine].[9]

Sue and his colleague "had similar negative reactions:"[10]

> First, balancing the weight on the plane seemed reasonable, but why were we being singled out? After all, we had boarded first and the three White men were the last passengers to arrive. Why were they not being asked to move? Were we being singled out because of our race? Was this just a random event with no racial overtones? Were we being oversensitive and petty?[11]

These are reasonable questions. It is easy to sympathize with Sue's anxiety as he wrestled with seemingly unanswerable questions. He and his colleague eventually "complied by moving to the back of the plane," but "felt resentment, irritation, and anger." Given their "everyday racial experiences," Sue and his colleague "came to the same conclusion: The flight attendant had treated us like second-class citizens because of our race."[12]

Feeling "my blood pressure rising, heart beating faster, and face flush with anger," Sue decided to confront the situation. As "the attendant walked back to make sure our seat belts were fastened," while "[s]truggling to control myself," Sue said to her: "Did you know that you asked two passengers of color to step to the rear of the 'bus'"?[13]

The attendant's reaction was predictable:

> For a few seconds she said nothing but looked at me with a horrified expression. Then she said in a righteously indignant tone, "Well, I have never been accused of that! How dare you? I don't see color! I only asked you to move to balance the plane. Anyway, I was only trying to give you more space and greater privacy."
>
> Attempts to explain my perceptions and feelings only generated greater defensiveness from her. For every allegation I made, she seemed to have a rational reason for her actions. Finally, she broke

> off the conversation and refused to talk about the incident any longer.[14]

This reaction is what DiAngelo has in mind when she talks about "[w]eaponized tears" and "[w]eaponized hurt feelings."[15] Thus, "white fragility actually functions as a kind of white racial bullying."[16] Indeed, Sue writes, "Were it not for my colleague who validated my experiential reality, I would have left that encounter wondering whether I was correct or incorrect in my perceptions. Nevertheless, for the rest of the flight, I stewed over the incident and it left a sour taste in my mouth."[17]

Granted, "white racial bullying" makes sense if we see Sue's anxiety as an example of what DiAngelo calls the "psychic burden of race" in chapter 4 of her book *White Fragility*, in which she explains how white people enjoy freedom from the burden of race: "Because I haven't been socialized to see myself or to be seen by other whites in racial terms," she writes, "I don't carry the psychic weight of race; I don't have to worry about how others feel about my race. Nor do I worry that my race will be held against me."[18]

Sue and his colleague did not have that luxury. They concluded instead that "[t]he flight attendant had treated us like second-class citizens because of our race." Their "everyday racial experiences" had convinced them that their impressions accurately reflected the attendant's implicit bias.[19]

Does this mean the attendant's reaction was implausible? No. As Sue acknowledges, "balancing the weight on the plane seemed reasonable."[20] The attendant may have asked Sue and his colleague to move to the back of the plane because they were closer to the back of the plane than the white men who, as Sue notes, sat in front of Sue and his colleague. The attendant may have thought it made sense to ask them simply because they were already closer to the back of the plane. If the white men sat behind Sue and his colleagues, maybe the attendant would have asked the white men to move to the back of the plane. It is equally plausible that the attendant was being honest about "trying to give you more space and greater privacy." "[F]or every allegation I made," Sue concedes, the attendant "seemed to have a rational reason for her actions."[21]

The point is not to agree or disagree with Sue or the flight attendant. It is to demonstrate that it's exceedingly hard, if not impossible, to answer these questions definitively. Any assessment of Sue's anecdote, and of similar anecdotes, involves speculation. This is not to make light of Sue's anxiety.

As a comprehensive critique of the microaggression research paradigm by Dr. Scott Lilienfeld says: "one point should not be in contention: Racial and cultural insensitivities persist in contemporary America, including college campuses. Nor should there be any doubt that prejudice at times manifests itself in subtle and indirect ways that have until recently received short shrift in psychological research."[22]

On the other hand, we should not overlook the reality that there are many things happening simultaneously in any social interaction. Personalities. Moods. Stress. Distractions. Perceptions. Intent. All sorts of things influence what we say and how we say it. This is why it is so important to be careful when interpreting social interactions. This includes being careful in our pushback against allegations of white fragility. We do not want to be *so* careful and scrupulous that skepticism also becomes dogmatic, preventing minorities from voicing their concerns about racial insensitivities.

White fragility theory, however, is careless rather than careful. It disregards due diligence altogether. "It's nice to know you had good intentions," DiAngelo says, "but the impact of what you did was harmful. And we need to let go of our intentions and attend to the impact, to focus on that."[23]

Certainly, we should be mindful of the impact of our actions. Moreover, it may be, as DiAngelo insists, that "[w]e're never going to be able to come to an agreement on intentions" because "[y]ou cannot prove somebody's intentions." But in keeping with the presumption of infallibility that permeates her work, she adds that people "might not even know their intentions," then asserts that "if they weren't good," people are "probably not going to admit that." Hence, she concludes, the question she asks is, "How does this function?" In other words, "[t]he impact of the action is what is relevant."[24]

BULLYING TACTIC

DiAngelo thus sidesteps sensible debate about the intent of our actions. But intent does matter, as it does in the courts (for instance, in tort law), where due process is crucial.[25] Proponents of white fragility theory, however, show little regard for due process. They seem to have no interest in asking, as Sue does, whether an alleged microaggression was "just a random event with no racial overtones" and whether Sue and his colleague were "being oversensitive and petty."[26]

They simply answer in the affirmative, seemingly without any doubt that the same results would be observed in similar states of affairs with different actors. This view presents any insistence on due process to determine whether the answers would be affirmative in the specific case, or generally, as "white racial bullying."

The theory of white fragility thus becomes a tactic for rhetorically bullying anyone who questions the theory. You do not agree? You have questions? You think the situation is more complex? You are not showing curiosity or healthy skepticism. You are demonstrating white fragility.

It would seem to be a natural conclusion that, when people are dealing with sensitive racial matters, silence from whites is appropriate. If they speak up to express skepticism or curiosity, they should be ignored or rejected. White people need to shut up and listen. But alas, shutting up is not enough.

White silence, according to DiAngelo, is not in order because silence in interracial discussions "functions to maintain white power and privilege."[27] It does not matter if you are an introvert. It does not matter if you are humble. It does not matter if you are trying to be polite. It does not matter if you are making an honest and good faith effort to shut up and listen. It does not matter if you are inclined toward skepticism about *any* idea until you have had time to think about the idea.

The only thing that distinguishes "constructive use of white silence from a reinforcement of white racism is that the person is using his or her best judgment, based in an antiracist framework and at each phase of the discussion, of how to engage with the goal of deepening racial self-knowledge, building antiracist community, and interrupting traditional racist power relations." If your silence "is not strategically enacted from [this] antiracist framework," white supremacy remains in place.[28]

Listening up, then, is not enough. You must actively join the endless conversation about how to fight Whiteness and white fragility. You must cultivate the stamina to deal with "race-based stress." You must suppress the tendency to look at any complexities that diverge from the narrative of white fragility.

If you point out that there is a distinction between rights and privileges (taken up in the next chapter), you are showing your white fragility. If you insist that intent matters, you are showing your white fragility. If you say that DiAngelo is being inconsistent by implying on the one hand that listening to feedback is necessary and sufficient, but arguing on the other hand that one must actively be involved in the dismantling of privilege, you are showing your white fragility. If you wonder if intent only seems to matter if you have "right" intent, you are showing your white fragility.

In the spring of 2016, I wrote an article in which I lamented Donald Trump's apparent refusal to disavow David Duke in a radio interview.[29] I described anecdotes in which people I know had shown their biases, which would seem to be the kinds of beliefs and behavior that underlie racism. The essay elicited a reader comment that shows us why white fragility theory is not a helpful guide:

> Did it ever cross your mind that racism is the act of implicitly to justify [*sic*] its benefit of the oppression of a group based on skin color (usual [*sic*] a minority) and in our country a group of folks who were denied resources, civil right [*sic*], economic opportunity, education and dignity. I'm not sure you even cracked the surface of your own implicit bias. I'm so disappointed I read this!

For this reader, I had not yet arrived. Was the reader right to be disappointed? Who is to decide? The reader? The editor who, as a committed social justice activist, was excited to publish the article? Perhaps DiAngelo would suggest that it was fine for the editor to be receptive, but what mattered is that the reader was disappointed. Does that mean that I will not arrive until every reader, or every person of color, decides that I have arrived? Somehow that seems unattainable.

We see that due process matters. Otherwise, we are left with a struggle in which a bully decides whether our behavior is racially sensitive enough, according to his or her own subjective or arbitrary standard. Lest this concern be construed as melodramatic, we need only keep in mind DiAngelo's own words: "Antiracist education seeks to interrupt these relations of inequality by educating people to identify, name, and challenge the norms, patterns, traditions, structures, and institutions that keep racism and white supremacy in place. A key aspect of this education process is to '*raise the consciousness*' [emphasis mine] of white people about what racism is and how it works."[30] Consciousness-raising calls to mind some of the worst practices of totalitarian regimes like Maoist China, vividly illustrated in Nien Cheng's memoir *Life and Death in Shanghai*.[31]

White fragility theory easily becomes a way to bully white people into agreeing with the claims of anyone who comes rallying under the banner of dismantling Whiteness and white privilege. What do we mean by Whiteness and white privilege? More on this in the next chapter, but according to white fragility theory, you are not supposed to ask. If you do, you are showing your white fragility. It is easy to see how this becomes a way for demagogues to bully opponents into submission.

10

A BETTER WAY TO THINK ABOUT WHITENESS AND WHITE PRIVILEGE

The previous chapters in this book may lead us to think that we should dispense entirely with the ideas of Whiteness, white privilege, and white fragility. We should not. White supremacy has been a force in American history, and its effects linger to this day. The problem with the theory of white fragility, and Whiteness Studies in general, is that it gives us ideas that are ill-suited to the analysis of racial inequality. It is also easily manipulated by political interests in a way that corrupts the integrity of education and undermines the fight against racial inequality, as we saw in chapter 7 when reviewing mandatory implicit bias trainings in New York City schools.

This chapter explains how economic theory provides us with a better way to think about Whiteness and white privilege. The basic insight harks back to the argument in chapter 3 that racism and racial inequality are not the same thing. Racism certainly can cause racial inequality, but racial inequality is not, by itself, evidence of racism. In other words, the quixotic quest to dismantle fictional ideologies and fanciful discourses associated with "Whiteness" leads us to conflate racism with the *legacy* of racism.

We must see "structural" racial inequality not as "systemic" racism that must be confronted with ceaseless "woke" consciousness raising about "reified" Whiteness. Instead, we must see racial inequality as a developmental challenge for society. First, we must acknowledge that Whiteness is a kind of public property historically owned by white people that gave rise to white privilege. Second, we must refine our understanding of white privilege. We must reform institutions to ensure that "privileges worth having" are not "club goods" for white people, but "public goods" for everyone. Moreover, we must dismantle "privileges not worth having" while finding a way to remedy the historical harms that resulted from white people benefitting from "privileges not worth having."

We will see that white fragility theory is decidedly unhelpful in attempting to meet these challenges.

THE THEORY OF WHITENESS AND WHITE PRIVILEGE

In her seminal paper on white privilege, Peggy McIntosh writes:

> I have come to see white privilege as an invisible package of unearned assets that I can count on cashing in each day, but about which I was "meant" to remain oblivious. White privilege is like an invisible weightless knapsack of special provisions, assurances, tools, maps, guides, codebooks, passports, visas, clothes, compass, emergency gear, and blank checks.[1]

Five years after McIntosh published her essay, Cheryl Harris wrote a paper titled *Whiteness as Property*, published in the *Harvard Law Review*. In this paper, Harris describes Whiteness as a form of public property. Whiteness is "constituted through the reification of expectations in the continued right of white-dominated institutions to control the legal meaning of group identity."[2]

"Whiteness as property," Harris continues, "is derived from the deep historical roots of systematic white supremacy that has given rise to definitions of group identity predicated on the racial subordination of the 'other,' and that has reified expectations of continued white privilege."[3] In Harris's formulation, having "white" skin means possessing a form of *property*, established and reinforced by law and custom. This "property interest in whiteness has proven to be resilient and adaptive to new conditions":[4]

> Over time it has changed in form, but it has retained its essential *exclusionary* [emphasis mine] character and continued to distort outcomes of legal disputes by favoring and protecting settled expectations of white privilege. The law expresses the dominant conception of "rights," "equality," "property," "neutrality," and "power": rights mean shields from interference; equality means formal equality; *property means the settled expectations* [emphasis mine] that are to be protected; neutrality means the existing distribution, which is natural; and, power is the mechanism for guarding all of this.[5]

Whiteness is property that only white people own. This property is the endowment of a society with a history of white supremacy. This history established "white" norms, habits, values, and beliefs. Since society's institutions are still anchored on Whiteness, white people continue to reinforce these "white" norms, habits, values, and beliefs. Whiteness is "reified." It perpetuates itself. Whiteness, and the privileges to which it gives rise, remains the public property of white people.

Economists view property as a right to make use of a resource. In this case, the resources in question are the advantages associated with being "white." Since the property belongs to all white people, it is publicly owned. This property generates the "invisible package of unearned assets" known as white privilege.[6]

WHITE PRIVILEGE: A CONCEPT IN NEED OF REFINEMENT

The main problem with McIntosh's definition of white privilege is that if we take a look inside this "invisible package of unearned assets," it is not exactly clear what we will find. We can certainly talk generally and meaningfully about the benefits of privilege, but the nature of "white privilege" can be as ambiguous as Whiteness.

One problem is concept creep,[7] the tendency for a concept to expand its meaning over time. For example, McIntosh constructs in her paper a long list of examples of white privilege. These include seemingly obvious examples, such as being able to "arrange to be in the company of people of my race most of the time" and being "reasonably sure that my neighbors in such a location will be neutral or pleasant to me." It also includes less obvious examples such as "flesh-colored" Band-Aids that match white flesh and being "pretty sure of finding a publisher for this piece on white privilege." It does not take much imagination to see this list expanding endlessly over a few glasses of wine.[8]

This "prevalence-induced concept change" is also the subject of a 2018 paper on how the definition of a concept can change as the frequency of incidents to which it applies declines: "When blue dots became rare, purple dots began to look blue; when threatening faces became rare, neutral faces began to appear threatening; and when unethical research proposals became rare, ambiguous research proposals began to seem unethical."[9] In other words, the more or less a concept is used, the more its meaning changes. Thus, "sexism and racism never diminish—even when everyone becomes less sexist and racist."[10]

There is also the problem of monocausality. This is the problem of attributing every instance of racial disparity to white privilege, ignoring the possibility that other factors might also provide insight.[11] It is also the problem of assuming white privilege is at work in any given social interaction.

An example pulls all this together. In a *New York Times* interview, sociologist Michael Eric Dyson talks about being outside Ben's Chili Bowl on U Street in Washington, DC, one night. He saw a drunk white kid harassing a police officer. He was immediately seized with fear that the officer would pull his gun. His dread quickly subsided, however, when the officer told the kid to go sleep it off. Dyson concluded that nothing happened because the kid was white. The drunk white kid *cashed in* an asset from his *white privilege* account and got off easy. A drunk black kid would not be so lucky.

The point is not to say Dyson is wrong. Instead, it is to emphasize how hard it is to conclude he is right. We do not know if a different officer would have acted differently. We do not know if the same police officer would have acted differently on a different night. We also do not know if the officer would have acted differently if the drunk kid were black. We also do not know the many reasons that influenced the police officer, in *that* moment, to decide not to draw his gun. Maybe he was working a late-night beat for the umpteenth time and was too tired or too jaded to bother.[12]

Similarly, McIntosh's list of forty-six examples of white privilege includes "I can be reasonably sure that my neighbors in such a location will be neutral or pleasant to me" and "I can go shopping alone most of the time, fairly well assured that I will not be followed or harassed by store detectives." One cannot know for certain, however, that any specific white person will be able to seamlessly move into a new neighborhood or stroll through a department without being followed by a store detective.[13] "Reasonably sure" and "fairly well assured" mean that white privilege is likely, not certain, to benefit a white person in these cases. To assume what is true on average is true in all cases is called the *ecological fallacy*.[14]

None of this is meant to imply that Dyson, or nonwhites in general, must always give police officers (or white people in general) the benefit of the doubt. This would have its own drawbacks. If we never know with certainty if a different police officer, or the same officer, might have acted differently, there is a causal indeterminacy that gives rise to interminable *search costs* associated with figuring out if a specific social interaction in a specific example of racial disparity is, or is not, a direct result of white privilege. Asking these questions can be exhausting, adding to what DiAngelo calls the "psychic weight of race" in chapter 4 of her book *White Fragility*, in which she describes how white people don't have to worry about whether their race will be held against them.[15]

Indeed, Dyson's anecdote is not only about what actually happened, but about the revelation that Mr. Dyson's reflexive thought was to *expect* police maltreatment when he saw a drunk white kid cursing the police. A white person is not likely to have the same reflexive expectation. In fact, I recall once being stopped by a cop while walking in a well-heeled Washington, DC, neighborhood where the police were searching for a robbery suspect. I instinctively cooperated by allowing the officer to search my backpack, and then was allowed to go free. I never felt panic. I thought to myself: cooperate, and all will be well. The same aplomb does not come as easy to a black person.[16]

We can appreciate the psychic weight of race, however, without allowing ourselves to fall prey to the pitfalls of confirmation bias and omitted variable bias. In contrast, DiAngelo makes no attempt to strike this careful balance. She simply dismisses outright any concern about omitted variable bias as an example of "aversive racism."[17] This reflexive commitment to monocausality not only exposes dogmatism in her thinking, but also prevents a more refined analysis of white privilege.

Though it can be hard to determine when white privilege is at work in practice, we have a plausible idea of what white privilege is in general. It refers to the ways in which white people benefit as a result of being white. One way is that white people do not regularly worry about whether their race is going to held against them. But an important question arises: is privilege necessarily a bad thing?

McIntosh draws a distinction "between positive advantages that we can work to spread, to the point where they are not advantages at all but simply part of the normal civic and social fabric, and negative types of advantage that unless rejected will always reinforce our present hierarchies." The feeling of belonging, for example, is "an entitlement that none of us should have to earn." On the other hand, the "negative 'privilege' that gave me cultural permission not to take darker-skinned Others seriously can be seen as arbitrarily conferred dominance and should not be desirable for anyone."[18]

This takes us to a critique of the ways we have come to understand white privilege. The philosopher Lawrence Blum, following McIntosh, distinguishes between *privileges worth having* and *privileges not worth having*.[19] The former can be divided into (1) "spared-injustice" privileges and (2) other privileges not related to injustice, while the latter can be more precisely described as "unjust enrichment" privileges.[20]

"Spared-injustice" privilege is when "a person of color suffer[s] an unjust treatment of some kind while a White person does not."[21] For example, "[t]he White person is spared the injustice of discrimination,"[22] as when "a Black person is stopped by the police without due cause but a White person is not."[23] Professor Blum writes, "In this case the privilege is simply in being spared an injustice suffered by the person of color, but without further benefiting from that injustice."[24]

"Non-injustice-related" privilege is "when one benefits from one's position, in a manner that one does not deserve from a moral point of view, but, in contrast to the previous two categories, the benefit is not related to an injustice suffered by the disadvantaged group."[25] One example is the "linguistic privilege" that comes with speaking a native language. Of course, there can be "discrimination against persons with 'accents' of various kinds, or violation of rights that should be independent of native language, such as voting rights or receiving of public services. But some advantages of being a native speaker do not involve discrimination."[26] Being able to fit in is not necessarily a bad thing.

A similar situation involves the "informal cultures of workplaces and professions," which "tend to have a partly ethno-cultural character, so that members of some ethnic or racial groups find them more comfortable than do others." In America, white people have been the majority, and these kinds of "biases have historically been shaped by exclusion, and in that respect are unjust."[27]

We can imagine, however, a "future in which the historical injustices have been rectified." Even so, it is possible "that some degree of ethnic bias in workplace culture would still remain, simply because of a majority/minority dynamic." But "[t]his would be a kind of unearned privilege not founded on injustice.[28]

Finally, there is "unjust enrichment." According to Blum, "the system of White privilege is so deeply entrenched in American life, institutions and history" that "it is difficult for Whites to escape unjust enrichment."[29] Thus "[w]hen Blacks are denied access to desirable homes, for example, this is not just an injustice to Blacks but a positive benefit to Whites who now have a wider range of domicile options than they would have if Blacks had equal access to housing." Moreover, "[w]hen urban schools do a poor job of educating their Latino/a and Black students, this benefits Whites in the sense that it unjustly advantages them in the competition for higher levels of education and jobs."[30]

In sum, "privileges worth having" are more like rights that should be expanded to people of color rather than entitlements which should be taken away from white people. As philosopher Lewis Gordon explains:

> A privilege is something that not everyone needs, but a right is the opposite. Given this distinction, an insidious dimension of the white-privilege argument emerges. It requires condemning whites for possessing, in the concrete, features of contemporary life that should be available to all, and if this is correct, how can whites be expected to give up such things?[31]

In contrast, "privileges not worth having" are advantages that unjustly enrich whites at the expense of people of color. Examples are residential segregation resulting from redlining, differences in the rate of police abuse, and biased white juries that exonerate a guilty white people and convict an innocent black person.

This distinction between "privileges worth having" and "privileges not worth having" tells us that privilege is not necessarily a bad thing. Whether it is good or bad depends on the nature of the privilege. As a matter of economics, "privileges worth having" are like public goods, while "privileges not worth having" are like public bads.

Public goods are things like the right to vote, national defense, and clean air. They are things we want to have. Public bads are things like pollution. We want to avoid them. Public goods and public bads are examples of "market failures." Public policy needs to step in and find a way to produce public goods while getting rid of public bads.

In the next few sections, we will see that "privileges worth having" are public goods that have historically been "club goods" for white people. Meanwhile "privileges not worth having" are public bads that must be avoided. We also see how "privileges not worth having" can result in tort harms. In general, we develop an economic theory of Whiteness that gives us a better way to think about the pursuit of racial justice. We will then see how the theory of white fragility gets in the way.

"PRIVILEGES WORTH HAVING" ARE PUBLIC GOODS

Economists define a public good as one that is *nonrivalrous* and *nonexcludable*. A good is nonrivalrous if one person's consumption of the good does not deplete the amount of the good available for consumption by others. It is nonexcludable if it is too costly to exclude people from consuming the good.

Classic examples are clean air and national defense. Once available, it is difficult, if not impossible, to charge a price because people benefit regardless of whether they pay, and thus the willingness to pay for some unit of the good cannot be easily determined. Moreover, it costs too much to exclude people from consumption. Public goods stand in contrast to private goods, which are both rivalrous and excludable.

Spared-injustice privileges and non-injustice-related privileges are public goods. The "privilege" of being spared injustices, such as discriminatory treatment by a police officer or a workplace supervisor, does not prevent others from being spared injustices such as discriminatory treatment by the same police officer or workplace supervisor. For example, a police officer who watches two cars drive by his cruiser simultaneously, both observing the speed limit and not violating any traffic laws, can decide not to stop either of them. Both drivers are spared injustice at the same time.

Similarly, the "privilege" of being a member of the majority, or being able to speak a native language, does not come at the expense of other members of the majority or other native speakers. All else equal, everyone who speaks the native language, or is a member of the majority, garners respect, comfort, and a sense of belonging at the same time. Everyone naturally fits in.

There is, however, no free lunch. These privileges, like rights and other advantages bestowed by law or custom or governance, require institutions that endow society with norms, habits, best practices, beliefs, and values that ensure everyone enjoys a high expectation of being spared injustice. Moreover, these institutions require ongoing maintenance. Finally, the ongoing norms, habits, beliefs, and values that underlie and reinforce a majority culture or native language should ensure that minorities or nonnative speakers can expect fair treatment from native speakers and members from the majority group.

Nevertheless, even in a society with well-designed institutions, one can expect instances of ill-treatment. Human imperfection provides a decisive economic reason that one should not expect that justice will always prevail. "Privilege" will not be guaranteed in all circumstances. Why is this? The reason is that society incurs costs in setting up and maintaining this institutional arrangement.

Police forces must be trained to treat everyone impartially. Courts must have procedures to facilitate the administration of justice. Schools must abide by curriculum standards while accommodating special needs and not cultivating or spreading discriminatory behavior. Workplaces must uphold standards of conduct that promote productive economic activity without compromising constructive cultural engagement. Community organizations must equitably deploy resources. Settled residents must have incentives to welcome new families who move into the neighborhood.

Institutional integrity depends on human behavior. Institutions must be well designed and have enough resources to carry out their missions. But their design, implementation, and everyday application depend on citizens' good-faith commitment to justice. Constitutions can be written. Legislation can be passed. But police officers, judges, juries, teachers, firms, community organizers, residents, and others must do their part. The public good of privilege depends on daily human effort.

As with other public goods (e.g., law enforcement), the optimal amount of privilege is where the marginal willingness of each citizen to pay for "privileges worth having" is equal to the marginal cost that society incurs in providing these "privileges worth having." Privileges worth having are earned privileges, not, as Peggy McIntosh describes them in her seminal paper, "unearned entitlement[s]" that "none of us should have to earn."[32] Privileges worth having are a public good for which people should be willing to pay. The provision of public goods such as privileges worth having confers benefits to society for which people are, and should, be willing to pay.

But what does it mean to pay? We can understand a willingness to pay for privileges worth having in terms of the human effort that is necessary and sufficient to ensure that institutions work for us. Police officers, judges, juries, teachers, human resource professionals, community organizers and citizens in general must all do their part to ensure that people are "spared injustice" and that they enjoy the benefits of non-injustice-related privileges. This collective commitment to such "privileges worth having" benefits everyone—including police officers, judges, juries, teachers, human resource professionals, community organizers, neighbors, and other citizens.

"Spared-injustice" and "non-injustice-related" privileges must be earned in the sense that these privileges can only survive as long as all members of society assume responsibility for upholding the institutions that protect these privileges. The cost of ensuring "privileges worth having" is thus a *civic duty*:

1. Citizens must collectively set up the just and fair institutional arrangement (form the social contract).
2. Citizens must collectively develop effective social and economic policies,
3. Citizens must collectively ensure the ongoing survival of "privileges worth having" by each fulfilling his or her "civic duty."

The problem with public goods is that free riding can occur. In this case, "privileges worth having" do not happen if citizens expect others to do their civic duty but fail to do their own civic duty, in which privileges do indeed become *unearned*. This can happen because the marginal cost of a citizen doing his duty outweighs the marginal benefit derived from *others* doing *their* duty.

Even if anyone can move into a new neighborhood facing the same (low) probability of harassment or bias from neighbors, any particular person may not feel compelled to exert the effort sufficient to ensure that other new neighbors are also welcomed into the community. He can expect to be well treated but may not "pay" for this treatment by putting in the effort to ensure others are also well-treated (the world is not without its grumps, curmudgeons, misanthropes, and free riders).

Similarly, a police officer may not feel especially compelled to treat everyone impartially if he is having a bad day or does not believe that his own professional behavior will affect the (low) probability with which *he* will not be treated impartially.

This is a calculation each individual makes. The social marginal benefit of each unit of "civic duty" exceeds the social marginal cost up to the optimal point. But at each level of production up to the optimal level, public goods generate "positive externalities"—when you do your civic duty, you do your part to make "privileges worth having" possible. Everyone benefits, at least up to the point where focusing so much on civic duty ends up becoming too tiresome. In economic-speak, the social benefit of each unit of "civic duty" exceeds the social cost up to the optimal point.

This works, then, if everyone does the civic duty expected of them. If they do, they ensure the optimal amount of "privileges worth having." In the case of private goods, a person can consume an additional unit only if he pays for it, because otherwise someone else will pay the price and consume it instead. The consumer thus reveals his willingness to pay for the good. With public goods, once the good is available, it is available to everyone at once, regardless of whether they pay a price. This is why people have an incentive to "free ride." Why pay when you don't have to? Of course, if everyone thinks like that, society is unable to make the public good available.

It is difficult, if not impossible, to determine each person's marginal willingness to pay for a public good. How much effort is a person willing to exert to ensure that institutions are set up—or in the present world, reformed—such that society provides an optimal amount of privilege? Once the institutions are set up, one can *free ride* on them. Many people are happy to be well-treated by others but may feel no special obligation or incentive to consciously "do unto others as you would have done unto you." Our actions benefit not only ourselves, but others, and thus everyone benefits when everyone does their civic duty. But then, people may neglect to do their civic duty while "free riding" on the civic duty of others.

For many people, the incremental cost of doing one's civic duty outweighs the incremental benefit of being "well-treated" by everyone else who does their duty. Think of a voter for whom the cost of getting to the polls outweighs the benefit of voting to elect a leader whose policies may only minimally affect his life.[33] The ideal arrangement is one in which everyone enjoys privileges worth having, and earns them by performing their civic duty. If not, the institutions break down—during social contract formation, social and economic policy development, or everyday social interactions. For example, if everyone fails to vote, what is the point of democracy?

The probability that any person will fail to fulfill his duty is probably not always one hundred percent. But free riding will likely lead to a suboptimal amount of "privileges worth having." To meet the costs, society must motivate citizens to reveal their willingness to pay for these services.

In practice, this means that society must motivate people to do their civic duty. In classic cases such as national defense, society collects taxes to pay for the provision of public goods. Here, progressive taxation is often recommended, because people with more income tend to want more of the public good.

America's founding fathers formed a Constitution that guaranteed to its citizenry certain inalienable rights (privileges worth having), designed to spare its citizens the injustices that stem from an oppressive government. It incurred great costs in terms of the American Revolutionary War and the formidable "transaction costs" associated with developing a constitution on which enough people could agree.

"Privileges worth having" became nonrivalrous once the institutions were established. In the United States, the system did not break down when it was formed—presumably because people revealed their willingness to pay by going to war to secure freedom from imperial rule. Subsequent events in American history, such as the Jacksonian expansion of suffrage (to all white men), demonstrated the substantial costs of developing the social and economic policy that spared citizens the injustice of not being able to vote because they did not own property. Once voting privileges were institutionalized, everyone benefited, as long as enough people fulfilled their civic duty to vote.

Of course, racism institutionalized the practice of excluding privileges worth having from nonwhite people. Whiteness made privilege available to white men at low marginal cost. Stated differently, Whiteness was a way for American society to provide a socially inefficient amount of privileges worth having. Though Civil Rights legislation brought an end to official discrimination, white persons are still more likely to be spared injustice and enjoy non-injustice-related privileges than nonwhite persons. They need only fulfill their civic duty to white people, rather than to all people. In sum, Whiteness resulted in a socially inefficient provision of "public good" privileges worth having.

CLUB GOODS THAT SHOULD BE PUBLIC GOODS

Some goods that are nonexcludable are rivalrous, and some goods that are nonrivalrous are excludable. These are hybrid goods.

An example of the former is the *tragedy of the commons*, which refers to a situation in which individuals overuse a common resource because they weigh only the benefits and costs they incur as individuals rather than as a community. As more users exploit the resources, failing to take into the account the collective depletion of the resource, the community eventually loses the resource.[34]

An example of the latter is broadcast television. Once a show is on broadcast television, it can be viewed by anyone with a television. But if the show is pay-per-view, the show becomes excludable. Another example is Whiteness. White people do not benefit from Whiteness at the expense of other white people (it is nonrivalrous), but people of color are excluded from the benefits of Whiteness by virtue of not being white (excludable).

In short, hybrid goods can be classified as commons goods or collective goods. Commons goods are nonexcludable and rivalrous, while collective goods are nonrivalrous and excludable.

Collective goods are also known as *club goods*. The economic theory of clubs was originally developed in a paper by James M. Buchanan.[35] Buchanan attempted to develop a general theory that "covers the whole spectrum of ownership-consumption possibilities, ranging from the purely private or individualized activity on the one hand to purely public or collectivized activity on the other." The theory of clubs is "a theory of co-operative membership" that includes "as a variable to be determined the extension of ownership-consumption rights over differing numbers of persons."[36]

In contrast to public goods, it is club members, not the public, that share the good.[37] The good could be a country club's golf course, a community center's swimming pool, or a gym's exercise equipment. The good is available to all members of the club, but "the utility that an individual receives from its consumption depends upon the number of other persons with whom he must share its benefits."[38]

Efficiency requires not only equating the marginal benefit and marginal cost at an optimal level of production of the good, but also requires equating the marginal benefit of some amount of the good with the marginal cost of allowing another person into the club in which the good can be consumed.

As the size of a club increases, the number of members at which congestion becomes a problem also increases. As Buchanan writes, "This reflects the fact that, normally for the type of good considered in this example, there will exist a complementary rather than a substitute relationship between increasing the quantity of the good and increasing the size of the sharing group."[39]

At some point, a club good may become a public good. It becomes an indivisible good that is available for everyone to consume. The benefit per person is not influenced by the number of consumers allowed to partake in consumption. There is no congestion, as in the case of a national defense.

As Buchanan writes, there is an "equilibrium only with respect to goods quantity [that] can be reached, defined with respect to the *all-inclusive* finite group." Congestion may be "possible over small sizes of facility, but if an equilibrium quantity is provided, there is no congestion, and, in fact, there remain economies of scale in club size."[40] Club goods become public goods when congestion is not a problem.

Ultimately, Buchanan writes, "Whether or not a particular good is purely private, purely public, or somewhere between these extremes" depends on the number of people who consume the good.[41] When the number of consumers is small, the good is largely private. When the number is big, the good is largely public. A public good is one for which "the all-inclusive club remains too small."[42]

When Whiteness is public property for white people, "privileges worth having" are denied to nonwhite people. The benefits associated with "privileges worth having" are *club goods* for white people rather than *public goods* for everyone. Like gyms, country clubs, and community centers with swimming pools that are available only to a community of people who pay a membership fee, Whiteness as public property gives rise to exclusive communities in which white people, but not people of color, can draw from an "invisible package of unearned assets" to "buy" their way into "clubs."

Think of redlined residential communities or majority cultures in workplaces. White privilege is a package of assets with which white people secure the benefits of membership in the club of Whiteness, while people of color are excluded because they lack the currency of being "white."

Racism made "privileges worth having" excludable. Only white people were able to "buy" them (free ride) by "cashing in" an asset from their (unearned) white privilege accounts. The social contract, formed by white ancestors and maintained by white contemporaries, "reified" Whiteness as public property.[43] Racism allowed white people to free-ride by relieving them of their civic duty to nonwhite people, turning what should have been a public good into a club good for white people only. "Privileges worth having" have been a public good for which "the all-inclusive club remains too small."

"PRIVILEGES NOT WORTH HAVING" ARE PUBLIC BADS[44]

A public bad is like the noise produced by a wind turbine company.[45] It is a public nuisance whose cost is born by nearby residents rather than the turbine company. In other words, it is what economists call a *negative externality*. It is a cost not for the company but for nearby residents. Noise does not affect the firm's profit.

Unjust enrichment is a "privilege not worth having." In this case, white privilege is a public bad. It benefits white people directly at the expense of people of color. White people have no incentive to alter their consumption of this "privilege not worth having" because only people of color incur the marginal cost of white people being unjustly enriched. For example, if an innocent black person is found guilty of a crime by a biased jury, the guilty white person thereby exonerated is unjustly enriched. The benefit of exoneration imposes a heavy cost on the innocent black person.

In the case of "privileges not worth having," we can analyze "systemic racial inequality" in terms of utility maximization in consumer theory. Systemic racial inequality typically, or at least often, focuses on metrics such as income and wealth. But Whiteness Studies, and white fragility theory, perceive socioeconomic measures of inequality as symptomatic rather than diagnostic.

Racial inequality encompasses a far broader set of realities that have their historical roots in norms, habits, beliefs, and practices that collectively place Whiteness at the center of social and cultural life. Racial inequality in income and wealth can only, or at least mostly, be addressed by *decentering* Whiteness, which principally, if not singlehandedly, explains all systemic disparities in the experiences of white and black people—differences in their interactions with the law, police officers, doctors, recruiters, bosses, colleagues, clients, teachers, neighbors, political representatives, store managers, cashiers, coaches, teammates, cultural media, and so on.

As a result, the life experiences of white and black people are different. If the "utility" of life experiences could be quantified, a higher value would be associated with the average white person than the average black person. In what economists call the *utility maximization problem*, the optimal "utility" derived from consumption of goods and services over a lifetime—happiness derived from "life experience"—is higher for the average white person than it is for the average black person.

This average difference is sustained over time. If it does not increase, it does not decline over time. Racial inequality is "structural" in the sense that utility (i.e., happiness and well-being) is higher for the average white person than the average black person, and this inequality persists over time.

Consider an "average" white consumer and "average" black consumer. Each consumer attempts to maximize utility (happiness) over a lifetime. Utility comes from consumption of a bundle of goods, services, and "unjust enrichment" privileges. In the case of "unjust enrichment" privileges, the average black consumer's utility does not depend on his *own* consumption of "unjust enrichment" privileges. It depends on the average white consumer's consumption of unjust enrichment.

The black consumer's utility rises or falls as the white person's consumption of "unjust enrichment" privileges falls or rises. As Blum writes, "When Blacks are denied access to desirable homes, for example, this is not just an injustice to Blacks but a positive benefit to Whites who now have a wider range of domicile options than they would have if Blacks had equal access to housing."[46] When the average white consumer benefits from unjust enrichment, the average black consumer loses.

If a white consumer enjoys "a wider range of domicile options"[47] because the black consumer does not have equal access to housing, the black consumer's utility falls while utility for the white consumer rises. This is similar to how someone suffers from second-hand smoke emitted by another person who enjoys smoking a cigarette. The white person, like the smoker, ignores the social cost of "unjust enrichment" privileges. His consumption of "unjust enrichment" privilege, like the smoker's consumption of cigarettes, imposes a cost on the black person. It creates a *negative externality*.

Notice that the white consumer's utility from consumption of "unjust enrichment" privilege comes at the expense of the black consumer but not the white consumer. Thus, "unjust enrichment" privilege is like smoking. It is an externality that has consequences for *many* people rather than a few. It is a public bad.

Like a public good, a public bad has features that make it nonrivalrous and nonexcludable. In the case of "unjust enrichment" privilege, it is more akin to a *collective* bad. Consider smoking. Smoking creates second-hand smoke, which is nonrivalrous. Many nonsmokers nearby suffer all at once, just as the "wider range of domicile options" for the white consumer benefits white consumers collectively (on average) while harming black consumers collectively (on average).

The average white consumer not only fails to fulfill his "civic duty" to ensure that the average black consumer has equal access to desirable homes. He also does not internalize the *social*, or *external*, cost of his privilege, which is incurred by the average black consumer who has fewer domicile options.

In cases involving public bads, compensation for damages as a result of negative externalities is usually considered a more efficient remedy than an injunction because of the number of people involved. An injunction provides an incentive for the parties involved to privately negotiate a solution. But in the case of public bads, collective bargaining may be too costly.

The courts can intervene to determine the damages from the externality.[48] In the context of racism, one can think of the debate about reparations as a debate about how to determine the damages associated with "unjust enrichment" privileges. This debate, or conversation, is costly, especially given that that the conversation involves millions of people discussing damages incurred across many generations.

The correct assessment of damages is neither clear nor obvious. The analysis is complex and variegated. It requires construction of a "but-for" world in which the externalities suffered by nonwhite people as a result of "unjust enrichment" privilege did not occur. This "but-for" world can then be compared with the actual world in which nonwhite people suffered the cost of these externalities. The difference in outcomes between the "but-for" and actual worlds is the estimate of damages.

But even before we can proceed to a comparison of the actual world and the "but-for" world to estimate the difference in outcomes in the actual and "but-for" worlds, we must be able to begin, and sustain, the conversation.

If the controversies on reparations in particular and race relations in general are any indication, it is obvious that the "transaction costs" of resolving disputes about the damages arising from "unjust enrichment" privilege are exceedingly high. As highlighted by the famous Coase theorem, when the transaction costs of negotiation exceed the gains, the possibility of dispute resolution breaks down.[49]

RACIAL HARMS AND EFFICIENT PRECAUTION

Human imperfection implies that the optimal institutional arrangement cannot be expected to eliminate abuses altogether. In seeking to optimize, we seek to minimize the probability that white people and people of color will suffer ill treatment. In other words, we seek to maximize the "privileges worth having" that we have identified as "spared-injustice" and "non-injustice-related" privileges, and to minimize the privileges of "unjust enrichment" that are not worth having.

This optimal institutional arrangement failed to materialize in American history. This takes us to what mathematicians call the *law of large numbers* and Bayesian analysis. Privilege can be understood in terms of systemic discrimination by pointing out that, while every individual has a different experience and every experience is subject to varying interpretations, privilege means that, *on average*, the black person can expect to encounter difficulties that a white person does not.[50]

The national conversation on race relations and racial justice should also focus both on developing the institutional arrangement to eliminate this disparity in probabilities, and to minimize the probability altogether for both white people and people of color. This conversation also may focus on remedies to compensate for past wrongs that stemmed from these disparities, as well as ongoing wrongs that occur as a result of human imperfection.

This brings us to torts, which are harms people inflict on each other that result in legal liability. As suggested in previous sections in this chapter, white privilege can be understood in terms of torts. "Spared-injustice" privilege implies that the probability of being followed in a department store by a store detective, or being abused by the police, is lower for white people than for people of color.

The cost, in terms of anxiety, from being followed by a store detective without cause, or being ill-treated by the police, is like a tort. The economic analysis of torts is concerned with liability rules that encourage potential offenders to exercise efficient levels of precaution. If these rules can be implemented, white people and people of color would be "spared injustice" with equally high probability.

According to one textbook in law and economics, tort law addresses "harm for which the laws of contracts and property offer no remedy."[51] Tort law applies to racial justice because the social contract underlying American institutions for much of American history has not guaranteed protections from, and provisions for redress for, the harms stemming from racial injustice, or not being well-treated by people who benefit from majority–minority dynamics or other "non-injustice-related" privileges.

As a matter of economics, the first thing we must address are the incentives that result in efficient or inefficient levels of precaution designed to prevent "accidents," or actions that result in harm.[52] The more precaution taken, either by a victim or perpetrator, the less likely an "accident," or action that results in harm, can be expected to occur. For much of American history, it was the burden of people of color to exert sufficient precaution to avoid conflicts with institutional representatives such as police officers that might result in harm. This is akin to a situation in law in which the law specifies no liability rule. In other words, the perpetrator is not liable for harm.

In such a case, the onus is on the victim to take precautions to avoid harm, for example, by avoiding certain behaviors around police officers that a white person could undertake without fear of retaliation. This precaution minimizes the probability of an action that results in harm. Alternatively, strict liability rules that mandate compensatory damages provide an incentive for the perpetrator to take precautions that minimize the probability of partaking in an action that results in harm.

In real life, it is often unclear who is at fault. Society must arrange incentives for both potential perpetrators and victims to take efficient precautions. For example, police officers must not assume the worst if black drivers who are pulled over express frustration about being pulled over, while black drivers understand that officers must follow protocol as part of their duty.

In these cases, negligence rules with a mandate for compensatory damages can be shown to provide efficient incentives for both parties.[53] A party to a dispute is held liable for harm only if he *neglected* to take sufficient precaution to avoid the action resulting in harm. In the case of torts, the national conversation on race relations must focus on cultivating incentives for everyone to take efficient levels of precaution in their social interactions to ensure that other people are spared injustice or otherwise not ill-treated in a context of majority–minority dynamics.

"REPARATIONS" AND THE POLITICAL COASE THEOREM

We now examine the collective "reparations" effort to address the wrongs of historical racism, in which racism is understood as:

1. Failure to maximize "privileges worth having" (i.e., to turn a club good for white people into a public good for everyone)
2. Failure to minimize "privileges not worth having" (i.e., to ensure that white people internalize the costs of "unjust enrichment")
3. Failure to establish rules to minimize the impact of racial tort harms

The Coase theorem is a famous theorem in the economic analysis of law and property that claims that, assuming zero transaction costs, the legal assignment of property rights does not matter.[54] Disputes over property rights can be adequately resolved as a result of private bargaining between parties involved in a dispute.

The textbook Coase story considers a conflict involving externalities that result from the exercise of property rights, such as the effects of pollution by a firm on a nearby residential community. If transaction costs are zero, private bargaining between the parties results in the *same* outcome regardless of which side wins the property rights in court, though who wins the rights can affect transfers of money.

For example, as explained by economist Jodi Beggs, consider a conflict between a wind turbine company and nearby residents who resent the noise that results from operating the turbine. Since it is likely that the company values operation of the turbine more than the residents value quiet, the company will pay residents for the right to continue operation if the courts rule in favor of the residents on the question of who owns the property rights.

If the courts instead bestow property rights to the company, the company continues operation and probably does not pay residents because "the households aren't willing to pay enough to convince the turbine company to cease operation." Thus "the assignment of rights . . . [doesn't] affect the outcome once the opportunity to bargain [is] introduced, but the property rights [do] affect the transfers of money between the two parties."[55]

In a paper on the "political Coase theorem,"[56] economist Daron Acemoglu explains that "[a]n extension of this reasoning to the political sphere suggests that political and economic transactions create a strong tendency towards policies and institutions that achieve the best outcomes given the varying needs and requirements of societies, irrespective of who, or which social group, has political power."[57]

Thus "policy and institutional differences are not the major determinant of the differences in economic outcomes, because societies choose, at least approximately, the appropriate policies and institutions for their conditions."[58] In a modified version of the political Coase theorem, "societies may choose different policies, with very different implications, because they or their leaders disagree about what would be good for the society ("theories of belief differences").[59]

In contrast to a pure or modified political Coase theorem, "theories of social conflict" claim that "societies choose different policies, some of which are disastrous for their citizens, because those decisions are made by political or politically powerful social groups that are interested in maximizing their own payoffs, not aggregate output or social welfare."[60] This inherent conflict arises whether "internal conflict within the society leads to inefficient choices" or "inefficient institutions and policies are imposed on societies from the outside, e.g., by colonial powers."[61]

This result contrasts with the prediction, under a standard application of the Coase theorem to politics, that efficient socioeconomic outcomes and redistribution of gains can arise from political and economic transactions among social groups regardless of which group has political power. If such outcomes do not arise, it is not conflict among groups that accounts for suboptimal outcomes, but disagreements about the efficacy of alternative policies and institutional arrangements.

Acemoglu's analysis implies that "conflicts of interest between different social groups"[62] impede political bargaining over the development of efficient policies and institutions because "parties holding political power cannot make commitments to bind their future actions because there is no outside agency with the coercive capacity to enforce such arrangements,"[63] as is assumed to be the case in a Coase model of negotiation between private parties with a third-party (e.g., the state) to enforce contracts.

Thus inefficient outcomes and absence of redistributive policies arise because groups in power lack a commitment to a social contract that is sufficient to ensure enforcement of the contract. This lack of commitment is a "transaction cost" that prevents resolution of disputes, or even formation of the social contract. We can view this "transaction cost" as an impediment to the "reparations" project of maximizing "privileges worth having," minimizing "privileges not worth having," and minimizing the impact of racial tort harms.

WHITE FRAGILITY THEORY UNDERMINES THE PURSUIT OF RACIAL JUSTICE

In the context of racial justice, Acemoglu's analysis implies that a failure of the political Coase theorem is the result of either (1) factional differences about the efficacy of various policies, or (2) factional conflicts between social groups that persist because the dominant social group has no coercive power to ensure it holds up its end of a bargain.[64]

Under (2), the lack of commitment is a sufficiently large "transaction cost" to preclude the collective bargaining necessary to maximize privileges worth having, minimize privileges not worth having, and establish rules to minimize the impact of racialized tort harms. This is the claim made by the theory of white fragility.

In this view, white fragility perpetuates white complicity.[65] This complicity is a complacency that quells any exhortation to address racial justice. White fragility functions as a lack of commitment to racial justice. Defined as a condition in which "even a minimum amount of racial stress becomes intolerable, triggering a range of defensive moves," such as an "outward display of emotions such as anger, fear, and guilt, and behaviors such as argumentation, silence, and leaving the stress-inducing situation,"[66] white fragility causes white people to perceive conversations about "institutional" racism and white moral responsibility[67] as an inconvenience at best and a hindrance at worst.

The perpetuation of racial inequality is the result of a commitment problem in which white people, as the dominant social group, are unwilling to part with the privileges that arise from being white in a society in which Whiteness is property. Controlling the levers of power, white people refuse to commit to the dismantling of white privilege, perceiving the costs of behavioral changes, policies, and reforms that might arise from such conversations as outweighing any gains, both to themselves and to people of color.

The cost of fulfilling their civic duty to everyone outweighs the benefits. If they signed off on policies to turn a club good into a public good, the absence of a neutral third-party to enforce policy implementation would cause a breakdown in commitment.

The previous sections in this chapter have paved the way for an alternative view in which the political Coase theorem breaks down under (1)—in other words, factional differences about the efficacy of various policies—and for the idea that the *theory* of white fragility, rather than what Robin DiAngelo calls *white fragility*, imposes a substantial transaction cost that militates against progress in the national conversation on how to address systemic racial inequality.

The fatal flaw in DiAngelo's theory is that it is plausible only if there is a widespread *explicit* effort by white people to retain control of institutional privilege at the expense of people of color, or if *implicit* bias obstructs an otherwise well-intended commitment to the expansion of privileges worth having and the dismantling of privileges not worth having—in other words, a commitment to racial justice.

But neither hypothesis holds up well under evidence. First, as discussed in chapter 2, changes in implicit bias do not necessarily lead to changes in explicit behavior. Second, explicit preferences for discrimination against blacks have declined dramatically among whites over the last half-century. Third, if white guilt among progressives is any indication, many white people are quite willing to put in the effort to ensure that nonwhite people are "spared injustice" or otherwise not victimized by "non-injustice-related" privileges. They are also quite willing to do away with "unjust enrichment" privileges.[68]

Finally, as Vincent Harinam and Rob Henderson explained in great detail in two articles for *Quillette*, "white progressives insist on spreading the gospel of white privilege."[69] Despite the rise of white identity politics, white people, by a large measure, support the pursuit of racial justice, despite the pessimism of critical race theorists who insist that such support does not exempt white people from "color-blind racism."[70]

These studies should not be taken to imply that the core tenets of Whiteness Studies are untenable. In their paper "An Empirical Assessment of Whiteness Theory," sociologists Douglas Hartmann, Joseph Gerteis, and Paul Croll draw on a "nationally representative survey (2003, N = 2081)" by the American Mosaic Project to "analyze three specific propositions relating to whites' awareness and conception of their own racial status: the invisibility of white identity; the understanding (or lack thereof) of racial privileges; and adherence to individualistic, color-blind ideals."[71]

They find "that white Americans are less aware of privilege than individuals from racial minority groups and consistently adopt color-blind, individualist ideologies," but "*also find that whites are both more connected to white identity and culture as well as more aware of the advantages of their race than many theoretical discussions suggest*."[72]

Hartmann and colleagues do a commendable service in articulating the difficulties of conducting a quantitative analysis of the core claims of Whiteness Studies. For example, they write that "claims about awareness of privilege—or, more precisely, the lack thereof—are extremely difficult to test with survey data for the obvious reason that it is essentially impossible to ask about a respondent's awareness of something like white advantage without calling attention to it in the question itself."[73] Nonetheless, they make an admirable attempt to conduct such a quantitative analysis:

> Overall, we find substantial support for key tenets of whiteness theory: whites' racial identities tend to be less visible than those of individuals from other racial groups, and whites are less likely to see ways

> that they have been actively advantaged by being white. At the same time, *we find that white identities and advantages are more salient than the whiteness literature typically assumes, and that color-blind, individualist ideologies and beliefs are by no means limited to whites.* Based upon these findings, we then estimate the number of white Americans that adhere uniformly and consistently to the core tenets of whiteness as theorized by scholars, a measure we call "categorical whiteness." [Their estimate is 15 percent.][74]

Indeed, "[a]lready in 2001," they write, "Frankenberg (2001) realized that the reality may be messier than the strong versions of the theory suggested. 'The more one scrutinizes it . . . the more the notion of whiteness as an unmarked norm is revealed to be a mirage.'"[75] Consistent with the lack of methodological rigor of Whiteness Studies in general and white fragility theory in particular, which we saw in chapter 4, Hartmann and colleagues "conclude by suggesting that these findings provide the basis for a more nuanced, contextualized understanding of whiteness as a social phenomenon."[76]

As this book has argued, one of the chief drawbacks of Whiteness Studies and white fragility theory is not that their concerns are entirely fabricated, but that the scholarship is undisciplined and doctrinaire. It could benefit from more humility and methodological rigor. Moreover, the central concept of white privilege is deeply ambiguous and in need of refinement. In this chapter, we have reviewed an alternative framework for understanding Whiteness and white privilege.

Unfortunately, as the fraught national conversation on race indicates, a principled commitment to racial equity does not necessarily imply an agreement about the specific policies that (1) will most effectively turn a club good for white people into a public good for everyone, (2) ensure that white people internalize the costs of "unjust enrichment," or (3) provide incentives for everyone to take efficient levels of precaution in their social interactions to ensure that other people are spared injustice or otherwise not ill-treated in a context of majority–minority dynamics.

Policy differences can be said to be a function of "belief differences" as mentioned in Acemoglu's analysis of the political Coase theorem, rather than a result of social conflict as the heart of Acemonglu's analysis covers, and which the theory of white fragility, in practice, contends.

A CASE STUDY: "PREFERENTIAL" VERSUS "DEVELOPMENTAL" AFFIRMATIVE ACTION

Perhaps no issue better illustrates how the commitment to racial justice does not imply agreement on remedies than the issue of affirmative action. Consider club goods, discussed in the third section of this chapter. Club goods can generate network externalities that arise from the acquisition of what economist Glenn Loury calls social capital.

Social capital consists of "familial and communal resources . . . [that] explicitly influence a person's acquisition of human capital."[77] In this view, "[s]ome important part of racial inequality . . . is seen to arise from the way that geographic and social segregation along racial lines makes an individual's opportunities to acquire skills depend on skill attainments by others in the same social group."[78] The role of social capital emphasizes the central importance of ensuring that privileges worth having are public goods for everyone rather than club goods for white people only.

It also highlights the importance of Professor Loury's distinction between *preferential* affirmative action and *developmental* affirmative action, which is discussed in further detail in a paper challenging economists to tackle social exclusion.[79] Privileges worth having, like being able to seamlessly move into residential communities with plentiful resources and civic commitment to propitious municipal policies, are public goods that generate positive externalities, chief among which is social capital.

The effort to turn club goods for white people into public goods for everyone is an effort to ensure equal access to social capital for everyone. As such, this effort should entail an effort to promote affirmative action programs that galvanize economic development of under-resourced communities rather than focusing more myopically, and less productively, on quotas. Society has an interest in cultivating the social capital that comes with full immersion in the network of opportunities that "privileges worth having" offer. This distinction would likely assuage much opposition among white people to affirmative action.

WHITE FRAGILITY THEORY EXACERBATES SOCIAL FRICTIONS

In addition to sober policy differences, there is also the social friction that results from white fragility theory's subservience to the reflexive tendency of social justice activism, cancel culture, and political correctness to attribute virtually anything that goes wrong to white privilege. The seeming arbitrariness with which white privilege is invoked to explain everything from differences in socioeconomic outcomes to alleged microaggressions to the latest headlines in the news greatly exacerbates the tensions already present in the sensitive national conversation on racial justice.

Earlier in the chapter, we discussed an interview of sociologist Michael Dyson on how the uneventful outcome of an interaction between a police officer and a drunk white kid immediately struck him as a manifestation of white privilege, without asking if a different police officer might have acted differently, or if the same police officer would have acted differently on a different night, or if the officer would have acted differently if the drunk kid were black. He also does not contemplate an alternative reason, or compilation of reasons, that factored into the specific decision of the police officer, in *that* moment, to not draw his gun on a drunk white kid who was lobbing insults. While Dyson's account certainly illustrates the anxieties still prevalent among racial and ethnic minorities, it also demonstrates the pitfalls of confirmation bias and omitted variable bias.[80]

Similarly, when McIntosh presents a list of forty-six examples of white privilege, including "I can be reasonably sure that my neighbors in such a location will be neutral or pleasant to me" and "I can go shopping alone most of the time, fairly well assured that I will not be followed or harassed by store detectives," one does not know for certain that a white person would be able to seamlessly move into a new neighborhood or stroll through a department without being followed by a store detective.[81] "Reasonably sure" and "fairly well assured" mean that white privilege is probabilistic in nature. To assume what is true on average is true in all cases is to commit the ecological fallacy.[82]

The essential point is that context matters. We can rarely be certain about the role of "white privilege" in *specific* social and economic outcomes. This indeterminateness gives rise to *search costs* associated with figuring out if a specific social interaction in a specific set of circumstances is or is not a manifestation of white privilege, especially if we are susceptible to errors in reasoning such as confirmation bias, omitted variable bias, availability bias, and base-rate neglect. The Kafka trap that arises with white fragility exacerbates the problem by antagonizing white people, thus making them less receptive to nonwhites who want to avoid the *search costs* of fretting in anxious silence about racial insensitivities and instead voice concerns about those insensitivities.

We should encourage rigorous examination of, rather than endless speculation about, claims that white privilege is manifest in specific situations. This is not what we get from Whiteness scholars like DiAngelo, who point nonchalantly and one-dimensionally to the obvious historical legacy of racial inequality. As labor historian Eric Arsenen has pointed out, "whiteness has become a blank screen onto which those who claim to analyze it can project their own meanings."[83]

This capriciousness gives rise to conversations on race relations that not only allows, but encourages, discussion about, as stated by DiAngelo, "whether in any given moment I'm behaving in anti-racist ways"[84] to be speculative rather than rigorous, a point we highlighted in chapter 9. It also makes the conversation never-ending. Indeed, DiAngelo and Sensoy have written that "racial justice learning is ongoing and our learning is never finished."[85] In sum, white fragility theory increases search costs by encouraging ceaseless, even arbitrary, speculation rather than due process aimed at a resolution.

CONCLUSION

The upshot is that white fragility *theory* poses a substantial transaction cost that sabotages progress in the conversation about racial justice. As a Kafka trap and bullying rhetorical tactic that relies on an erroneous conception of Whiteness as reified dominance, white fragility theory impedes reform efforts by depicting whites as incorrigibly committed to the ongoing reification of white supremacy *in spite of* the increasing prominence and prevalence of white progressives who, according to research by political science graduate student Zach Goldberg, "are leading a 'woke' revolution that is transforming American politics."[1] DiAngelo, in contrast, *blames* white progressives, whom she condescendingly calls her "specialty" and whom she sees as "the most difficult and [who] land the most harshly on people of color day in and day out."[2]

White liberals may be good sports about their own supposed shortcomings, but their cult-like devotion to self-improvement according to the gospel of Robin DiAngelo's white fragility theory has divisive consequences. It should come as little surprise that a recent paper provides evidence that while "social liberals were overall more sympathetic to poor people than social conservatives, reading about White privilege decreased their sympathy for a poor White (vs. Black) person."[3]

The paper's authors suggest that white liberals "draw upon default hierarchies of groups in order to mentally rank who is worst off." Given that whites as a group are better off, the poor white person is seen as more responsible for his predicament. The authors point out that this reasoning falls prey to the ecological fallacy: "[T]he average white person is more likely to have increased inherited wealth, more economic opportunities, and more educational opportunities" than the average person of color, but what is true on average is not necessarily true for each individual.[4]

According to Erin Cooley, one of the authors of the paper, "what we found is that when liberals read about white privilege . . . it didn't significantly change how they empathized with a poor black person—but it did significantly bump *down* their sympathy for a poor white person."[5] The theory of white fragility invariably treats all disagreements about the nature of racism and how it can be addressed as disagreements in bad faith. In so doing, it is the kind of acrimonious "us versus them" approach that can explain why diversity training can make people more biased,[6] or how social liberals reading about White privilege can end up having less sympathy for a poor white person versus a poor black person.

The rise of Donald Trump has certainly not helped ameliorate racial tensions,[7] but neither has DiAngelo and her theory of white fragility. Intended as disruptive, white fragility theory undermines its own project not only by trivializing racial inequality—for example, by drawing what one *Slate* writer calls "spindly connections between social etiquette and institutional power"[8]—but doing so intentionally as part of a proselytization effort that incites racial conflict. How? By deploying a Kafka trap to bully any objectors into silence, even when objectors seek to point out factual errors on issues like the story of Jackie Robinson or the Mexican–American War (see chapter 5).

DiAngelo has explicitly said that it is "less relevant to me whether we agree or disagree" because "I don't really need everyone to agree with me." She clarifies, "[Malcolm Gladwell's] tipping point theory says you just need 30 per cent to change culture."[9] Given the pious divinity with which she colors her writing and her speeches, she is presumably less concerned with proving she is right than she is with gaining adherents because she is already convinced that she is right.

Her inquisitor-like presumption of omniscience is groundless, given how her theory's numerous shortcomings obscure a more refined understanding of white privilege and how white privilege relates to racial inequality. Her pugnacious arrogance serves only to raise transaction costs and contribute to a breakdown in collective negotiations on how to address racial inequality.

NOTES

INTRODUCTION

1. Robin DiAngelo, "White Fragility: Why It's So Hard to Talk to White People about Racism," *The Good Men Project*, April 9, 2015, https://goodmen-project.com/featured-content/white-fragility-why-its-so-hard-to-talk-to-white-people-about-racism-twlm/.

2. Robin DiAngelo, "White Fragility," *International Journal of Critical Pedagogy* 3, no. 3, (2011): 57.

3. DiAngelo, "White Fragility," *International Journal of Critical Pedagogy*.

4. Robin DiAngelo, *White Fragility: Why It's So Hard for White People to Talk about Racism* (Boston: Beacon, 2018); Robin DiAngelo, *What Does It Mean to Be White? Developing White Racial Illiteracy*, rev ed. (New York: Peter Lang, 2016); Özlem Sensoy and Robin DiAngelo, *Is Everyone Really Equal? An Introduction to Key Concepts in Social Justice Education* (New York: Teachers College Press, 2012). For a list of Robin DiAngelo's linked publications, see https://robindiangelo.com/publications/.

5. DiAngelo, "White Fragility," *International Journal of Critical Pedagogy*, 57.

6. Robin DiAngelo, "White Fragility: Why It's So Hard to Talk to White People about Racism," *The Good Men Project*.

7. Kelefa Sanneh, "The Fight to Redefine Racism," *New Yorker*, August 12, 2019, https://www.newyorker.com/magazine/2019/08/19/the-fight-to-redefine-racism.

8. Beacon Broadside, "Robin DiAngelo's 'White Fragility' Celebrates More Than 6 Months as a *New York Times* Bestseller," February 28, 2019, https://www.beaconbroadside.com/broadside/2019/02/robin-diangelos-white-fragility-celebrates-more-than-6-months-as-a-new-york-times-bestseller.html.

9. White Fragility workshop with Dr. Robin DiAngelo, The Nancy R. Chandler Visiting Scholar Program at COCC Foundation, January 31, 2019, https://www.eventbrite.com/e/white-fragility-workshop-with-dr-robin-diangelo-tickets-53886405690; "White Fragility," A conversation with Dr. Robin DiAngelo, Goldsmiths' Center for Feminist Research and Race Critical Studies Network, February 18, 2019, https://www.eventbrite.com/e/white-fragility-a-conversation-with-robin-diangelo-tickets-55719752279.

10. "Book Review: White Fragility: Why It's So Hard for White People to Talk about Racism by Robin DiAngelo," *LSE Review of Books*, January 27, 2019, https://blogs.lse.ac.uk/usappblog/2019/01/27/book-review-white-fragility-why-its-so-hard-for-white-people-to-talk-about-racism-by-robin-diangelo/; Edward J. Blum, "Identifying White Fragility," *The Christian Century*, December 18, 2018, https://www.christiancentury.org/review/books/identifying-white-fragility; K. Biswas, "How Not to Be a Racist," *New Statesman America*, March 27, 2019, https://www.newstatesman.com/obin-diangelo-white-fragility-why-its-so-hard-for-white-people-to-talk-about-racism.

11. Robin DiAngelo, White Fragility book Talk, Urban Grace, 902 Market Street, Tacoma, WA 98402, United States, https://www.brownpapertickets.com/event/3492403?cookie_header=1; "Dr. Robin DiAngelo Discusses 'White Fragility,'" Seattle Central Library, June 28, 2018, https://www.youtube.com/watch?v=45ey4jgoxeU.

12. Nosheen Iqbal, "Academic Robin DiAngelo: 'We Have to Stop Thinking about Racism as Someone Who Says the N-word," *The Guardian*, February 16, 2019, https://www.theguardian.com/world/2019/feb/16/white-fragility-racism-interview-robin-diangelo; Katy Waldman, "A Sociologist Examines the 'White Fragility' That Prevents White Americans from Confronting Racism," *New Yorker*, July 23, 2018, https://www.newyorker.com/books/page-turner/a-sociologist-examines-the-white-fragility-that-prevents-white-americans-from-confronting-racism.

13. Sarah McKibben, "Robin DiAngelo on Educators' 'White Fragility,'" *Educational Leadership* 76, no. 7 (April 2019): http://www.ascd.org/publications/educational-leadership/apr19/vol76/num07/Robin-DiAngelo-on-Educators'-£White-Fragility£.aspx; Sarah Rimer, "Why Is It So Hard for White Peo-

ple to Talk about Race?" *BU Today*, February 28, 2019, https://www.bu.edu/articles/2019/white-fragility; "NPR's Jennifer Ludden Talks to Author Robin DiAngelo about Her Latest Book, White Fragility: Why It's So Hard for White People to Talk about Racism," August 18, 2018, https://www.npr.org/2018/08/18/639822895/robin-diangelo-on-white-peoples-fragility; "Robin DiAngelo on 'White Fragility,'" *Amanpour and Co.*, September 21, 2018, http://www.pbs.org/wnet/amanpour-and-company/video/robin-diangelo-on-white-fragility/; Adrienne van der Valk and Anya Malley, "What's My Complicity? Talking White Fragility with Robin DiAngelo," *Teaching Tolerance* no. 62 (Summer 2019): https://www.tolerance.org/magazine/summer-2019/whats-my-complicity-talking-white-fragility-with-robin-diangelo; "Critical Conversations: Dr. Robin DiAngelo on White Fragility and Why It's So Hard for White People to Talk about Racism," *The Conscious Kid*, https://www.theconsciouskid.org/white-fragility.

14. "White Fragility," C-SPAN, June 30, 2018, https://www.c-span.org/video/?447421-2/robin-diangelo-white-fragility; "Author Robin DiAngelo: Debunking the Most Common Myths White People Tell about Race," September 25, 2018, https://www.nbcnews.com/think/video/debunking-the-most-common-myths-white-people-tell-about-race-1328672835886; "Deconstructing White Privilege with Dr. Robin DiAngelo," Religion and Race: The United Methodist Church, http://www.gcorr.org/video/vital-conversations-racism-dr-robin-diangelo/.

15. Robin DiAngelo, "White People Are Still Raised to Be Racially Illiterate. If We Don't Recognize the System, Our Inaction Will Uphold It," NBC News, September 16, 2018, https://www.nbcnews.com/think/opinion/white-people-are-still-raised-be-racially-illiterate-if-we-ncna906646; Robin DiAngelo, "White Fragility: Why It's So Hard to Talk to White People about Racism," *The Good Men Project.*

16. Tim Chan, "'White Fragility,' 'The New Jim Crow' Top Amazon Best Sellers List Following Week of Unrest," *Rolling Stone*, June 4, 2020, https://www.rollingstone.com/culture/culture-news/books-race-sell-out-amazon-george-floyd-protest-1008220/.

17. Heather MacDonald, "The Cost of America's Cultural Revolution," *City Journal*, December 9, 2019, https://www.city-journal.org/social-justice-ideology.

18. "White Fragility in America Tour with Robin DiAngelo and Jack Hill," Friends Select, April 17, 2019, https://www.friends-select.org/school-news/

post/~board/all-school-news/post/white-fragility-tour-with-robin-diangelo-and-jack-hill.

19. Jonathan Church and Christopher Paslay, "How 'White Fragility' Theory Turns Classrooms Into Race-Charged Power Struggles," *The Federalist*, February 28, 2020, https://thefederalist.com/2020/02/28/how-white-fragility-theory-turns-classrooms-into-race-charged-power-struggles/; Christopher Paslay, *White Fragility Explored: Examining the Effects of Whiteness Studies on America's Schools* (Lanham, MD: Rowman & Littlefield, 2021).

20. New Business Item 11, National Education Association, Houston 2019 Representative Assembly, George R. Brown Convention Center, https://ra.nea.org/business-item/2019-nbi-011/.

21. Jerrica Thurman, "AACTE Announces Robin DiAngelo as 2020 Opening Keynote Speaker," American Association of Colleges for Teacher Education, October 2, 2019, https://edprepmatters.net/2019/10/aacte-announces-robin-diangelo-as-2020-opening-keynote-speaker/.

1. "WHITE FRAGILITY" IS A TRAP

1. Jonathan Church, "How One Man Discovered He Might Be More Sexist Than He Thought," *The Good Men Project*, July 26, 2018 (originally published May 1, 2016), https://goodmenproject.com/guy-talk/how-one-man-discovered-he-might-be-more-sexist-than-he-thought-wcz/.

2. Jonathan Church, "Men Should Not Be Asking Themselves What They Have Done Right but What They Have Done Wrong," *The Good Men Project*, December 10, 2017, https://goodmenproject.com/featured-content/men-asking-not-done-right-wcz/.

3. Jonathan Church, "The Problem with Having Changing Tables in Men's Restrooms," *The Good Men Project*, June 18, 2017, https://goodmenproject.com/families/the-problem-with-having-changing-tables-in-mens-restrooms-wcz/.

4. Jonathan Church, "And Then Charlottesville Happened," *The Good Men Project*, August 27, 2017, https://goodmenproject.com/featured-content/and-then-charlottesville-happened-wcz/.

5. Jonathan Church, "*The Adventures of Huckleberry Finn* Promotes the Cause of Black Lives Matter," *The Good Men Project*, April 30, 2017, https://

goodmenproject.com/social-justice-2/the-adventures-of-huckleberry-finn-promotes-the-cause-of-black-lives-matter-wcz/.

6. Jonathan Church, "The Persistence of Discriminatory Job Advertisements," *The Good Men Project*, April 23, 2017, https://goodmenproject.com/social-justice-2/the-persistence-of-discriminatory-job-advertisements-wcz/.

7. Jonathan Church, "Are Microaggressions Really a Thing?" *The Good Men Project*, April 16, 2017, https://goodmenproject.com/featured-content/are-micro-aggressions-really-a-thing-wcz/; Scott Lilienfeld, "Microaggressions: Strong Claims, Inadequate Evidence," *Perspectives on Psychological Science* 12, no. 1 (2017): 138–69.

8. Jonathan Church, "The Problem I Have with the Concept of White Privilege," *The Good Men Project*, March 19, 2017, https://goodmenproject.com/featured-content/the-problem-i-have-with-the-concept-of-white-privilege-wcz/.

9. Jonathan Church, "Is Walter White Simply a Poor White Guy Trying to Take Care of His Family?" *The Good Men Project*, December 4, 2016, https://goodmenproject.com/arts/walter-white-simply-poor-white-guy-trying-take-care-family-wcz/.

10. Jonathan Church, "Is Confirmation Bias the Dark Side of Social Justice Activism?" *The Good Men Project*, August 9, 2018, https://goodmenproject.com/featured-content/is-confirmation-bias-the-dark-side-of-social-justice-activism-wcz/; Shahram Heshmat, "What Is Confirmation Bias?" *Psychology Today*, April 23, 2015, https://www.psychologytoday.com/us/blog/science-choice/201504/what-is-confirmation-bias.

11. For example, as of March 2020, the black unemployment rate is 6.7 percent compared with 3.5 percent for whites, and the employment-to-population ratio for blacks is 57.6 percent, compared with 60.8 percent for whites. "Table A-2: Employment Status of the Civilian Population by Race, Sex, and Age," US Bureau of Labor Statistics Economic News Release on Employment, https://www.bls.gov/news.release/empsit.t02.htm. In the fourth quarter of 2019, data from the US Bureau of Labor Statistics show that the median nominal usual weekly earnings of blacks sixteen years and over employed full-time was $756, compared with $967 for whites. See data retrieval tool for Labor Force Statistics at the US Bureau of Labor Statistics website: https://www.bls.gov/webapps/legacy/cpswktab3.htm. Finally, a summary of "[d]emographic trends and economic well-being" by the Pew Research Center shows, among other things, that "blacks still trail whites in college completion,"

blacks are "more than twice as likely as whites to be poor," the net worth of white households was "roughly 13 times that of black households" in 2013, and blacks are "significantly less likely than whites to be homeowners." Pew Research Center, "On Views of Race and Inequality, Blacks and Whites Are Worlds Apart," June 27, 2016, https://www.pewsocialtrends.org/2016/06/27/1-demographic-trends-and-economic-well-being/.

12. Robin DiAngelo, "How White People Handle Diversity Training in the Workplace," *Medium*, June 27, 2018, https://gen.medium.com/how-white-people-handle-diversity-training-in-the-workplace-e8408d2519f.

13. Robin DiAngelo and Darlene Flynn, "Showing What We Tell: Facilitating Antiracist Education in Cross-Racial Teams," *Journal of Understanding and Dismantling Privilege* 1, no. 1 (August 2010): 19.

14. Robin DiAngelo, "White Fragility: Why It's So Hard to Talk to White People about Racism," *The Good Men Project*, April 9, 2015, https://goodmenproject.com/featured-content/white-fragility-why-its-so-hard-to-talk-to-white-people-about-racism-twlm/.

15. Katy Waldman, "A Sociologist Examines the "White Fragility" That Prevents White Americans from Confronting Racism," *The New Yorker*, July 23, 2018, https://www.newyorker.com/books/page-turner/a-sociologist-examines-the-white-fragility-that-prevents-white-americans-from-confronting-racism.

16. Robin DiAngelo, "White Fragility: Why It's So Hard to Talk to White People about Racism," *The Good Men Project*; Robin DiAngelo, "White Fragility," *International Journal of Critical Pedagogy* 3, no. 3 (2011): 57.

2. BEHIND THE CURVE ON IMPLICIT BIAS

1. Robin DiAngelo, *White Fragility: Why It's So Hard for White People to Talk about Racism* (Boston: Beacon, 2018), 71.

2. DiAngelo, *White Fragility*, 76.

3. DiAngelo, *White Fragility*, 73.

4. DiAngelo, *White Fragility*, 76.

5. DiAngelo, *White Fragility*, 79.

6. DiAngelo, *White Fragility*, 81–82.

7. Robin DiAngelo, "White Fragility: Why It's So Hard to Talk to White People about Racism," *The Good Men Project*, April 9, 2015, https://goodmen-

project.com/featured-content/white-fragility-why-its-so-hard-to-talk-to-white-people-about-racism-twlm/.

8. Anthony G. Greenwald, Debbie E. McGhee, and Jordan L. K. Schwartz, "Measuring Individual Differences in Implicit Cognition: The Implicit Association Test," *Journal of Personality and Social Psychology* 74, no. 6, 1464–80.

9. Scott Sleek, "The Bias Beneath: Two Decades of Measuring Implicit Associations," Association for Psychological Science, February 2018, https://www.psychologicalscience.org/observer/the-bias-beneath-two-decades-of-measuring-implicit-associations.

10. Jesse Singal, "Psychology's Favorite Tool for Measuring Racism Isn't Up to the Job," *The Cut*, https://www.thecut.com/2017/01/psychologys-racism-measuring-tool-isnt-up-to-the-job.html.

11. Tom Bartlett, "Can We Really Implicit Bias? Maybe Not," *The Chronicle of Higher Education*, January 5, 2017, https://www.chronicle.com/article/Can-We-Really-Measure-Implicit/238807.

12. Scott Sleek, "The Bias Beneath: Two Decades of Measuring Implicit Associations," Association for Psychological Science, February 2018, https://www.psychologicalscience.org/observer/the-bias-beneath-two-decades-of-measuring-implicit-associations.

13. Hart Blanton and James Jaccard, "Unconscious Racism: A Concept in Pursuit of a Measure," *Annual Review of Sociology* 34 (June 2008): 284–85.

14. Blanton and Jaccard, "Unconscious Racism," 282.

15. Blanton and Jaccard, "Unconscious Racism," 283.

16. Melanie Funchess, "Implicit Bias—How It Affects Us and How We Push Through," TEDxFlourCity, https://www.youtube.com/watch?v=Fr8G7MtRNlk; Dushaw Hockett, "We All Have Implicit Biases. So What Can We Do about It?" TEDxMidAtlanticSalon, https://www.youtube.com/watch?v=kKHSJHkPeLY.

17. Gregory Mitchell, "An Implicit Bias Primer," *Virginia Journal of Social Policy and the Law* (Winter 2018): 2.

18. Singal, "Psychology's Favorite Tool"; Bartlett, "Can We Really Measure Implicit Bias?'"; Olivia Goldhill, "The World Is Relying on a Flawed Psychological Test to Fight Racism," *Quartz*, December 3, 2017, https://qz.com/1144504/the-world-is-relying-on-a-flawed-psychological-test-to-fight-racism/; Bertram Gawronski, "Six Lessons for a Cogent Science of Implicit Bias and Its Criticism," *Perspectives on Psychological Science* 14, no. 4 (2019).

19. Blanton and Jaccard, "Unconscious Racism," 277–97.

20. Blanton and Jaccard, "Unconscious Racism," 279.

21. Blanton and Jaccard, "Unconscious Racism," 277.

22. Mitchell, "An Implicit Bias Primer," 5.

23. Mitchell, "An Implicit Bias Primer," 3, 6.

24. Lee Jussim, Akeela Careem, Zach Goldberg, Nathan Honeycutt, and Sean T. Stevens, "IAT Scores, Racial Gaps, and Scientific Gaps," in *The Future of Research on Implicit Bias*, eds. J. A. Krosnick, T. H. Stark, and A. L. Scott (Cambridge, UK: Cambridge University Press, in press).

25. Jussim et al., "IAT Scores, Racial Gaps, and Scientific Gaps."

26. Mitchell, "An Implicit Bias Primer," p. 5.

27. Olivier Corneille and Mandy Hutter, "Implicit? What Do You Mean? A Comprehensive Review of the Delusive Implicitness Construct in Attitude Research," *Personality and Social Psychology Review*, in press.

28. Philip Tetlock and Gregory Mitchell, "Calibrating Prejudice in Milliseconds," *Social Psychology Quarterly* 71 (2008): 12.

29. Tetlock and Mitchell, "Calibrating Prejudice," 12–13.

30. Tetlock and Mitchell, "Calibrating Prejudice," 13–14.

31. Philip Tetlock and Gregory Mitchell, "Popularity as a Poor Proxy for Utility: The Case of Implicit Prejudice," in *Psychological Science under Scrutiny: Recent Challenges and Proposed Solutions*, eds. Scott Lilienfeld and Irwin D. Waldman (Chichester, West Chester, UK: Wiley, Blackwell), 2017. Tetlock and Mitchell have not been without a strong response from IAT defenders. John T. Jost, Laurie A. Rudman, Irene V. Blair, Dana R. Carney, Nilanjana Dasgupta, Jack Glaser, and Curtis D. Hardin, "The Existence of Implicit Bias Is beyond Reasonable Doubt: A Refutation of Ideological and Methodological Objections and Executive Summary of Ten Studies That No Manager Should Ignore," *Research in Organizational Behavior* 29 (2009): 39–69.

32. Jussim et al., "IAT Scores, Racial Gaps, and Scientific Gaps."

33. Jussim et al., "IAT Scores, Racial Gaps, and Scientific Gaps."

34. Tetlock and Mitchell, "Calibrating Prejudice," 13.

35. Singal, "Psychology's Favorite Tool."

36. Mathias Bluemke and Klaus Fiedler, "Base Rate Effects on the IAT," *Consciousness and Cognition* 18, no. 4 (December 2009): 1029–38.

37. Jack Cao and Mahzarin R. Banaji, "The Base Rate Principle and the Fairness Principle in Social Judgment," Proceedings of the National Academy of Sciences, July 5, 2016.

38. Project Implicit website: https://implicit.harvard.edu/implicit/ethics.html.

39. Singal, "Psychology's Favorite Tool."

40. Singal, "Psychology's Favorite Tool."

41. Mitchell, "An Implicit Bias Primer," 7.

42. Mitchell, "An Implicit Bias Primer," 6.

43. Patrick S. Forscher, Calvin K. Lai, Jordan R. Axt, Charles R. Ebersole, Michelle Herman, Patricia G. Devine, and Brian A. Nosek, "A Meta-Analysis of Procedures to Change Implicit Measures," *Journal of Personality and Social Psychology* 117, no. 3 (September 2019); Patrick Forscher, Calvin K. Lai, Jordan R. Axt, and Charles R. Ebersole, "A Meta-Analysis of Change in Implicit Bias," May 2016.

44. Patrick S. Forscher, May 13, 2019, https://twitter.com/psforscher/status/1127971450269380612.

45. "Project Implicit was founded in 1998 by three scientists—Tony Greenwald (University of Washington), Mahzarin Banaji (Harvard University), and Brian Nosek (University of Virginia). Project Implicit Mental Health launched in 2011, led by Bethany Teachman (University of Virginia) and Matt Nock (Harvard University). Project Implicit also provides consulting services, lectures, and workshops on implicit bias, diversity and inclusion, leadership, applying science to practice, and innovation." Project Implicit, "About Us," https://implicit.harvard.edu/implicit/aboutus.html.

46. Katie Herzog, "Is Starbucks Implementing Flawed Science in Their Anti-Bias Training?" *The Stranger*, April 17, 2018, https://www.thestranger.com/slog/2018/04/17/26052277/is-starbucks-implementing-flawed-science-in-their-anti-bias-training.

47. Frederick L. Oswald, Gregory Mitchell, Hart Blanton, James Jaccard, Philip E. Tetlock, "Predicting Ethnic and Racial Discrimination: A Meta-Analysis of IAT Criterion Studies," *Journal of Personality and Social Psychology* 105, no. 2 (June 2013).

48. Hart Blanton, James Jaccard, Jonathan Klick, Barbara Mellers, Gregory Mitchell, and Phillip. E. Tetlock, "Strong Claims and Weak Evidence: Reassessing the Predictive Validity of the IAT," *Journal of Applied Psychology* 94, no. 3 (2009): 567–82.

49. Lois James, Stephen M. James, and Bryan J. Vila, "The Reverse Racism Effect: Are Cops More Hesitant to Shoot Black Than White Suspects?" *Criminology and Public Policy* 15, no. 2 (January 2016).

50. Mitchell, "An Implicit Bias Primer," 6.

51. Mitchell, "An Implicit Bias Primer," 4.

52. "The Race IAT: A Case Study of the Validity Crisis in Psychology," Replicability Index, February 6, 2019, https://replicationindex.com/2019/02/06/the-race-iat-a-case-study-of-the-validity-crisis-in-psychology/.

53. Chloe Fitzgerald, Angela Martin, Delphine Berner, and Samia Hurst, "Interventions Designed to Reduce Implicit Prejudices and Implicit Stereotypes in Real World Contexts: A Systematic Review," *BMC Psychology* 7, no. 29 (2019).

54. David Rock, "Is Your Company's Diversity Training Making You More Biased?" *Psychology Today*, June 7, 2017, https://www.psychologytoday.com/gb/blog/your-brain-work/201706/is-your-company-s-diversity-training-making-you-more-biased; Frank Dobbin and Alexandra Kalev, "Why Diversity Programs Fail," *Harvard Business Review*, July–August 2016, https://hbr.org/2016/07/why-diversity-programs-fail; Julia Belluz, "Companies Like Starbucks Love Anti-bias Training. But It Doesn't Work—and May Backfire," *Vox*, March 29, 2018, https://www.vox.com/science-and-health/2018/4/19/17251752/philadelphia-starbucks-arrest-racial-bias-training; Tomas Chamorro-Premuzic, "Implicit Bias Training Doesn't Work," *Bloomberg Opinion*, January 4, 2020, https://www.bloomberg.com/opinion/articles/2020-01-04/implicit-bias-training-isn-t-improving-corporate-diversity; Gabriel Andrade, "What DARE and Diversity Training Programs Have in Common," *Areo Magazine*, April 23, 2019, https://areomagazine.com/2019/04/23/what-dare-and-diversity-training-programs-have-in-common/; Patricia G. Devine, Patrick S. Forscher, Anthony J. Austin, and William T. L. Cox, "Long-term Reduction in Implicit Race Bias: A Prejudice Habit-breaking Intervention," *Journal of Experimental Social Psychology* 48, no. 6 (November 2012): 1267–78; Elizabeth Levy Paluck and Donald P. Green, "Prejudice Reduction: What Works? A Review and Assessment of Research and Practice," *Annual Review of Psychology* 60, 339–67, January 10, 2009; Mike Noon, "Pointless Diversity Training: Unconscious Bias, New Racism and Agency," British Sociological Association, September 1, 2017; Christy K. Boscardin, "Reducing Implicit Bias through Curricular Interventions," *Journal of General Internal Medicine*, 30, no. 12, (December 2015); Laura Glasman and Dolores Albarracin, "Forming Attitudes That Predict Future Behavior: A Meta-Analysis of the Attitude–Behavior Relation," *Psychological Bulletin* 132, no. 5 (October 2006), 778–822.

55. Mitchell, "An Implicit Bias Primer," 8.

56. Lee Jussim, "Mandatory Implicit Bias Training Is a Bad Idea," *Psychology Today*, December 2, 2017, https://www.psychologytoday.com/us/blog/rabble-rouser/201712/mandatory-implicit-bias-training-is-bad-idea.

57. Jussim et al., "IAT Scores, Racial Gaps, and Scientific Gaps."

58. Jussim et al., "IAT Scores, Racial Gaps, and Scientific Gaps."

59. Jussim, "Mandatory Implicit Bias Training Is a Bad Idea."

3. REINVENTING RACISM

1. Ian Haney Lopez, *White by Law* (New York: New York University Press, 2006), 121, 126.

2. Sofia Leung, "Whiteness as Collections," April 15, 2019, https://sleung.wordpress.com/2019/04/15/whiteness-as-collections/.

3. Leung, "Whiteness as Collections."

4. Marcos Gonsalez, "Recognizing the Enduring Whiteness of Jane Austen," *Lit Hub*, December 11, 2019, https://lithub.com/recognizing-the-enduring-whiteness-of-jane-austen/?fbclid=IwAR3LboQl-aHN0iDumdgNe6BE_cZ6HeE6FclAzm4ujyJpexcEaQofcIof2K8.

5. Douglas Hartmann, Joseph Gerteis, and Paul R. Croll, "An Empirical Assessment of Whiteness Theory: Hidden from How Many?" *Social Problems* 56, no. 3 (August 2009).

6. Robin DiAngelo and David Allen, "'My Feelings Are Not about You': Personal Experience as a Move of Whiteness," *UCLA Journal of Education and Information Studies* 2, no. 2. DiAngelo and her co-author David Allen write, "In interracial discussions of racism, White participants in our study used the discourse of personal experience to inoculate their racial claims against *interrogation* or critique."

7. According to Encyclopedia.com, *reification* is "[t]he error of regarding an abstraction as a material thing, and attributing causal powers to it—in other words the fallacy of misplaced concreteness. An example would be treating a model or ideal type as if it were a description of a real individual or society. In Marxist theory, reification is linked to people's alienation from work and their treatment as objects of manipulation rather than as human beings, and was popularized by György Lukács, but the term is given a variety of meanings by different schools of Marxist thought." https://www.encyclopedia.com/social-sciences/dictionaries-thesauruses-pictures-and-press-releases/reification. The

website *Logically Fallacious* notes, "When an abstraction (abstract belief or hypothetical construct) is treated as if it were a concrete, real event or physical entity—when an idea is treated as if had a real existence." "Reification," *Logically Fallacious*, https://www.logicallyfallacious.com/tools/lp/Bo/LogicalFallacies/154/Reification.

8. Venita Blackburn, "White People Must Save Themselves from Whiteness," *Paris Review*, March 25, 2019, https://www.theparisreview.org/blog/2019/03/25/white-people-must-save-themselves-from-whiteness/.

9. Blackburn, "White People Must Save Themselves."

10. Coleman Hughes, "The Racism Treadmill," *Quillette*, May 14, 2018, https://quillette.com/2018/05/14/the-racism-treadmill/.

11. Robin DiAngelo, *White Fragility: Why It's So Hard for White People to Talk about Racism* (Boston: Beacon Press, 2018), 43.

12. DiAngelo, *White Fragility: Why It's So Hard for White People to Talk about Racism*, p. 44; Robin DiAngelo, *What Does It Mean to Be White? Developing White Racial Illiteracy* (New York: Peter Lang, 2016), 132.

13. Ruth Frankenberg, *White Women, Race Matters: The Social Construction of Whiteness* (Minneapolis: University of Minnesota Press, 1993), 1.

14. Robin DiAngelo, "White Fragility," *International Journal of Critical Pedagogy* 3, no. 3 (2011): 56.

15. Blackburn, "White People Must Save Themselves."

16. Blackburn, "White People Must Save Themselves."

17. Frankenberg, *White Women, Race Matters*, 6.

18. Frankenberg, *White Women, Race Matters*, 6.

19. Frankenberg, *White Women, Race Matters*, 242.

20. Frankenberg, *White Women, Race Matters*, 242–43.

21. Blackburn, "White People Must Save Themselves."

22. Robin DiAngelo and Özlem Sensoy, "'We Are All for Diversity, but . . .': How Faculty Hiring Committees Reproduce Whiteness and Practical Suggestions for How They Can Change," *Harvard Educational Review* 87, no. 4 (Winter 2017): 575.

23. Peggy McIntosh, "White Privilege and Male Privilege: A Personal Account of Coming to See Correspondences through Work in Women's Studies," Working Paper 189, Wellesley Centers for Women, Wellesley, MA, 1988, 2.

24. Lopez, *White by Law*, 137.

25. "White Fragility: The New Racism, and More Effective Steps to Undoing Racism." Lecture by University of Michigan School of Social Work gradu-

ate and therapist Andy Horning. See around 13:15 at https://www.youtube.com/watch?v=05hU4QKBhss.

26. Robin DiAngelo and Darlene Flynn, "Showing What We Tell: Facilitating Antiracist Education in Cross-Racial Teams," *Journal of Understanding and Dismantling Privilege* 1, no. 1 (August 2010): 15; Robin DiAngelo and Özlem Sensoy, "Calling In: Strategies for Cultivating Humility and Critical Thinking in Antiracism Education," *Journal of Understanding and Dismantling Privilege* 4, no. 2 (2014): 195: "[A]ntiracism education is a complex, life-long process rather than a singular event"; Özlem Sensoy and Robin DiAngelo, *Is Everyone Really Equal? An Introduction to Key Concepts in Social Justice Education*, (New York: Teachers College Press, 2012), xviii.

27. Frankenberg, *White Women, Race Matters*, 236.

28. DiAngelo, "White Fragility," *International Journal of Critical Pedagogy*, 56.

29. Blackburn, "White People Must Save Themselves."

30. Frankenberg, *White Women, Race Matters*, 236.

31. Bettina Bergo and Tracey Nicholls, "Introduction," in *"I Don't See Color": Personal and Critical Perspectives on White Privilege*, edited by Bettina Bergo and Tracey Nicholls (University Park: Pennsylvania State University Press, 2015).

32. Table A-2 in the US Bureau of Labor Statistics Economic News Release on Employment, https://www.bls.gov/news.release/empsit.t02.htm; Labor Force Statistics at the US Bureau of Labor Statistics website: https://www.bls.gov/webapps/legacy/cpswktab3.htm; Pew Research Center, "On Views of Race and Inequality, Blacks and Whites Are Worlds Apart," June 27, 2016, https://www.pewsocialtrends.org/2016/06/27/1-demographic-trends-and-economic-well-being/.

33. Alexa Lardieri, "Despite Diverse Demographics, Most Politicians Are Still White Men," *US News and World Report*, October 24, 2017, https://www.usnews.com/news/politics/articles/2017-10-24/despite-diverse-demographics-most-politicians-are-still-white-men; Sinduja Rangarajan, "Here's the Clearest Picture of Silicon Valley's Diversity Yet: It's Bad. But Some Companies Are Doing Less Bad," *Reveal News*, June 25, 2018, https://www.revealnews.org/article/heres-the-clearest-picture-of-silicon-valleys-diversity-yet/?utm_source=Reveal&utm_medium=social_media&utm_campaign=twitter; "Race/Ethnicity of College Faculty," US Department of Education, National Center for Education Statistics (2018), data for fall

2016, https://nces.ed.gov/fastfacts/display.asp?id=61; *The Status of Women in the US Media 2014*, Women's Media Center, https://wmc.3cdn.net/6dd3de8ca65852dbd4_fjm6yck9o.pdf.

34. Manisha Krishnan, "Dear White People, Please Stop Pretending Reverse Racism Is Real," *Vice*, October 2, 2016, https://www.vice.com/en_us/article/kwzjvz/dear-white-people-please-stop-pretending-reverse-racism-is-real.

35. DiAngelo and Sensoy, "We Are All for Diversity, but . . . ," 575.

36. Jonathan Church, "The Problem I Have with the Concept of White Privilege," *The Good Men Project*, March 19, 2017, https://goodmenproject.com/featured-content/the-problem-i-have-with-the-concept-of-white-privilege-wcz/.

37. Blackburn, "White People Must Save Themselves."

38. Samuel Kronen, "#ItsOkayToBeWhite," *Areo*, February 17, 2020, https://areomagazine.com/2020/02/17/itsokaytobewhite.

39. György Lukács, *History and Class Consciousness* (London: Merlin Press, 1967).

40. Nikole Hannah-Jones, "America Wasn't a Democracy, Until Black Americans Made It One," *New York Times*, August 14, 2019, https://www.nytimes.com/interactive/2019/08/14/magazine/black-history-american-democracy.html?mtrref=www.google.com&gwh=F1DFCB3AAE870D364A50A17705CCAFCF&gwt=pay&assetType=REGIWALL; Adam Serwer, "The Fight Over the 1619 Project Is Not about the Facts," *Atlantic*, December 23, 2019, https://www.theatlantic.com/ideas/archive/2019/12/historians-clash-1619-project/604093/.

41. Tom Mackaman, "An Interview with Historian James Oakes on the New York Times' 1619 Project," World Socialist Website, November 18, 2019, https://www.wsws.org/en/articles/2019/11/18/oake-n18.html.

42. Derrick Bell, *Faces at the Bottom of the Well: The Permanence of Racism* (New York: Basic, 1993).

43. Coleman Hughes, "Let's Arm Black Children with Lessons That Can Improve Their Lives," *Woodson Center*, February 2020, https://1776unites.com/scholars/coleman-cruz-hughes/essay/525116945. This article has been removed from the website.

44. Blackburn, "White People Must Save Themselves."

45. Sean Wilentz, *No Property in Man* (Cambridge, MA: Harvard University Press, 2018).

46. Kenneth M. Stampp, *The Peculiar Institution* (New York: Alfred A. Knopf, 1956). The Peculiar Institution, https://www.ushistory.org/us/27.asp.

47. Hughes, "The Racism Treadmill."

48. Jonathan Church, "A Personal Awakening in America," *The Good Men Project*, March 12, 2016, https://goodmenproject.com/featured-content/a-personal-awakening-on-racism-in-america-wcz/.

49. "CBS Fires Don Imus over Racial Slur," *CBS News*, April 12, 2007, https://www.cbsnews.com/news/cbs-fires-don-imus-over-racial-slur/.

50. Hughes, "The Racism Treadmill"; Derrick Bell, *And We Are Not Saved* (New York: Basic, 1987).

51. Hughes, "The Racism Treadmill"; Steven Pinker, "Why Do Progressives Hate Progress?" https://www.youtube.com/watch?v=PnitLNObR7c.

52. Hughes, "The Racism Treadmill."

53. "'When I See Racial Disparities, I See Racism.' Discussing Race, Gender and Mobility," *New York Times*, March 27, 2018, https://www.nytimes.com/interactive/2018/03/27/upshot/reader-questions-about-race-gender-and-mobility.html.

54. Kronen, "#ItsOkayToBeWhite"; Gustavo Lopez, Neil G. Ruiz, and Eileen Patten, "Key Facts about Asian Americans, a Diverse and Growing Population," Pew Research Center, September 8, 2017, https://www.pewresearch.org/fact-tank/2017/09/08/key-facts-about-asian-americans/; "Indians in the US Fact Sheet," Pew Research Center, September 8, 2017, https://www.pewsocialtrends.org/fact-sheet/asian-americans-indians-in-the-u-s/; US Census Bureau, American Fact Finder, Selected Population Profile in the United States, 2014 American Community Survey 1-Year Estimates, https://archive.vn/20200213015935/http://factfinder.census.gov/bkmk/table/1.0/en/ACS/14_1YR/S0201//popgroup~-07#.

55. US Census Bureau, Historical Income Tables: Households, https://www.census.gov/data/tables/time-series/demo/income-poverty/historical-income-households.html.

56. Vincent Harinam and Rob Henderson, "Why White Privilege Is Wrong—Part 1," *Quillette*, August 22, 2019, https://quillette.com/2019/08/22/why-white-privilege-is-wrong-part-1/.

57. Anna Maria Barry-Jester, "Attitudes toward Racism and Inequality Are Shifting," *FiveThirtyEight*, June 23, 2015, https://fivethirtyeight.com/features/attitudes-toward-racism-and-inequality-are-shifting/; Maria Krysan and Sarah Moberg, "A Portrait of African American and White Racial Attitudes," Univer-

sity of Illinois Institute of Government and Public Affairs, Trends in Racial Attitudes, September 9, 2016, https://igpa.uillinois.edu/sites/igpa.uillinois.edu/files/reports/A-Portrait-of-Racial-Attitudes.pdf; Astead W. Herndon, "How 'White Guilt' in the Age of Trump Shapes the Democratic Primary," *New York Times*, October 13, 2019, https://www.nytimes.com/2019/10/13/us/politics/democratic-candidates-racism.html; Harinam and Henderson, "Why White Privilege Is Wrong—Part 1."

58. Eduardo Bonilla-Silva, *Racism without Racists* (Lanham, MD: Rowman & Littlefield, 2010), 4. Bonilla-Silva's book, however, addresses the shortcomings of racial optimism, particularly with respect to so-called colorblind racism (131).

59. Hughes, "The Racism Treadmill."

60. Hughes, "The Racism Treadmill."

61. DiAngelo and Sensoy, "'We Are All for Diversity, but . . . .'" 576.

62. Hughes, "The Racism Treadmill"; Julia Edwards, "Justice Department Mandates 'Implicit Bias' Training for Agents, Lawyers," *Reuters*, June 27, 2016, https://www.reuters.com/article/us-usa-justice-bias-exclusive-idUSKCN0ZD251.

63. Hughes, "The Racism Treadmill."

64. Scott Lilienfeld, "Microaggressions: Strong Claims, Inadequate Evidence," *Perspectives on Psychological Science* 12, no. 1 (2017): 148; Jonathan Church, "Are Microaggressions Really a Thing?" *The Good Men Project*, April 16, 2017, https://goodmenproject.com/featured-content/are-micro-aggressions-really-a-thing-wcz/.

65. Orlando Patterson, "Race, Gender, and Liberal Fallacies," *New York Times*, October 20, 1991, https://www.nytimes.com/1991/10/20/opinion/op-ed-race-gender-and-liberal-fallacies.html.

66. DiAngelo, *White Fragility: Why It's So Hard for White People to Talk about Racism*, 71.

67. DiAngelo, *White Fragility: Why It's So Hard for White People to Talk about Racism*, 71.

68. DiAngelo, *White Fragility: Why It's So Hard for White People to Talk about Racism*, 43–44; Coleman Hughes, "Black American Culture and the Racial Wealth Gap," *Quillette*, July 19, 2018, https://quillette.com/2018/07/19/black-american-culture-and-the-racial-wealth-gap/.

69. DiAngelo, *What Does It Mean to Be White?* 108–109.

70. DiAngelo, *White Fragility: Why It's So Hard for White People to Talk about Racism*, 72; Omowale Akintunde, "White Racism, White Supremacy, White Privilege, and the Social Construction of Race: Moving from Modernist to Postmodernist Multiculturalism," *Multicultural Education* 7, no. 2 (Winter 1999): 2–8.

71. DiAngelo, *White Fragility: Why It's So Hard for White People to Talk about Racism*, 27.

72. Barbara Applebaum, "Critical Whiteness Studies," *Oxford Research Encyclopedias*, June 2016, https://oxfordre.com/education/view/10.1093/acrefore/9780190264093.001.0001/acrefore-9780190264093-e-5.

73. Applebaum, "Critical Whiteness Studies."

74. Frankenberg, *White Women, Race Matters.*

75. John T. Warren, "Whiteness and Cultural Theory: Perspectives on Research and Education," *Urban Review* 31, no. 2 (1999): 189.

76. Robin DiAngelo, "White Fragility," *International Journal of Critical Pedagogy*, 56. In this paper, DiAngelo cites Frankenberg's book, *White Women, Race Matters: The Social Construction of Whiteness*, as well as Ruth Frankenberg "Introduction: Local Whitenesses, Localizing Whiteness," in *Displacing Whiteness: Essays in Social and Cultural Criticism*, ed. Ruth Frankenberg, 1–33 (Durham, NC: Duke University Press, 1997). Robin DiAngelo, *White Fragility: Why It's So Hard for White People to Talk about Racism*, 27. In her book, DiAngelo cites Frankenberg, "Local Whiteness, Localizing Whiteness," 1.

77. Frankenberg, *White Women, Race Matters*, 20.

78. Warren, "Whiteness and Cultural Theory," 189; Frankenberg, *White Women, Race Matters*, 142.

79. Warren, "Whiteness and Cultural Theory," 189–91.

80. Warren, "Whiteness and Cultural Theory," 193.

81. Warren, "Whiteness and Cultural Theory," 191.

82. Warren, "Whiteness and Cultural Theory," 197.

83. Warren, "Whiteness and Cultural Theory," 198.

84. As cited by Warren: David R. Roediger, "White Looks: Hairy Apes, True Stories, and Limbaugh's Laughs," *Whiteness: A Critical Reader*, ed. Mike Hill (New York: New York University Press, 1997).

85. Warren, "Whiteness and Cultural Theory," 192; Michael E. Staub, "The Whitest I: On Reading the Hill–Thomas Transcripts," in *Whiteness: A Critical Reader*, ed. Mike Hill (New York: New York University Press, 1997).

86. John A. Powell, Director, Haas Diversity Research Center (HDRC), Berkeley Law, University of California, https://works.bepress.com/john_powell/.

87. Douglas Hartmann, Joseph Gerteis and Paul R. Croll, "An Empirical Assessment of Whiteness Theory: Hidden from How Many?" *Social Problems* 56, no. 3 (August 2009): 403–24.

88. Hartmann, Gerteis, and Croll, "An Empirical Assessment of Whiteness Theory," 412–14.

89. John A. Powell and Jason Reece, "The Future of Fair Housing and Fair Credit: From Crisis to Opportunity, Symposium: New Strategies in Fair Housing," *Cleveland State Law Review* 57, no. 2 (2009): https://engagedscholarship.csuohio.edu/clevstlrev/vol57/iss2/4/.

90. John A. Powell, "Post-Racialism or Targeted Universalism?" *Denver University Law Review* 86 (2009): 789–90. The distinction between the design and effects of policy is voluminously addressed in the discourse on so-called "color-blind racism." A seminal book is Eduardo Bonilla-Silva, *Racism without Racists* (Lanham, MD: Rowman & Littlefield, 2010); DiAngelo, *White Fragility: Why It's So Hard for White People to Talk about Racism*, 40–43; DiAngelo, *What Does It Mean to Be White?* 122, 129–32, 199–200; Sensoy and DiAngelo, *Is Everyone Really Equal?* 108–10, 172; Michelle Alexander, *The New Jim Crow: Mass Incarceration in the Age of Colorblindness* (New York: The New Press, 2010, 2012).

91. Jonathan Church, "The Puzzling Irony of Censoring the Adventures of Huckleberry Finn," *The Good Men Project*, June 16, 2017, https://goodmenproject.com/featured-content/the-puzzling-irony-of-censoring-the-adventures-of-huckleberry-finn-wcz/.

92. Hughes, "The Racism Treadmill."

93. John A. Powell, "Whites Will Be Whites: The Failure to Interrogate Racial Privilege," *University of San Francisco Law Review*, Vol. 34, 2000, p. 422.

94. Hartmann, Gerteis, and Croll, "An Empirical Assessment of Whiteness Theory," 415.

95. Hartmann, Gerteis, and Croll, "An Empirical Assessment of Whiteness Theory," 417.

96. Austin Cline, "Hypostatization Fallacy: Ascribing Reality to Abstractions," *ThoughtCo*, updated October 28, 2019, https://www.thoughtco.com/reification-hypostatization-fallacy-250333.

97. McIntosh, "White Privilege and Male Privilege," 5.

98. Howard Zinn, *People's History of the United States* (New York, NY: HarperCollins, 1980, 1995, 1998, 1990, 2003).

99. Jonathan Church, "The Problem I Have."

100. Michael Kazin, "Howard Zinn's History Lessons," *Dissent Magazine*, Spring 2004, https://www.dissentmagazine.org/article/howard-zinns-history-lessons.

101. "An Expert's History of Howard Zinn," *Los Angeles Times*, February 1, 2010, https://www.latimes.com/archives/la-xpm-2010-feb-01-la-oe-miller1-2010feb01-story.html.

102. Scott Jaschik, "Making a Point by Moving Shakespeare's Portrait," *Inside Higher Education*, December 14, 2016, https://www.insidehighered.com/news/2016/12/14/students-penn-remove-portrait-shakespeare.

103. Özlem Sensoy and Robin DiAngelo, "Respect Differences? Challenging the Common Guidelines in Social Justice Education," *Democracy and Education* 22, no. 1 (2014): 3; DiAngelo and Sensoy, "Calling In," 197.

104. DiAngelo and Sensoy, "Calling In," 197.

105. Sensoy and DiAngelo, "Respect Differences?" 1.

106. Frederick Douglass, *The Narrative of the Life of Frederick Douglass, an American Slave*, (New York: Barnes and Noble Classics, 2003).

107. Toni Morrison, *Song of Solomon* (New York: Alfred A. Knopf, 1977).

108. Eric Arsenen, "Whiteness and Historians' Imagination," *International Labor and Working-Class History Society* 60 (October 2001): 3–32.

109. Sarah Jeong, quoted in Jon Sharman, "Sarah Jeong: New York Times Journalist Who Tweeted 'Cancel White People' Is Victim of 'Dishonest' Trolls, Claims Former Employer," *The Independent*, August 3, 2018, https://www.independent.co.uk/news/media/ny-times-journalist-sarah-jeong-racist-tweets-white-people-trolls-verge-a8475596.html.

110. Andrew Sullivan, "When Racism Is Fit to Print," *New York Intelligencer*, August 3, 2018, http://nymag.com/intelligencer/2018/08/sarah-jeong-new-york-times-anti-white-racism.html.

111. Shannon Sullivan, *Good White People* (Albany: State University of New York Press, 2014), 4; "Good White," *New Discourses Social Justice Encyclopedia*, https://newdiscourses.com/tftw-good-white/.

112. DiAngelo, *White Fragility: Why It's So Hard for White People to Talk about Racism*, 71; Akintunde, "White Racism, White Supremacy, White Privilege," 2–8; DiAngelo, *What Does It Mean to Be White?* 108–109.

113. Gabriel Andrade, "What DARE and Diversity Training Programs Have in Common," *Areo*, April 23, 2019, https://areomagazine.com/2019/04/23/what-dare-and-diversity-training-programs-have-in-common/.

114. Helen Pluckrose, James Lindsay, and Peter Boghossian, "Academic Grievance Studies and the Corruption of Scholarship," *Areo*, October 2, 2018, https://areomagazine.com/2018/10/02/academic-grievance-studies-and-the-corruption-of-scholarship/.

115. Helen Pluckrose and James A. Lindsay, "The Influence of Anti-Racist Scholarship-Activism on Evergreen College," *Areo*, January 20, 2019, https://areomagazine.com/2019/01/20/the-influence-of-anti-racist-scholarship-activism-on-evergreen-college/; Maria Krysan and Sarah Moberg, "A Portrait of Africa American and White Racial Attitudes," University of Illinois Institute of Government and Public Affairs, Trends in Racial Attitudes, September 9, 2016, https://igpa.uillinois.edu/programs/racial-attitudes, https://igpa.uillinois.edu/report/portrait-african-american-and-white-racial-attitudes, and https://igpa.uillinois.edu/sites/igpa.uillinois.edu/files/reports/A-Portrait-of-Racial-Attitudes.pdf; J. C. Pan, "Why Diversity Training Isn't Enough," *The New Republic*, January 7, 2020, https://newrepublic.com/article/156032/diversity-training-isnt-enough-pamela-newkirk-robin-diangelo-books-reviews.

116. David Rock, "Is Your Company's Diversity Training Making You More Biased?" *Psychology Today*, June 7, 2017, https://www.psychologytoday.com/gb/blog/your-brain-work/201706/is-your-company-s-diversity-training-making-you-more-biased.

117. Jay Van Bavel, Social Identity and Morality Lab, New York University Department of Psychology, https://www.psych.nyu.edu/vanbavel/lab/research.html.

118. Rock, "Is Your Company's Diversity Training Making You More Biased?"

119. DiAngelo, *White Fragility: Why It's So Hard for White People to Talk about Racism*, xiv.

120. Kimberlé Crenshaw, "Why Intersectionality Can't Wait," *Washington Post*, September 24, 2015, https://www.washingtonpost.com/news/in-theory/wp/2015/09/24/why-intersectionality-cant-wait/; Kimberlé Crenshaw, "Demarginalizing the Intersection of Race and Sex: A Black Feminist Critique of Antidiscrimination Doctrine, Feminist Theory and Antiracist Politics," *University of Chicago Legal Forum* 1989, no. 1, Article 8, http://chicagounbound.uchicago.edu/cgi/viewcontent.cgi?article=1052&context=uclf; "Kim-

berlé Crenshaw on Intersectionality, More than Two Decades Later," Columbia Law School, June 8, 2017, https://www.law.columbia.edu/pt-br/news/2017/06/kimberle-crenshaw-intersectionality.

121. Venita Blackburn, "White People Must Save Themselves," *Paris Review*, March 25, 2019, https://www.theparisreview.org/blog/2019/03/25/white-people-must-save-themselves-from-whiteness/.

122. Lawrence Blum, "Moral Asymmetry: A Problem for the Protected Categories Approach," *Lewis and Clark Law Review* 16, no. 2 (Summer 2012): 652–53, 655. Blum emphasizes that discrimination against blacks is not morally equivalent to discrimination against whites because race "has a social and historical meaning" that transcends skin color and is rooted in the historical injustices of slavery, Jim Crow, and violent disenfranchisement.

4. FLAWED METHODOLOGY

1. Jonathan Church, "How Critical Theory Came to Be Skeptical of Science," *Areo*, February 12, 2020, https://areomagazine.com/2020/02/12/how-critical-theory-came-to-be-skeptical-of-science/.

2. Robin DiAngelo, *White Fragility: Why It's So Hard for White People to Talk about Racism* (Boston: Beacon, 2018), xiv.

3. Robin DiAngelo and Özlem Sensoy, "'We Are All for Diversity, but . . .': How Faculty Hiring Committees Reproduce Whiteness and Practical Suggestions for How They Can Change," *Harvard Educational Review* 87, no. 4 (Winter 2017): 561.

4. Robin DiAngelo, "My Class Didn't Trump My Race: Using Oppression to Face Privilege," *Multicultural Perspectives* 8, no. 1 (2006): 54.

5. The skepticism about objectivity can also be traced to ideas surrounding the development of postmodernism and poststructuralism, beginning at least with the philosophy of Friedrich Nietzsche, and continuing with Jacques Derrida, Michel Foucault, and many others.

6. Robin DiAngelo, "White Fragility," *International Journal of Critical Pedagogy* 3, no. 3 (2011): 57.

7. To cite only one example, economist Michael Reich's 1981 book, *Racial Inequality: A Political-Economic Analysis*, reviews various classical models developed by economists over several decades to explain racial inequality, going all the way back to Nobel Laureate Gary Becker's famous *The Economics of*

Discrimination. Reich provides a useful overview of their pros and cons. The review is useful also as a way of illustrating how many factors must be considered, and how hard it is to come to a definitive conclusion about why racial inequality persists. Michael Reich, *Racial Inequality: A Political-Economic Analysis* (Princeton, NJ: Princeton University Press, 1981); Gary Becker, *The Economics of Discrimination* (Chicago: The University of Chicago Press, 1957, 1971).

8. John McWhorter, *Winning the Race: Beyond the Crisis in Black America* (New York: Penguin, 2006); John McWhorter, "Stop Policing the N-Word," *Time*, May 3, 2016, https://time.com/4316322/larry-wilmore-obama-n-word/; Glenn Loury, "Why Does Racial Inequality Persist? Culture, Causation, and Responsibility," *The Manhattan Institute*, May 7, 2019, https://www.manhattan-institute.org/racial-inequality-in-america-post-jim-crow-segregation; William Voegeli, "Thomas Sowell's Inconvenient Truths," *Claremont Review of Books* 18, no. 3 (Summer 2018): https://www.claremont.org/crb/article/thomas-sowells-inconvenient-truths/; Jason Riley, *False Black Power* (West Conshohocken, PA: Templeton, 2017).

9. Roland G. Fryer and Steven D. Levitt, "The Causes and Consequences of Distinctively Black Names," *The Quarterly Journal of Economics* 119, no. 3 (August 2004): 767–805.

10. Robin DiAngelo and Darlene Flynn, "Showing What We Tell: Facilitating Antiracist Education in Cross-Racial Teams," *Journal of Understanding and Dismantling Privilege* 1, no. 1 (August 2010): 2–3.

11. Robin DiAngelo and David Allen, "'My Feelings Are Not About You': Personal Experience as a Move of Whiteness," *UCLA Journal of Education and Information Studies* 2, no. 2 (2006).

12. Robin DiAngelo and Özlem Sensoy, "'We Don't Want Your Opinion': Knowledge Construction and the Discourse of Opinion in the Equity Classroom," *Equity and Excellence in Education* 42, no. 4 (2009): 444.

13. Robin DiAngelo, "Nothing to Add: A Challenge to White Silence in Racial Discussions," *Journal of Understanding and Dismantling Privilege* 2, no. 1 (February 2012).

14. Jacques Derrida, *Of Grammatology* (Baltimore: Johns Hopkins University Press, 1967, 1974, 1976, 1997, 2016). Michel Foucault, *The Order of Things: An Archaeology of the Human Sciences* (New York: Random House, 1970; Vintage Books Edition, 1994).

15. Özlem Sensoy and Robin DiAngelo, *Is Everyone Really Equal? An Introduction to Key Concepts in Social Justice Education* (New York: Teachers College, 2012), 52–53.

16. Sensoy and DiAngelo, *Is Everyone Really Equal?* 53.

17. Sensoy and DiAngelo, *Is Everyone Really Equal?* 54.

18. Sensoy and DiAngelo, *Is Everyone Really Equal?* 54.

19. Michel Foucault, *The Order of Things: An Archaeology of the Human Sciences* (New York: Random House, 1970; Vintage Books Edition, April 1994), p. xi.

20. Michel Foucault, *Discipline and Punish: The Birth of the Prison* (New York: Pantheon Books, 1977); Michel Foucault, *Birth of the Clinic: An Archaeology of Medical Perception* (London: Tavistock, 1973; Vintage Books, 1994); Michel Foucault, *Madness and Civilization* (New York: Random House; Vintage Books Edition 1988).

21. Foucault, *The Order of Things*, xi.

22. In a paper on interrogating white racial privilege and how it contributes to the "othering" of marginalized groups, John Powell argues that "[t]he recently popular but subsequently disfavored term 'underprivileged' functions problematically as a linguistic companion to privilege; it reifies the notion of privilege as normal and unquestionable." John A. Powell, "Whites Will Be Whites: The Failure to Interrogate Racial Privilege," *University of San Francisco Law Review* 34 (2000): 422.

23. DiAngelo and Allen, "'My Feelings Are Not about You,'" section on the Theory of Experience.

24. DiAngelo and Allen, "'My Feelings Are Not about You,'" Discussion section.

25. Robin DiAngelo, "Whiteness in Racial Dialogue: A Discourse Analysis" (PhD diss., University of Washington, 2004), abstract.

26. For example, see Robin DiAngelo and Özlem Sensoy, "Calling In: Strategies for Cultivating Humility and Critical Thinking in Antiracism Education," *Journal of Understanding and Dismantling Privilege* 4, no. 2 (August 2014): 194.

27. For a list of Robin DiAngelo's publications provided by Robin DiAngelo, see her website: https://robindiangelo.com/publications/.

28. "Deconstructing White Privilege with Dr. Robin DiAngelo," at https://www.youtube.com/watch?v=h7mzj0cVL0Q; "White Fragility" C-SPAN, June 30, 2018, at https://www.c-span.org/video/?447421-2/robin-diangelo-white-fra-

gility; "Dr. Robin DiAngelo Discusses 'White Fragility.'" YouTube, July 3, 2018, https://www.youtube.com/watch?v=45ey4jgoxeU.

29. Robin DiAngelo, "How White People Handle Diversity Training in the Workplace," *Medium*, June 27, 2018, https://gen.medium.com/how-white-people-handle-diversity-training-in-the-workplace-e8408d2519f; Robin DiAngelo, "White Fragility: Why It's So Hard to Talk to White People about Racism," *The Good Men Project*, April 9, 2015, https://goodmenproject.com/featured-content/white-fragility-why-its-so-hard-to-talk-to-white-people-about-racism-twlm/.

30. Robin DiAngelo, *What Does It Mean to Be White? Developing White Racial Illiteracy*, rev. ed. (New York: Peter Lang, 2016), 107, 110–14.

31. DiAngelo, *White Fragility: Why It's So Hard for White People to Talk about Racism*, 31.

32. DiAngelo, *White Fragility: Why It's So Hard for White People to Talk about Racism*, 44.

33. DiAngelo, *What Does It Mean to Be White?* 188–89.

34. Lincoln Quillian, "Why Is Black-White Residential Segregation So Persistent? Evidence on Three Theories from Migration Data," *Social Science Research* 31, no. 2 (June 2002), 197–229, https://www.sciencedirect.com/science/article/abs/pii/S0049089X01907264.

35. Quillian, "Why Is Black-White Residential Segregation So Persistent?" abstract.

36. Maria Krysan, "Does Race Matter in the Search for Housing? An Exploratory Study of Search Strategies, Experiences, and Locations," *Social Science Research* 37, no. 2 (2008), 581–603, https://www.ncbi.nlm.nih.gov/pmc/articles/PMC2597838/.

37. Leah Platt Boustan, "Was Postwar Suburbanization 'White Flight'? Evidence from the Black Migration," Working Paper 13543, National Bureau of Economic Research, October 2007, https://www.nber.org/papers/w13543.pdf.

38. Boustan, "Was Postwar Suburbanization 'White Flight'?" 21–22.

39. Leah Boustan, "The Culprits behind White Flight," *New York Times*, May 15, 2017, https://www.nytimes.com/2017/05/15/opinion/white-flight.html.

40. DiAngelo, *What Does It Mean to Be White?* 108.

41. DiAngelo, "Whiteness in Racial Dialogue," chapter 2.

42. DiAngelo, *White Fragility: Why It's So Hard for White People to Talk about Racism*, 12.

43. DiAngelo, "Whiteness in Racial Dialogue," 48.

44. DiAngelo, "Whiteness in Racial Dialogue," 48.

45. DiAngelo, "White Fragility," *International Journal of Critical Pedagogy*, 56.

46. DiAngelo, "White Fragility," *International Journal of Critical Pedagogy*, 47.

47. DiAngelo, "White Fragility," *International Journal of Critical Pedagogy*, 47.

48. James Lindsay and Helen Pluckrose, *Cynical Theories: How Activist Scholarship Made Everything about Race, Gender, and Identity—and Why This Harms Everybody* (Durham, NC: Pitchstone, 2020).

49. "Dr. Robin DiAngelo Discusses 'White Fragility.'" YouTube, July 3, 2018, https://www.youtube.com/watch?v=45ey4jgoxeU, 14:30; "White Fragility" C-SPAN, June 30, 2018, at https://www.c-span.org/video/?447421-2/robin-diangelo-white-fragility, 11:30.

50. Robin DiAngelo, *White Fragility: Why It's So Hard for White People to Talk about Racism*, 8.

51. Karl Popper, *Stanford Encyclopedia of Philosophy*, first published November 13, 1997, substantive revision August 7, 2018, https://plato.stanford.edu/entries/popper/.

52. DiAngelo, "White Fragility," *International Journal of Critical Pedagogy*, 56.

53. Paul Koks, "Six Challenges of Qualitative Data Analysis," *Online Metrics*, July 14, 2015, https://online-metrics.com/qualitative-data/.

54. Robin DiAngelo, "My Class Didn't Trump My Race: Using Oppression to Face Privilege," *Multicultural Perspectives* 8, no. 1 (2006): 54, Part IV: Personal Perspective.

55. DiAngelo, "White Fragility," *International Journal of Critical Pedagogy*, 56.

5. EXPLOITING NARRATIVES AT THE EXPENSE OF FACTS

1. "White Fragility: Robin DiAngelo Explored the Challenges in Discussing Race with White Americans," June 30, 2018, C-SPAN, https://www.c-span.org/video/?447421-2/robin-diangelo-white-fragility, 24:15. DiAngelo also presents this episode as an example of "the white disconnect from our shared

history" in *What Does It Mean to Be White? Developing White Racial Illiteracy*, rev. ed. (New York: Peter Lang, 2016), 149–50.

2. Shahram Heshmat, "What Is Confirmation Bias?" *Psychology Today*, April 23, 2015, https://www.psychologytoday.com/us/blog/science-choice/201504/what-is-confirmation-bias.

3. "Jeopardy Contestants Painfully Avoid Black History Questions as Long as They Can," *Huffington Post*, February 19, 2014, updated February 17, 2015, https://www.huffpost.com/entry/jeopardy-black-history-month_n_4815162?guccounter=1. If she is referring to the 2014 episode, she inaccurately states in her June 2018 C-SPAN talk that the *Jeopardy!* episode is from the previous year (i.e., 2017). "White Fragility," C-SPAN, at around 24:00. She also inaccurately states in her book *What Does It Mean to Be White?* that the episode occurred in 2015. DiAngelo, *What Does It Mean to Be White?* 149.

4. "Jeopardy Contestants Painfully Avoid Black History Questions."

5. Phillis Wheatley, 1753–1784, *Poetry Foundation*, https://www.poetryfoundation.org/poets/phillis-wheatley.

6. Apollo Theater History, https://www.apollotheater.org/about/history/.

7. "Who Were the Scottsboro Boys?" https://www.pbs.org/wgbh/american-experience/features/scottsboro-boys-who-were-the-boys/; "Scottsboro Boys," History.com, February 22, 2018, updated June 10, 2019, https://www.history.com/topics/great-depression/scottsboro-boys.

8. Elliot Partin, "1st Rhode Island Regiment," *Blackpast*, November 17, 2010, https://www.blackpast.org/african-american-history/first-rhode-island-regiment/.

9. Robin DiAngelo, *What Does It Mean to Be White? Developing White Racial Illiteracy*, rev. ed. (New York: Peter Lang, 2016), 149.

10. "White Fragility," C-SPAN, 25:30. Robin DiAngelo, *What Does It Mean to Be White? Developing White Racial Illiteracy* (New York, NY: Peter Lang Publishing, Revised Edition, 2016), p. 149. Robin DiAngelo, *White Fragility: Why It's So Hard for White People to Talk about Racism* (Boston, MA: Beacon Press, 2018), p. 26.

11. Robin DiAngelo, *White Fragility: Why It's So Hard for White People to Talk about Racism* (Boston: Beacon, 2018), 26.

12. DiAngelo, *What Does It Mean to Be White?* 149.

13. DiAngelo, *White Fragility: Why It's So Hard for White People to Talk about Racism*, 26.

14. Susan King, "The Hard Run to First," *Los Angeles Times*, April 14, 1996, https://www.latimes.com/archives/la-xpm-1996-04-14-tv-58266-story.html.

15. Negro Leagues, https://www.u-s-history.com/pages/h2079.html.

16. Arnold Rampersad, *Jackie Robinson: A Biography* (New York: Alfred A. Knopf, 1997), 126–27.

17. Rampersad, *Jackie Robinson*, 121–22.

18. Rampersad, *Jackie Robinson*, 154.

19. Rampersad, *Jackie Robinson*, 160.

20. National Baseball Hall of Fame, Wesley Branch Rickey, https://baseballhall.org/hall-of-famers/rickey-branch; The Jackie Robinson Story, https://www.youtube.com/watch?v=5-BWnSjlXL0; Rampersad, *Jackie Robinson*; David Falkner, *Great Time Coming* (New York: Touchstone, 1995).

21. DiAngelo, *White Fragility: Why It's So Hard for White People to Talk about Racism*, 26.

22. DiAngelo, *What Does It Mean to Be White?* 149.

23. DiAngelo, *What Does It Mean to Be White?* 149.

24. DiAngelo, *What Does It Mean to Be White?* 149.

25. DiAngelo, *What Does It Mean to Be White?* 149.

26. Chris Chavez, "How the Red Sox Will Try to Enforce a Lifetime Ban on the Fan Who Used a Racial Slur," *Sports Illustrated*, May 8, 2017, https://www.si.com/mlb/2017/05/08/red-sox-fan-lifetime-ban-racial-slur-enforced; Amita Kelly, "Orioles' Adam Jones Receives Ovation at Fenway after Alleged Epithets," *NPR*, May 3, 2017, https://www.npr.org/2017/05/03/526710441/watch-orioles-adam-jones-receives-ovation-at-fenway-after-alleged-epithets.

27. Robin DiAngelo and Darlene Flynn, "Showing What We Tell: Facilitating Antiracist Education in Cross-Racial Teams," *Journal of Understanding and Dismantling Privilege* 1, no. 1 (August 2010): 15. "A basic premise of antiracist education is that it is lifelong work; the process of identifying and challenging patterns of racism is always evolving and never finished."

28. Robin DiAngelo, *White Fragility: Why It's So Hard for White People to Talk about Racism*, 15–16.

29. Allan Nevins and Henry Steele Commager, *A Pocket History of the United States*, 9th ed. (New York: Pocket Books, 1992), 189; "The Annexation of Texas, the Mexican–American War, and the Treaty of Guadalupe-Hidalgo, 1845–1848," Department of State, United States of America, Office of the Historian, https://history.state.gov/milestones/1830-1860/texas-annexation.

30. John M. Blum, William S. McFeely, Edmund S. Morgan, Arthur M. Schlesinger, Jr., Kenneth M. Stampp, C. Vann Woodward, *The National Experience: A History of the United States*, 8th ed. (Harcourt Brace Jovanovic, 1993, 1989, 1985, 1981, 1977, 1973, 1968, 1963), 292–96; Nevins and Commager, *A Pocket History of the United States*, 190–92; "Mexican–American War 1846–1848," *Encyclopedia Britannica*, https://www.britannica.com/event/Mexican-American-War/Invasion-and-war.

31. Nevins and Commager, *A Pocket History of the United States*, 190.

32. Alexander Hamilton, James Madison, and John Jay, *The Federalist Papers*. See, in particular, Federalist Paper #10: https://avalon.law.yale.edu/18th_century/fed10.asp.

33. Robin DiAngelo and Özlem Sensoy, "'OK, I Get It! Now Tell Me How to Do It!': Why We Can't Just Tell You How to Do Critical Multicultural Education," *Multicultural Perspectives* 12, no. 2 (2010): 100.

34. Sean Wilentz, *No Property in Man* (Cambridge, MA: Harvard University Press, 2018).

35. Abraham Lincoln, "Slavery as the Fathers Viewed It," Address at Cooper Union, New York, February 27, 1860, in *The Works of Abraham Lincoln, Vol. III, Speeches and Presidential Addresses, 1859–1865, Anecdotes and Conversations of Lincoln by F. B. Carpenter* (New York: Newton and Cartwright; Current Literature Publishing Company, 1907), 37–38. See also http://www.abrahamlincolnonline.org/lincoln/speeches/cooper.htm.

36. Lincoln, "Slavery as the Fathers Viewed It," 28–29.

37. US Library of Congress, Today in History—September 17, https://www.loc.gov/item/today-in-history/september-17/.

38. "Abraham Lincoln, First Inaugural Address, Delivered at Washington, DC, March 4, 1861," in *The Works of Abraham Lincoln, Vol. III, Speeches and Presidential Addresses, 1859–1865, Anecdotes and Conversations of Lincoln by F. B. Carpenter* (New York: Newton and Cartwright; Current Literature Publishing Company, 1907), 138. See also https://avalon.law.yale.edu/19th_century/lincoln1.asp.

6. THE CRITIQUE OF REASON

1. Özlem Sensoy and Robin DiAngelo, *Is Everyone Really Equal? An Introduction to Key Concepts in Social Justice Education* (New York: Teachers College Press, 2012), xviii.

2. Sensoy and DiAngelo, *Is Everyone Really Equal?* 1.

3. Sensoy and DiAngelo, *Is Everyone Really Equal?* 2.

4. Sensoy and DiAngelo, *Is Everyone Really Equal?* 4.

5. Sensoy and DiAngelo, *Is Everyone Really Equal?* 5.

6. Sensoy and DiAngelo, *Is Everyone Really Equal?* 5.

7. Sensoy and DiAngelo, *Is Everyone Really Equal?* 5.

8. M. A. Rafey Habib, "The Myth of Liberal Humanim," Rutgers University, 2019, https://habib.camden.rutgers.edu/publications/essays/the-myth-of-liberal-humanism/.

9. Max Horkheimer, *Critical Theory: Selected Essays* (New York: Continuum, 1999), 178.

10. Sensoy and DiAngelo, *Is Everyone Really Equal?* 4.

11. Max Horkheimer, *Eclipse of Reason* (New York: Oxford University Press, 1947; New York: Continuum, 1974), 3.

12. Horkheimer, *Eclipse of Reason*, 7.

13. Immanuel Kant, "What Is Enlightenment?" Konigsberg in Prussia, September 30, 1784, http://www2.idehist.uu.se/distans/ilmh/Ren/idehist-enlighten-kant02.htm; Immanuel Kant, "An Answer to the Question: What Is Enlightenment?" 1784, trans. Ted Humphrey (Hackett Publishing, 1992), https://www.stmarys-ca.edu/sites/default/files/attachments/files/Kant--What%20Is%20Enlightenment_.pdf.

14. Max Horkheimer and Theodor Adorno, *Dialectic of Enlightenment* (New York: Continuum, 1998). See also, English translation, 2002, by the Board of Trustees of the Leland Stanford Junior University, https://monoskop.org/images/2/27/Horkheimer_Max_Adorno_Theodor_W_Dialectic_of_Enlightenment_Philosophical_Fragments.pdf.

15. Horkheimer and Adorno, *Dialectic of Enlightenment*, 106.

16. Horkheimer and Adorno, *Dialectic of Enlightenment*, xvi.

17. Horkheimer and Adorno, *Dialectic of Enlightenment*, 2.

18. Curtis Bowman, "Odysseus and the Siren Call of Reason: The Frankfurt School Critique of Enlightenment," *Other Voices* 1, no. 1 (March 1997); Jonathan Church, "The Specter of Marxism Haunts the Social Justice Movement," *The Good Men Project*, July 9, 2017, https://goodmenproject.com/featured-content/the-specter-of-marxism-haunts-the-social-justice-movement-wcz/.

19. Horkheimer and Adorno, *Dialectic of Enlightenment*, xviii.

20. Peter Harrison, "The Enlightenment of Steven Pinker," *ABC Religion and Ethics*, February 20, 2018, https://www.abc.net.au/religion/the-enlightenment-of-steven-pinker/10094966?fbclid=IwAR3JAxoRzBjs2haTkNk6iFxs0uUAsL0mAZVxKv4auXoRQHoUEZ3Acr8r-PY.

7. RUNNING AFOUL OF REASON AND LOGIC

1. Robin DiAngelo, *White Fragility: Why It's So Hard for White People to Talk about Racism*, (Boston: Beacon, 2018), 9.

2. DiAngelo, *White Fragility: Why It's So Hard for White People to Talk about Racism*, 9. Note that she demonstrates incoherence in seemingly asserting as an objective truth that objectivity is not possible. In another paper, for example, DiAngelo states, "But there is no objective, neutral reality. Human objectivity is not actually possible, but as long as we construct the world as if it is, and then ascribe it only to ourselves, we keep White experience and people centered and people of color in the margins." Robin DiAngelo, "My Class Didn't Trump My Race: Using Oppression to Face Privilege," *Multicultural Perspectives* 8, no. 1 (2006): 54. To see where this leads us, one can anticipate DiAngelo's pushback on this point, to which one might reply, "Well, that's according to your view, which does not reflect an objective evaluation because human objectivity is not actually possible." Circularity ensues.

3. DiAngelo, *White Fragility: Why It's So Hard for White People to Talk about Racism*, 10.

4. DiAngelo, *White Fragility: Why It's So Hard for White People to Talk about Racism*, 10.

5. DiAngelo, *White Fragility: Why It's So Hard for White People to Talk about Racism*, 10.

6. DiAngelo, *White Fragility: Why It's So Hard for White People to Talk about Racism*, 11.

7. DiAngelo, *White Fragility: Why It's So Hard for White People to Talk about Racism*, 10.

8. DiAngelo, *White Fragility: Why It's So Hard for White People to Talk about Racism*, 11.

9. DiAngelo, *White Fragility: Why It's So Hard for White People to Talk about Racism*, 11.

10. DiAngelo, *White Fragility: Why It's So Hard for White People to Talk about Racism*, 11.

11. DiAngelo, *White Fragility: Why It's So Hard for White People to Talk about Racism*, 11. Conversely, however, insisting that we have them presumes an aura of omniscience that demands acquiescence, guaranteeing that critique is unidirectional, or in other words, aimed at the presumed ghosts of racism within us that necessarily "reify" the norms and habits that underlie a supposedly racist society, rather than at the possibility that "racism" is not monocausal, or in other words, solely, or at least fundamentally, the result of Whiteness and white privilege (however defined).

12. DiAngelo, *White Fragility: Why It's So Hard for White People to Talk about Racism*, 10.

13. DiAngelo, *White Fragility: Why It's So Hard for White People to Talk about Racism*, 10.

14. I leave to the (individual) reader to determine for himself or herself whether it is internally coherent or contradictory to say that it is *not the case* that one is *taught* to believe that they matter naturally, but it *is the case* that one is *taught* that they matter socially. Perhaps what DiAngelo is saying is that what we think we are aware of having been taught is wrong, and that, in fact, we are not aware that we have been taught something else. We should be grateful that we have DiAngelo to psychoanalyze our unconscious biases.

15. DiAngelo, *White Fragility: Why It's So Hard for White People to Talk about Racism*, 11.

16. DiAngelo, *White Fragility: Why It's So Hard for White People to Talk about Racism*, 12.

17. DiAngelo, *White Fragility: Why It's So Hard for White People to Talk about Racism*, 12.

18. DiAngelo, *White Fragility: Why It's So Hard for White People to Talk about Racism*, 12.

19. DiAngelo, *White Fragility: Why It's So Hard for White People to Talk about Racism*, 11.

20. Douglas Hartmann, Joseph Gerteis and Paul R. Croll, "An Empirical Assessment of Whiteness Theory: Hidden from How Many?" *Social Problems* 56, no. 3 (August 2009): 403–24.

21. Hartmann, Gerteis, and Croll, "An Empirical Assessment," 415.

22. Özlem Sensoy and Robin DiAngelo, *Is Everyone Really Equal? An Introduction to Key Concepts in Social Justice Education* (New York: Teachers College, 2012), 4.

23. David Hume, *An Enquiry Concerning Human Understanding*, ed. Tom L. Beauchamp (New York: Oxford University Press, 1999).

24. Hume, *An Enquiry*, 150, 157.

25. Hume, *An Enquiry*, Sections 7 and 8.

26. Hume, *An Enquiry*, 141.

27. Hume, *An Enquiry*, 144.

28. Hume, *An Enquiry*, 144.

29. Hume, *An Enquiry*, 149–50.

30. Internet Encyclopedia of Philosophy (IEP), "David Hume: Causation," https://www.iep.utm.edu/hume-cau/.

31. IEP, "David Hume."

32. IEP, "David Hume."

33. IEP, "David Hume."

34. IEP, "David Hume."

35. IEP, "David Hume."

36. DiAngelo, *White Fragility: Why It's So Hard for White People to Talk about Racism*, 11.

37. IEP, "David Hume."

38. "All people are individuals, but they are also members of social groups." Sensoy and DiAngelo, *Is Everyone Really Equal?* xviii.

39. DiAngelo, *White Fragility: Why It's So Hard for White People to Talk about Racism*, 13.

40. DiAngelo, *White Fragility: Why It's So Hard for White People to Talk about Racism*, 13.

41. As defined at Logically Fallacious (https://www.logicallyfallacious.com/tools/lp/Bo/LogicalFallacies/99/Genetic-Fallacy), the genetic fallacy refers to the practice of "[b]asing the truth claim of an argument on the origin of its claims or premises." According to the *Internet Encyclopedia of Philosophy*

(https://www.iep.utm.edu/fallacy/#Genetic), "A critic uses the Genetic Fallacy if the critic attempts to discredit or support a claim or an argument because of its origin (genesis) when such an appeal to origins is irrelevant."

42. Sensoy and DiAngelo, *Is Everyone Really Equal?* 4.

43. Max Horkheimer, *Eclipse of Reason* (New York: Oxford University Press, 1947; New York: The Continuum Publishing Company, 1974).

44. Hartmann, Gerteis, and Croll, "An Empirical Assessment," 404.

45. Hartmann, Gerteis, and Croll, "An Empirical Assessment," 405.

46. Wikipedia defines *presentism* as follows: "In literary and historical analysis, presentism is the anachronistic introduction of present-day ideas and perspectives into depictions or interpretations of the past." https://en.wikipedia.org/wiki/Presentism_(literary_and_historical_analysis). Merriam-Webster defines *presentism* as follows: "an attitude toward the past dominated by present-day attitudes and experiences." https://www.merriam-webster.com/dictionary/presentism.

47. "Publisher Places a Politically Correct Warning Label on Kant's *Critiques*," *Open Culture*, March 20, 2014, http://www.openculture.com/2014/03/publisher-places-a-politically-correct-warning-label-on-kants-critiques.html.

48. Immanuel Kant, *Kant's Critiques* (Radford, VA: A and D, 2008).

49. "Publisher Places," *Open Culture*; Kant, *Kant's Critiques.*

50. "Immanuel Kant: The Crisis of the Enlightenment," *Stanford Encyclopedia of Philosophy*, May 20, 2010, substantive revision January 25, 2016, https://plato.stanford.edu/entries/kant/#CriEnl.

51. "Michael Ayers on Locke and Berkeley (1987)," YouTube, https://www.youtube.com/watch?v=WJzQF7eknKA, 30:40.

52. "Michael Ayers," YouTube, 31:00.

53. Friedrich Nietzsche, *Will to Power*, ed. Walter Kauffmann (New York: Vintage, 1967); Friedrich Nietzsche, *The Birth of Tragedy* and *Genealogy of Morals* (New York: Doubleday, 1956).

54. Susan Edelman, Selim Algar, and Aaron Feis, "Richard Carranza Held 'White Supremacy Culture' Training for School Admins," *New York Post*, May 20, 2019, https://nypost.com/2019/05/20/richard-carranza-held-doe-white-supremacy-culture-training/; Bob McManus, "Fixated on Race," *City Journal*, August 28, 2018, https://www.city-journal.org/html/richard-carranza-16136.html.

55. Susan Edelman, "Teachers Allegedly Told to Favor Black Students in 'Racial Equity' Training," *New York Post*, May 25, 2019, https://nypost.com/

2019/05/25/teachers-allegedly-told-to-treat-black-students-as-victims-punish-whites/.

56. Joe R. Feagin, *The White Racial Frame* (New York: Routledge, 2013).

57. Robin DiAngelo, "White Fragility," *International Journal of Critical Pedagogy* 3, no. 3 (2011): 57.

58. Robin DiAngelo, "White Fragility: Why It's So Hard to Talk to White People about Racism," *The Good Men Project*, April 9, 2015, https://goodmen-project.com/featured-content/white-fragility-why-its-so-hard-to-talk-to-white-people-about-racism-twlm/.

59. According to Logically Fallacious (https://www.logicallyfallacious.com/tools/lp/Bo/LogicalFallacies/89/Fallacy-of-Division): "Inferring that something is true of one or more of the parts from the fact that it is true of the whole." According to the *Internet Encyclopedia of Philosophy* (https://www.iep.utm.edu/fallacy/#Division): "Merely because a group as a whole has a characteristic, it often doesn't follow that individuals in the group have that characteristic."

60. DiAngelo, *White Fragility: Why It's So Hard for White People to Talk about Racism*, 11–12.

61. DiAngelo, "White Fragility," *International Journal of Critical Pedagogy*, 56.

62. DiAngelo, *White Fragility: Why It's So Hard for White People to Talk about Racism*, 56; Feagin, *The White Racial Frame*.

63. Jonathan Church, "White Privilege, the Law of Large Numbers, and a Little Bit of Bayes," *The Good Men Project*, August 14, 2016, https://goodmen-project.com/featured-content/white-privilege-law-large-numbers-little-bit-bayes-wcz/.

64. Peggy McIntosh, "White Privilege and Male Privilege: A Personal Account of Coming to See Correspondences through Work in Women's Studies," Working Paper 189, Wellesley Centers for Women, Wellesley, MA, 1988, 4.

65. According to Logically Fallacious (https://www.logicallyfallacious.com/tools/lp/Bo/LogicalFallacies/232/Ecological-Fallacy), the *ecological fallacy* refers to "[t]he interpretation of statistical data where inferences about the nature of individuals are deduced from inference for the group to which those individuals belong." According to David A. Freedman, "The ecological fallacy consists in thinking that relationships observed for groups necessarily hold for individuals." David A. Freeman, "Ecological Inference and Ecological Falla-

cy," Technical Report No. 549, October 15, 1999, https://web.stanford.edu/class/ed260/freedman549.pdf.

66. According to Logically Fallacious (https://www.logicallyfallacious.com/tools/lp/Bo/LogicalFallacies/88/Fallacy-of-Composition), "Inferring that something is true of the whole from the fact that it is true of some part of the whole." According to the *Internet Encyclopedia of Philosophy* (https://www.iep.utm.edu/fallacy/#Composition): "The Composition Fallacy occurs when someone mistakenly assumes that a characteristic of some or all the individuals in a group is also a characteristic of the group itself, the group 'composed' of those members."

67. Robin DiAngelo, "Whiteness in Racial Dialogue: A Discourse Analysis," (PhD diss., University of Washington, 2004), abstract.

68. Niccolò Machiavelli, *Discourses on the First Ten Books of Titus Livius*, trans. Christian E. Detmold (New York: Random House, 1950), 233.

8. SERMONIZING, NOT SCHOLARSHIP

1. Robin DiAngelo, "White Fragility," *International Journal of Critical Pedagogy* 3, no. 3 (2011): 56.

2. Özlem Sensoy and Robin DiAngelo, *Is Everyone Really Equal? An Introduction to Key Concepts in Social Justice Education* (New York: Teachers College, 2012), 4.

3. Sensoy and DiAngelo, *Is Everyone Really Equal?* 6.

4. Sensoy and DiAngelo, *Is Everyone Really Equal?* 4.

5. Sensoy and DiAngelo, *Is Everyone Really Equal?* 6.

6. Sensoy and DiAngelo, *Is Everyone Really Equal?* 19–20.

7. Gregory Mitchell, "An Implicit Bias Primer," *Virginia Journal of Social Policy and the Law* (Winter 2018): 8.

8. Roland G. Fryer and Steven D. Levitt, "The Causes and Consequences of Distinctively Black Names," *Quarterly Journal of Economics* 119, no. 3 (August 2004): 767–805.

9. Fryer and Levitt, "The Causes and Consequences," 771.

10. Fryer and Levitt, "The Causes and Consequences," 771–72.

11. Fryer and Levitt, "The Causes and Consequences," 774–76.

12. Fryer and Levitt, "The Causes and Consequences," 779–80.

13. Fryer and Levitt, "The Causes and Consequences," 783.

14. Fryer and Levitt, "The Causes and Consequences," 783.

15. Fryer and Levitt, "The Causes and Consequences," 786.

16. George A. Akerlof and Rachel E. Kranton, *Identity Economics: How Our Identities Shape Our Work, Wages, and Well-Being* (Princeton, NJ: Princeton University Press, 2010), https://press.princeton.edu/books/paperback/9780691152554/identity-economics.

17. Fryer and Levitt, "The Causes and Consequences," 791–792.

18. Fryer and Levitt, "The Causes and Consequences," 792.

19. Fryer and Levitt, "The Causes and Consequences," 793.

20. Fryer and Levitt, "The Causes and Consequences," 793.

21. Fryer and Levitt, "The Causes and Consequences," 793.

22. Fryer and Levitt, "The Causes and Consequences," 793.

23. Fryer and Levitt, "The Causes and Consequences," 793–794.

24. Fryer and Levitt, "The Causes and Consequences," 794.

25. Fryer and Levitt, "The Causes and Consequences," 794.

26. Fryer and Levitt, "The Causes and Consequences," 795.

27. Fryer and Levitt, "The Causes and Consequences," 795.

28. Fryer and Levitt, "The Causes and Consequences," 795.

29. Matt Teffer, "White Fragility: Are White People Inherently Racist?" *Australian Financial Review*, January 4, 2019, https://www.afr.com/life-and-luxury/arts-and-culture/white-fragility-are-white-people-inherently-racist-20190102-h19mh9. According to the *Australian Financial Review*, "Matt Teffer is a journalist and production editor with The Australian Financial Review, and reviews live music for The Sydney Morning Herald." https://www.afr.com/by/matt-teffer-gy15ky.

30. Teffer, "White Fragility."

31. Teffer, "White Fragility."

32. Teffer, "White Fragility."

33. For a list of Robin DiAngelo's linked publications, see her website: https://robindiangelo.com/publications/.

9. A RHETORICAL WEAPON FOR ACTIVIST BULLIES

1. Nosheen Iqbal, "Academic Robin DiAngelo: 'We Have to Stop Thinking about Racism as Someone Who Says the N-word," *The Guardian*, February 16,

2019, https://www.theguardian.com/world/2019/feb/16/white-fragility-racism-interview-robin-diangelo.

2. Joe R. Feagin, *The White Racial Frame* (New York: Routledge, 2013).

3. Robin DiAngelo, "White Fragility," *International Journal of Critical Pedagogy* 3, no. 3 (2011): 57.

4. Adrienne Van Der Valk and Anya Malley, "What's My Complicity? Talking White Fragility with Robin DiAngelo," *Teaching Tolerance* no. 62 (Summer 2019): https://www.tolerance.org/magazine/summer-2019/whats-my-complicity-talking-white-fragility-with-robin-diangelo.

5. DiAngelo and her co-author Darlene Flynn write in one paper that a "basic premise of antiracist education is that it is lifelong work; the process of identifying and challenging patterns of racism is always evolving and never finished." Robin DiAngelo and Darlene Flynn, "Showing What We Tell: Facilitating Antiracist Education in Cross-Racial Teams," *Journal of Understanding and Dismantling Privilege* 1, no. 1 (August 2010): 15. DiAngelo and Sensoy write that "antiracism education is a complex, life-long process rather than a singular event." Robin DiAngelo and Özlem Sensoy, "Calling In: Strategies for Cultivating Humility and Critical Thinking in Antiracism Education," *Journal of Understanding and Dismantling Privilege* 4, no. 2 (2014): 195.

6. Derald Wing Sue, Christina M. Capodilupo, Gina C. Torino, Jennifer M. Bucceri, Aisha M. B. Holder, Kevin L. Nadal, and Marta Esquilin, "Racial Microaggressions in Everyday Life," *American Psychologist*, May–June 2007.

7. Sue et al., "Racial Microaggressions," 271.

8. Sue et al., "Racial Microaggressions," 275.

9. Sue et al., "Racial Microaggressions," 275.

10. Sue et al., "Racial Microaggressions," 275.

11. Sue et al., "Racial Microaggressions," 275.

12. Sue et al., "Racial Microaggressions," 275.

13. Sue et al., "Racial Microaggressions," 275.

14. Sue et al., "Racial Microaggressions," 275.

15. Van Der Valk and Malley, "What's My Complicity?"

16. Van Der Valk and Malley, "What's My Complicity?"

17. Sue et al., "Racial Microaggressions," 275.

18. Robin DiAngelo, *White Fragility: Why It's So Hard for White People to Talk about Racism* (Boston: Beacon, 2018), 54; Jonathan Church, "Robin Di-Angelo Is Correct about the Psychic Weight of Race," *Merion West*, March 24,

2020, https://merionwest.com/2020/03/24/robin-diangelo-is-correct-about-the-psychic-weight-of-race/.

19. Sue et al., "Racial Microaggressions," 275.

20. Sue et al., "Racial Microaggressions," 275.

21. Sue et al., "Racial Microaggressions," 275.

22. Scott Lilienfeld, "Microaggressions: Strong Claims, Inadequate Evidence," *Perspectives on Psychological Science* 12, no. 1 (2017): 139.

23. Van Der Valk and Malley, "What's My Complicity?"

24. Van Der Valk and Malley, "What's My Complicity?"

25. "In Tort Law, intent plays a key role in determining the civil liability of persons who commit harm." "Intent," The Free Dictionary, https://legal-dictionary.thefreedictionary.com/intent. "In tort cases, intent is the key factor in determining liability." "Understanding the Intent in Tort Laws," LAWS, https://tort.laws.com/intentional-interference/with-a-person/meaning-of-intent. Moreover, the second edition of a textbook in law and economics by Robert Cooter and Thomas Ulen addresses tort law at length from an economic standpoint in chapter 8. Intent (and lack of intent) figures prominently in discussions of liability rules. Robert Cooter and Thomas Ulen, *Law and Economics*, 2nd ed. (Boston: Addison-Wesley, 1997).

26. Sue et al., "Racial Microaggressions," 275.

27. Robin DiAngelo, "Nothing to Add: A Challenge to White Silence in Racial Discussions," *Journal of Understanding and Dismantling Privilege* 2, no. 1 (February 2012): abstract.

28. DiAngelo, "Nothing to Add," 6.

29. Jonathan Church, "A Personal Awakening on Racism in America," *The Good Men Project*, March 12, 2016, https://goodmenproject.com/featured-content/a-personal-awakening-on-racism-in-america-wcz/.

30. DiAngelo, "Nothing to Add," 4.

31. Nien Cheng, *Life and Death in Shanghai* (New York: Grove Press, 1986; Penguin Books, 1988).

10. A BETTER WAY TO THINK ABOUT WHITENESS AND WHITE PRIVILEGE

1. Peggy McIntosh, "White Privilege and Male Privilege: A Personal Account of Coming to See Correspondences through Work in Women's Studies," Working Paper 189, Wellesley Centers for Women, Wellesley, MA, 1988, 2.

2. Cheryl Harris, "Whiteness as Property," *Harvard Law Review* 106, no. 8 (June 1993): 1761.

3. Harris, "Whiteness as Property," 1785.

4. Harris, "Whiteness as Property," 1778.

5. Harris, "Whiteness as Property," 1778.

6. McIntosh, "White Privilege and Male Privilege," 2.

7. Nick Haslam, "Concept Creep: Psychology's Expanding Concepts of Harm and Pathology," *Psychological Inquiry* 27, no. 1 (2016). Haslam writes, "I contend that the expansion primarily reflects an ever-increasing sensitivity to harm, reflecting a liberal moral agenda. Its implications are ambivalent, however. Although conceptual change is inevitable and often well motivated, concept creep runs the risk of pathologizing everyday experience and encouraging a sense of virtuous but impotent victimhood." Gregg Henriques, "The Concept of Concept Creep," *Psychology Today*, January 4, 2017, https://www.psychologytoday.com/us/blog/theory-knowledge/201701/the-concept-concept-creep.

8. McIntosh, "White Privilege and Male Privilege," 4–7.

9. "Prevalence-induced concept change in human judgment" is the subject of a 2018 paper on how the definition of a concept can change as the frequency of incidents to which it applies declines: "When blue dots became rare, purple dots began to look blue; when threatening faces became rare, neutral faces began to appear threatening; and when unethical research proposals became rare, ambiguous research proposals began to seem unethical"—or alternatively, "why sexism and racism never diminish—even when everyone becomes less sexist and racist." David E. Levari, Daniel T. Gilbert, Timothy D. Wilson, Beau Sievers, David M. Amodio, and Thalia Wheatley, "Prevalence-Induced Concept Change in Human Judgment," *Science* 360, no. 6396 (June 29, 2018): 1465–67, https://science.sciencemag.org/content/360/6396/1465/tab-pdf; Alex Tabarrok, "Why Sexism and Racism Never Diminish—Even When Everyone Becomes Less Sexist and Racist," *Marginal Revolution*, June

30, 2018, https://marginalrevolution.com/marginalrevolution/2018/06/sexism-racism-never-diminishes-even-everyone-becomes-less-sexist-racist.html.

10. Tabarrok, "Why Sexism and Racism Never Diminish."

11. Vincent Harinam and Rob Henderson, "Why White Privilege Is Wrong—Part 1," *Quillette*, August 22, 2019, https://quillette.com/2019/08/22/why-white-privilege-is-wrong-part-1/; Vincent Harinam and Rob Henderson, "Why White Privilege Is Wrong—Part 2," *Quillette*, October 16, 2019, https://quillette.com/2019/10/16/why-white-privilege-is-wrong-part-2/.

12. Jonathan Church, "The Problem I Have with the Concept of White Privilege," *The Good Men Project*, March 19, 2017, https://goodmenproject.com/featured-content/the-problem-i-have-with-the-concept-of-white-privilege-wcz/; Ana Marie Cox, "Michael Eric Dyson Believes in Individual Reparations," *New York Times*, January 4, 2017, https://www.nytimes.com/2017/01/04/magazine/michael-eric-dyson-believes-in-individual-reparations.html.

13. McIntosh, "White Privilege and Male Privilege, 4–7.

14. According to Logically Fallacious (https://www.logicallyfallacious.com/tools/lp/Bo/LogicalFallacies/232/Ecological-Fallacy), the ecological fallacy refers to "[t]he interpretation of statistical data where inferences about the nature of individuals are deduced from inference for the group to which those individuals belong." David A. Freedman writes, "The ecological fallacy consists in thinking that relationships observed for groups necessarily hold for individuals." David A. Freedman, "Ecological Inference and Ecological Fallacy," Technical Report No. 549, October 15, 1999, https://web.stanford.edu/class/ed260/freedman549.pdf.

15. Robin DiAngelo, *White Fragility: Why It's So Hard for White People to Talk about Racism* (Boston: Beacon, 2018), 54. Jonathan Church, "Robin DiAngelo Is Correct about the Psychic Weight of Race," *Merion West*, March 24, 2020, https://merionwest.com/2020/03/24/robin-diangelo-is-correct-about-the-psychic-weight-of-race/.

16. Church, "The Problem I Have"; Jonathan Church, "White Privilege, the Law of Large Numbers, and a Little Bit of Bayes," *The Good Men Project*, August 14, 2016, https://goodmenproject.com/featured-content/white-privilege-law-large-numbers-little-bit-bayes-wcz/.

17. DiAngelo, *White Fragility: Why It's So Hard for White People to Talk about Racism*, 43–44.

18. McIntosh, "White Privilege and Male Privilege," 10.

19. Lawrence Blum, "'White Privilege': A Mild Critique," *Theory and Research in Education* 6, no. 3 (2008): 310.

20. Blum, "'White Privilege,'" 310–311.

21. Blum, "'White Privilege,'" 311.

22. Blum, "'White Privilege,'" 311.

23. Blum, "'White Privilege,'" 311.

24. Blum, "'White Privilege,'" 311.

25. Blum, "'White Privilege,'" 311.

26. Blum, "'White Privilege,'" 312.

27. Blum, "'White Privilege,'" 312.

28. Blum, "'White Privilege,'" 312.

29. Blum, "'White Privilege,'" 311.

30. Blum, "'White Privilege,'" 311.

31. From the Introduction to *"I Don't See Color": Personal and Critical Perspectives on White Privilege*, edited by Bettina Bergo and Tracey Nicholls, (University Park, PA: The Pennsylvania State University Press, 2015).

32. McIntosh, "White Privilege and Male Privilege," 10.

33. As economics professor Louis Putterman writes at *Psychology Today*, "Among the many reasons one ought to vote, despite the relative unlikelihood of any single vote changing the outcome, is that reasoning from individual cost and benefit fails to consider the positive externality of one's vote to society as a whole." Louis Putterman, "Why You Should Vote," *Psychology Today*, November 2, 2018, https://www.psychologytoday.com/gb/blog/the-good-the-bad-the-economy/201811/why-you-should-vote.

34. Garret Hardin, "The Tragedy of the Commons," *Science* 162 (December 13, 1968), 1243–48, https://science.sciencemag.org/content/sci/162/3859/1243.full.pdf. Garrett Hardin, "Tragedy of the Commons," The Library of Economics and Liberty, https://www.econlib.org/library/Enc/TragedyoftheCommons.html.

35. James M. Buchanan, "An Economic Theory of Clubs," *Economica*, 32, no. 125 (February 1965): 1–14.

36. Buchanan, "An Economic Theory of Clubs," 1.

37. Buchanan, "An Economic Theory of Clubs," 3. Club goods are "available for consumption to the whole membership unit of which the reference individual is a member."

38. Buchanan, "An Economic Theory of Clubs," 3.

39. Buchanan, "An Economic Theory of Clubs," 10.

40. Buchanan, "An Economic Theory of Clubs," 11.

41. Buchanan, "An Economic Theory of Clubs," 6.

42. Buchanan, "An Economic Theory of Clubs," 5.

43. Harris, "Whiteness as Property," 1761; Charles W. Mills, *The Racial Contract* (Ithaca, NY: Cornell University Press, 1997).

44. For a textbook discussion of "externalities" and "public bads," see Robert Cooter and Thomas Ulen, *Law and Economics*, 2nd ed. (Boston: Addison-Wesley, 1997): 139–46.

45. Jodi Beggs, "An Introduction to the Coase Theorem," *ThoughtCo*, January 17, 2019, https://www.thoughtco.com/introduction-to-the-coase-theorem-1147386.

46. Blum, "'White Privilege,'" 311.

47. Blum, "'White Privilege,'" 311.

48. Cooter and Ulen, *Law and Economics*, 140–42.

49. Beggs, "An Introduction"; Cooter and Ulen, *Law and Economics*, chapter 4; Ronald H. Coase, "The Problem of Social Cost," *The Journal of Law and Economics* 3 (October 1960): 1–44.

50. Church, "White Privilege."

51. Cooter and Ulen, *Law and Economics*, 261.

52. Cooter and Ulen, *Law and Economics*, chapter 8.

53. Cooter and Ulen, *Law and Economics*, 275–79.

54. Beggs, "An Introduction"; Cooter and Ulen, *Law and Economics*, chapter 4; Coase, "The Problem of Social Cost," 1–44.

55. Beggs, "An Introduction."

56. Daron Acemoglu, "Why Not a Political Coase Theorem? Social Conflict, Commitment, and Politics," *Journal of Comparative Politics* 31 (2003): 620–52.

57. Acemoglu, "Why Not a Political Coase Theorem?" 621.

58. Acemoglu, "Why Not a Political Coase Theorem?" 621.

59. Acemoglu, "Why Not a Political Coase Theorem?" 621.

60. Acemoglu, "Why Not a Political Coase Theorem?" 621.

61. Acemoglu, "Why Not a Political Coase Theorem?" 621.

62. Acemoglu, "Why Not a Political Coase Theorem?" 649.

63. Acemoglu, "Why Not a Political Coase Theorem?" abstract.

64. Acemoglu, "Why Not a Political Coase Theorem?" abstract, 621.

65. Barbara Applebaum, *Being White, Being Good: White Complicity, White Moral Responsibility, and Social Justice Pedagogy* (Lanham, MD: Rowman & Littlefield, 2010).

66. Robin DiAngelo, "White Fragility," *International Journal of Critical Pedagogy* 3, no. 3 (2011): 57.

67. Barbara Applebaum, "On 'Glass Snakes,' White Moral Responsibility, and Agency Under Complicity," *Philosophy of Education Yearbook*, 2005.

68. Anna Maria Barry-Jester, "Attitudes toward Racism and Inequality Are Shifting," *FiveThirtyEight*, June 23, 2015, https://fivethirtyeight.com/features/attitudes-toward-racism-and-inequality-are-shifting/; Maria Krysan and Sarah Moberg, "A Portrait of Africa American and White Racial Attitudes," University of Illinois Institute of Government and Public Affairs, Trends in Racial Attitudes, September 9, 2016, https://igpa.uillinois.edu/sites/igpa.uillinois.edu/files/reports/A-Portrait-of-Racial-Attitudes.pdf; Astead W. Herndon, "How 'White Guilt' in the Age of Trump Shapes the Democratic Primary," *New York Times*, October 13, 2019.

69. Harinam and Henderson, "Why White Privilege Is Wrong—Part 1"; Harinam and Henderson, "Why White Privilege Is Wrong—Part 2."

70. Ashley Jardina, *White Identity Politics* (Cambridge, NY: Cambridge University Press, 2019); Eduardo Bonilla-Silva, *Racism without Racists* (Lanham, MD: Rowman & Littlefield, 2010), 4, 131.

71. Douglas Hartmann, Joseph Gerteis, and Paul R. Croll, "An Empirical Assessment of Whiteness Theory: Hidden from How Many?" *Social Problems* 56, no. 3 (August 2009): 403, 405.

72. Hartmann, Gerteis, and Croll, "An Empirical Assessment," 403.

73. Hartmann, Gerteis, and Croll, "An Empirical Assessment," 407.

74. Hartmann, Gerteis, and Croll, "An Empirical Assessment," 403, 405.

75. Hartmann, Gerteis, and Croll, "An Empirical Assessment," 407.

76. Hartmann, Gerteis, and Croll, "An Empirical Assessment," 403.

77. Glenn Loury, "Social Exclusion and Ethnic Groups: The Challenge to Economics," Paper prepared for the Annual World Bank Conference on Development Economics, Washington, DC, April 28–30, 1999, 13, https://www.brown.edu/Departments/Economics/Faculty/Glenn_Loury/louryhomepage/papers/Loury%20-%20Social%20Exclusion.pdf.

78. Loury, "Social Exclusion and Ethnic Groups," 13.

79. Loury, "Social Exclusion and Ethnic Groups," 31–34.

80. Church, "The Problem I Have"; Cox, "Michael Eric Dyson."

81. McIntosh, "White Privilege and Male Privilege," 4–7.

82. According to Logical Fallacy (https://www.logicallyfallacious.com/tools/lp/Bo/LogicalFallacies/232/Ecological-Fallacy), the *ecological fallacy* refers to

"[t]he interpretation of statistical data where inferences about the nature of individuals are deduced from inference for the group to which those individuals belong"; David A. Freedman writes, "The ecological fallacy consists in thinking that relationships observed for groups necessarily hold for individuals." David A. Freedman, "Ecological Inference and Ecological Fallacy," Technical Report No. 549, October 15, 1999, https://web.stanford.edu/class/ed260/freedman549.pdf.

83. Eric Arsenen, "Whiteness and Historians' Imagination," *International Labor and Working-Class History Society* 60 (October 2001): 3–32.

84. Adrienne Van Der Valk, Anya Malley, "What's My Complicity? Talking White Fragility with Robin DiAngelo," *Teaching Tolerance* no. 62 (Summer 2019): https://www.tolerance.org/magazine/summer-2019/whats-my-complicity-talking-white-fragility-with-robin-diangelo.

85. Robin DiAngelo and Özlem Sensoy, "'We Are All for Diversity, but . . .': How Faculty Hiring Committees Reproduce Whiteness and Practical Suggestions for How They Can Change," *Harvard Educational Review* 87, no. 4 (Winter 2017): 576.

CONCLUSION

1. Zach Goldberg, "America's White Saviors," *Tablet Magazine*, June 5, 2019, https://www.tabletmag.com/jewish-news-and-politics/284875/americas-white-saviors.

2. "White Fragility: Robin DiAngelo Explored the Challenges in Discussing Race with White Americans," June 30, 2018, C-SPAN, https://www.c-span.org/video/?447421-2/robin-diangelo-white-fragility, 13:00.

3. Tom Jacobs, "Talking about White Privilege Can Reduce Liberals' Sympathy for Poor White People," *Pacific Standard*, May 30, 2019, https://psmag.com/news/talking-about-white-privilege-can-reduce-liberal-sympathy-for-poor-white-people; Erin Cooley, Jazmin L. Brown-Iannuzzi, Ryan F. Lei, William Cipolli III, "Complex Intersections of Race and Class: Among Social Liberals, Learning about White Privilege Reduces Sympathy, Increases Blame, and Decreases External Attributions for White People Struggling with Poverty," Journal of Experimental Psychology: General 148, no. 12 (2019): 2218–28.

4. Tom Jacobs, "Talking about White Privilege"; Cooley, Brown-Iannuzzi, Lei, Cipolli, "Complex Intersections of Race and Class." According to Logically

Fallacious (https://www.logicallyfallacious.com/tools/lp/Bo/LogicalFallacies/232/Ecological-Fallacy), the ecological fallacy refers to "[t]he interpretation of statistical data where inferences about the nature of individuals are deduced from inference for the group to which those individuals belong." David A. Freedman writes, "The ecological fallacy consists in thinking that relationships observed for groups necessarily hold for individuals." David A. Freedman, "Ecological Inference and Ecological Fallacy," Technical Report No. 549, October 15, 1999, https://web.stanford.edu/class/ed260/freedman549.pdf.

5. Zaid Jilani, "What Happens When You Educate Liberals about White Privilege?" *Greater Good Magazine*, May 20, 2019, https://greatergood.berkeley.edu/article/item/what_happens_when_you_educate_liberals_about_white_privilege.

6. David Rock, "Is Your Company's Diversity Training Making You More Biased?" *Psychology Today*, June 7, 2017, https://www.psychologytoday.com/us/blog/your-brain-work/201706/is-your-company-s-diversity-training-making-you-more-biased.

7. Jonathan Church, "A Personal Awakening on Racism in America," *The Good Men Project*, March 12, 2016, https://goodmenproject.com/featured-content/a-personal-awakening-on-racism-in-america-wcz/; Jonathan Church, "And Then Charlottesville Happened," *The Good Men Project*, August 27, 2017, https://goodmenproject.com/featured-content/and-then-charlottesville-happened-wcz/; Jonathan Church, "The Best Response to This Weekend's 'Unite the Right' Rally in Washington, D.C. (take down the Confederate Monuments)," *The Good Men Project*, August 11, 2018, https://goodmenproject.com/featured-content/the-best-response-to-this-weekends-unite-the-right-rally-in-washington-d-c-wcz/.

8. Lauren Michele Jackson, "What's Missing from 'White Fragility,'" *Slate*, September 4, 2019, https://slate.com/human-interest/2019/09/white-fragility-robin-diangelo-workshop.html.

9. Matt Teffer, "White Fragility: Are White People Inherently Racist?" *Australian Financial Review*, January 4, 2019, https://www.afr.com/life-and-luxury/arts-and-culture/white-fragility-are-white-people-inherently-racist-20190102-h19mh9.

REFERENCES

Acemoglu, Daron. "Why Not a Political Coase Theorem? Social Conflict, Commitment, and Politics." *Journal of Comparative Politics* 31 (2003): 620–52, https://economics.mit.edu/files/4461.

Akerlof, George A., and Rachel E. Kranton. *Identity Economics: How Our Identities Shape Our Work, Wages, and Well-Being*. Princeton, NJ: Princeton University Press, 2010.

Akintunde, Omowale. "White Racism, White Supremacy, White Privilege, and the Social Construction of Race: Moving from Modernist to Postmodernist Multiculturalism." *Multicultural Education* 7, no. 2 (Winter 1999).

Alexander, Michelle. *The New Jim Crow: Mass Incarceration in the Age of Colorblindness*. New York: The New Press, 2010, 2012.

Andrade, Gabriel. "What DARE and Diversity Training Programs Have in Common." *Areo*, April 23, 2019, https://areomagazine.com/2019/04/23/what-dare-and-diversity-training-programs-have-in-common/.

Apollo Theater History, Apollo 85, https://www.apollotheater.org/about/history/.

Applebaum, Barbara. "Education: Critical Whiteness Studies." *Oxford Research Encyclopedias*, June 2016, https://oxfordre.com/education/view/10.1093/acrefore/9780190264093.001.0001/acrefore-9780190264093-e-5.

———. "On 'Glass Snakes,' White Moral Responsibility, and Agency Under Complicity," Philosophy of Education Yearbook, 2005, http://connection.ebscohost.com/c/articles/19271323/on-glass-snakes-white-moral-responsibility-agency-under-complicity.

———. *Being White, Being Good: White Complicity, White Moral Responsibility, and Social Justice Pedagogy*. Lanham, MD: Rowman & Littlefield, 2010.

Arsenen, Eric. "Whiteness and Historians' Imagination." *International Labor and Working-Class History* no. 60 (Fall, 2001): 3–32, https://www.jstor.org/stable/27672732?seq=1#page_scan_tab_contents.

"Author Robin DiAngelo: Debunking the Most Common Myths White People Tell about Race." NBC News, September 25, 2018, https://www.nbcnews.com/think/video/debunking-the-most-common-myths-white-people-tell-about-race-1328672835886.

Barry-Jester, Anna Maria. "Attitudes toward Racism and Inequality Are Shifting." *FiveThirtyEight*, June 23, 2015, https://fivethirtyeight.com/features/attitudes-toward-racism-and-inequality-are-shifting/.

Bartlett, Tom. "Can We Really Measure Implicit Bias? Maybe Not." *The Chronicle Review*, The Chronicle of Higher Education, January 5, 2017, https://www.chronicle.com/article/Can-We-Really-Measure-Implicit/238807.

Becker, Gary. *The Economics of Discrimination*. Chicago: The University of Chicago Press, 1957, 1971.

Beggs, Jodi. "An Introduction to the Coase Theorem." *ThoughtCo*, January 17, 2019, https://www.thoughtco.com/introduction-to-the-coase-theorem-1147386.

Bell, Derrick. *And We Are Not Saved*. New York: Basic, 1987.

———. *Faces at the Bottom of the Well: The Permanence of Racism*. New York: Basic, 1993.

Biswas, K. "How Not to Be a Racist." *New Statesman America*, March 27, 2019, https://www.newstatesman.com/obin-diangelo-white-fragility-why-its-so-hard-for-white-people-to-talk-about-racism.

Blackburn, Venita. "White People Must Save Themselves from Whiteness." *The Paris Review*, March 25, 2019, https://www.theparisreview.org/blog/2019/03/25/white-people-must-save-themselves-from-whiteness/.

Blanton, Hart, James Jaccard, Jonathan Klick, Barbara Mellers, Gregory Mitchell, and Philip E. Tetlock. "Strong Claims and Weak Evidence: Reassessing the Predictive Validity of the IAT." *Journal of Applied Psychology* 94, no. 3 (2009): 567–82.

Blum, Edward J. "Identifying White Fragility." *The Christian Century*, December 18, 2018, https://www.christiancentury.org/review/books/identifying-white-fragility.

Blum, John M., William S. McFeely, Edmund S. Morgan, Arthur M. Schlesinger Jr., Kenneth M. Stampp, and C. Vann Woodward. *The National Experience: A History of the United States*, 8th edition. New York: Harcourt Brace Jovanovich, 1993, 1989, 1985, 1981, 1977, 1973, 1968, 1963.

Blum, Lawrence. "'White Privilege': A Mild Critique." *Theory and Research in Education* 6, no. 3 (2008).

———. "Moral Asymmetry: A Problem for the Protected Categories Approach." *Lewis and Clark Law Review* 16, no. 2 (2012).

Bonilla-Silva, Eduardo. *Racism without Racists*. Lanham, MD: Rowman & Littlefield, 2010.

"Book Review: White Fragility: Why It's So Hard for White People to Talk about Racism by Robin DiAngelo." *LSE Review of Books*, January 27, 2019, https://blogs.lse.ac.uk/usappblog/2019/01/27/book-review-white-fragility-why-its-so-hard-for-white-people-to-talk-about-racism-by-robin-diangelo/.

Boustan, Leah. "Was Postwar Suburbanization 'White Flight'? Evidence from the Black Migration." Working Paper 13543, National Bureau of Economic Research, October 2007.

———. "The Culprits behind White Flight." *New York Times*, May 15, 2017, https://www.nytimes.com/2017/05/15/opinion/white-flight.html.

Bowman, Curtis. "Odysseus and the Siren Call of Reason: The Frankfurt School Critique of Enlightenment." *Other Voices, The (e) Journal of Cultural Criticism* 1, no. 1 (March 1997).

Buchanan, James M. "An Economic Theory of Clubs." *Economica* 32, no. 125 (February 1965): 1–14.

Casella, George, and Roger L. Berger, *Statistical Inference*, 2nd edition. Belmont, CA: Wadsworth, 2002.

"CBS Fires Don Imus Over Racial Slur." CBS News, April 12, 2007, https://www.cbsnews.com/news/cbs-fires-don-imus-over-racial-slur/.

Chan, Tim. "'White Fragility,' 'The New Jim Crow' Top Amazon Best Sellers List Following Week of Unrest." *Rolling Stone*, June 4, 2020, https://www.rollingstone.com/culture/culture-news/books-race-sell-out-amazon-george-floyd-protest-1008220/.

Chavez, Chris. "How the Red Sox Will Try to Enforce a Lifetime Ban on the Fan Who Used a Racial Slur." *Sports Illustrated*, May 8, 2017, https://www.si.com/mlb/2017/05/08/red-sox-fan-lifetime-ban-racial-slur-enforced.

Cheng, Nien. *Life and Death in Shanghai.* New York: Grove, 1986; Penguin Books, 1988.

Church, Jonathan. Essays linked at www.jonathandavidchurch.com.

Cline, Austin. "Hypostatization Fallacy: Ascribing Reality to Abstractions." *ThoughtCo*, October 28, 2019, https://www.thoughtco.com/reification-hypostatization-fallacy-250333.

Coase, Ronald H. "The Problem of Social Cost." *The Journal of Law and Economics* 3 (October 1960): 1–44.

Cooley, Erin, Jazmin L. Brown-Iannuzzi, Ryan F. Lei, and William Cipolli III. "Complex Intersections of Race and Class: Among Social Liberals, Learning about White Privilege Reduces Sympathy, Increases Blame, and Decreases External Attributions for White People Struggling with Poverty." *Journal of Experimental Psychology*: General 148, no. 12 (2019): 2218–28.

Cooter, Robert, and Thomas Ulen. *Law and Economics*, 2nd edition. Boston: Addison-Wesley, 1997.

Cox, Ana Marie. "Michael Eric Dyson Believes in Individual Reparations." *New York Times*, January 4, 2017, https://www.nytimes.com/2017/01/04/magazine/michael-eric-dyson-believes-in-individual-reparations.html.

Crenshaw, Kimberlé. "Demarginalizing the Intersection of Race and Sex: A Black Feminist Critique of Antidiscrimination Doctrine, Feminist Theory and Antiracist Politics." University of Chicago Legal Forum 1989, no. 1, Article 8, http://chicagounbound.uchicago.edu/cgi/viewcontent.cgi?article=1052&context=uclf.

———. "Why Intersectionality Can't Wait." *Washington Post*, September 24, 2015, https://www.washingtonpost.com/news/in-theory/wp/2015/09/24/why-intersectionality-cant-wait.

"Critical Conversations: Dr. Robin DiAngelo on White Fragility and Why It's So Hard for White People to Talk about Racism," *the conscious kid*, https://www.theconsciouskid.org/white-fragility.

Deconstructing White Privilege with Dr. Robin DiAngelo, https://www.youtube.com/watch?v=h7mzj0cVL0Q.

"Deconstructing White Privilege with Dr. Robin DiAngelo," Religion and Race: The United Methodist Church. See: http://www.gcorr.org/video/vital-conversations-racism-dr-robin-diangelo/.

Office of the Historian, "The Annexation of Texas, the Mexican–American War, and the Treaty of Guadalupe Hidalgo, 1845–1848." US Department of State, https://history.state.gov/milestones/1830-1860/texas-annexation.

Derin, Jacob. "The Progressive Case against White Privilege." *Areo*, January 7, 2019, https://areomagazine.com/2019/01/07/the-progressive-case-against-white-privilege/.

Derrida, Jacques. *Of Grammatology*. Baltimore, MD: Johns Hopkins University Press, 1974, 1976, 1997, 2016.

DiAngelo, Robin: books and academic publications linked at https://robindiangelo.com/publications/.

———. "How White People Handle Diversity Training in the Workplace." *Medium*, June 27, 2018, https://gen.medium.com/how-white-people-handle-diversity-training-in-the-workplace-e8408d2519f.

———. *White Fragility: Why It's So Hard to Talk to White People about Racism.* Boston: Beacon, 2018.

———. "White Fragility: Why It's So Hard to Talk to White People about Racism." *The Good Men Project*, April 9, 2015, https://goodmenproject.com/featured-content/white-fragility-why-its-so-hard-to-talk-to-white-people-about-racism-twlm/.

———. "White People Are Still Raised to Be Racially Illiterate. If We Don't Recognize the System, Our Inaction Will Uphold It." NBC News, September 16, 2018, https://www.nbcnews.com/think/opinion/white-people-are-still-raised-be-racially-illiterate-if-we-ncna906646.

———. "Whiteness in Racial Dialogue: A Discourse Analysis." PhD dissertation, University of Washington, 2004.

Douglass, Frederick. *The Narrative of the Life of Frederick Douglass, an American Slave*, New York: Barnes and Noble Classics, 2003.

"Dr. Robin DiAngelo discusses 'White Fragility,'" June 28, 2018, https://www.youtube.com/watch?v=45ey4jgoxeU.

Edelman, Susan. "Teachers Allegedly Told to Favor Black Students in 'Racial Equity' Training." *New York Post*, May 25, 2019, https://nypost.com/2019/05/25/teachers-allegedly-told-to-treat-black-students-as-victims-punish-whites/.

Edwards, Julia. "Justice Department Mandates 'Implicit Bias' Training for Agents, Lawyers." *Reuters*, June 27, 2016, https://www.reuters.com/article/us-usa-justice-bias-exclusive-idUSKCN0ZD251.

Falkner, David. *Great Time Coming.* New York: Touchstone, 1995.

Feagin, Joe R. *The White Racial Frame.* New York: Rutledge, Taylor and Francis, 2013.

Fitzgerald, Chloe, Angela Martin, Delphine Berner, and Samia Hurst. "Interventions Designed to Reduce Implicit Prejudices and Implicit Stereotypes in Real World Contexts: A Systematic Review." *BMC Psychology* 7 (2019): article 29.

Forscher, Patrick S., Calvin K. Lai, Jordan R. Axt, Charles R. Ebersole, Michelle Herman, Patricia G. Devine, and Brian A. Nosek. "A Meta-Analysis of Procedures to Change Implicit Measures." *Journal of Personality and Social Psychology* 117, no. 3 (September 2019).

Foucault, Michel. "What Is Enlightenment?" In *The Foucault Reader*, edited by Paul Rabinow, 32–50. New York: Pantheon, 1984.

———. *The Order of Things: An Archaeology of the Human Sciences.* New York: Vintage, 1994.

Frankenberg, Ruth. "White Women, Race Matters: The Social Construction of Whiteness." Minneapolis: University of Minnesota Press, 1993.

Freedman, David A. "Ecological Inference and Ecological Fallacy." Technical Report No. 549, October 15, 1999, https://web.stanford.edu/class/ed260/freedman549.pdf.

Fryer, Roland G., and Steven D. Levitt. "The Causes and Consequences of Distinctively Black Names." *Quarterly Journal of Economics* 119, no. 3 (August 2004).

Gawronski, Bertram. "Six Lessons for a Cogent Science of Implicit Bias and Its Criticism." *Perspectives on Psychological Science* 14, no. 4 (2019).

Goldberg, Zach. "America's White Saviors." *Tablet*, June 5, 2019, https://www.tabletmag.com/jewish-news-and-politics/284875/americas-white-saviors.

Goldhill, Olivia. "The World Is Relying on a Flawed Psychological Test to Fight Racism." *Quartz*, December 3, 2017, https://qz.com/1144504/the-world-is-relying-on-a-flawed-psychological-test-to-fight-racism/.

Habib, M. A. Rafey. "The Myth of Liberal Humanism." Rutgers University, 2019, https://habib.camden.rutgers.edu/publications/essays/the-myth-of-liberal-humanism/.

Hamilton, Alexander, James Madison, and John Jay. *The Federalist Papers.* In particular, Federalist Paper #10: https://avalon.law.yale.edu/18th_century/fed10.asp.

Hannah-Jones, Nikole. "America Wasn't a Democracy, until Black Americans Made It One." *New York Times*, August 14, 2019, https://www.nytimes.com/interactive/2019/08/14/magazine/black-history-american-democracy.html?mtrref=www.google.com&gwh=F1DFCB3AAE870D364A50A17705CCAFCF&gwt=pay&assetType=REGIWALL.

Hardin, Garret. "The Tragedy of the Commons," *Science* 162 (December 13, 1968): 1243–48, https://science.sciencemag.org/content/sci/162/3859/1243.full.pdf.

———. "Tragedy of the Commons." The Library of Economics and Liberty, https://www.econlib.org/library/Enc/TragedyoftheCommons.html.

Harinam, Vincent, and Rob Henderson. "Why White Privilege Is Wrong—Part 1." *Quillette*, August 22, 2019, https://quillette.com/2019/08/22/why-white-privilege-is-wrong-part-1/.

———. "Why White Privilege Is Wrong—Part 2." *Quillette*, October 16, 2019, https://quillette.com/2019/10/16/why-white-privilege-is-wrong-part-2/.

Harris, Cheryl. "Whiteness as Property." *Harvard Law Review* 106, no. 8 (June 1993).

Harrison, Peter. "The Enlightenment of Steven Pinker." *ABC Religion and Ethics*, February 20, 2018, https://www.abc.net.au/religion/the-enlightenment-of-steven-pinker/10094966?fbclid=IwAR3JAxoRzBjs2haTkNk6iFxs0uUAsL0mAZVxKv4auXoRQHoUEZ3Acr8r-PY.

Hartmann, Douglas, Joseph Gerteis, and Paul R. Croll. "An Empirical Assessment of Whiteness Theory: Hidden from How Many?" *Social Problems* 56, no. 3 (August 2009).

Haslam, Nick. "Concept Creep: Psychology's Expanding Concepts of Harm and Pathology." *Psychological Inquiry* 27, no. 1 (2016).

Henriques, Gregg. "The Concept of Concept Creep." *Psychology Today*, January 4, 2017, https://www.psychologytoday.com/us/blog/theory-knowledge/201701/the-concept-concept-creep.

Herndon, Astead W. "How 'White Guilt' in the Age of Trump Shapes the Democratic Primary." *New York Times*, October 13, 2019, https://www.nytimes.com/2019/10/13/us/politics/democratic-candidates-racism.html.

Herzog, Katie. "Is Starbucks Implementing Flawed Science in Their Anti-Bias Training?" *The Stranger*, April 17, 2018, https://www.thestranger.com/slog/2018/04/17/26052277/is-starbucks-implementing-flawed-science-in-their-anti-bias-training.

Heshmat, Shahram. "What Is Confirmation Bias?" *Psychology Today*, April 23, 2015, https://www.psychologytoday.com/us/blog/science-choice/201504/what-is-confirmation-bias.

Horkheimer, Max. *Eclipse of Reason.* New York: Oxford University Press, 1947; New York: Continuum, 1974.

Horkheimer, Max, and Theodor Adorno. *Dialectic of Enlightenment.* New York: Continuum, 1998. See also the English translation © 2002, by the Board of Trustees of the Leland Stanford Junior University.

Hughes, Coleman. "Black American Culture and the Racial Wealth Gap." *Quillette*, July 19, 2018, https://quillette.com/2018/07/19/black-american-culture-and-the-racial-wealth-gap.

———. "Let's Arm Black Children with Lessons That Can Improve Their Lives." *Woodson Center*, February 2020, https://1776unites.com/scholars/coleman-cruz-hughes/essay/525116945.

———. "The Racism Treadmill." *Quillette*, May 14, 2018, https://quillette.com/2018/05/14/the-racism-treadmill/.

Hume, David. *An Enquiry Concerning Human Understanding*, edited by Tom L. Beauchamp. New York: Oxford University Press, 1999.

"'I Am Not De Problem:' Benjamin Zephaniah on Modern Racism." https://www.youtube.com/watch?v=RXDxMH2EUTY.

"I Don't See Color": Personal and Critical Perspectives on White Privilege, edited by Bettina Bergo and Tracey Nicholls (University Park: Pennsylvania State University Press, 2015).

Immanuel Kant, "An Answer to the Question: What Is Enlightenment?" 1784, translated by Ted Humphrey. Indianapolis, IN: Hackett, 1992.

———. *Kant's Critiques.* Radford, VA: A and D; Wilder Publications, 2008).

———. "What Is Enlightenment?" Konigsberg in Prussia, September 30, 1784, http://www2.idehist.uu.se/distans/ilmh/Ren/idehist-enlighten-kant02.htm.

"Indians in the US Fact Sheet." Pew Research Center, September 8, 2017, https://www.pewsocialtrends.org/fact-sheet/asian-americans-indians-in-the-u-s/.

Iqbal, Nosheen. "Academic Robin DiAngelo: 'We Have to Stop Thinking about Racism as Someone Who Says the N-word." *The Guardian*, February 16, 2019, https://www.theguardian.com/world/2019/feb/16/white-fragility-racism-interview-robin-diangelo.

Jackson, Lauren Michele. "What's Missing from 'White Fragility.'" *Slate*, September 4, 2019, https://slate.com/human-interest/2019/09/white-fragility-robin-diangelo-workshop.html.

Jacobs, Tom. "Talking about White Privilege Can Reduce Liberals' Sympathy for Poor White People." *Pacific Standard*, May 30, 2019, https://psmag.com/news/talking-about-white-privilege-can-reduce-liberal-sympathy-for-poor-white-people.

Jardina, Ashley. *White Identity Politics.* Cambridge, UK: Cambridge University Press, 2019.

Jaschik, Scott. "Making a Point by Moving Shakespeare's Portrait." *Inside Higher Education*, December 14, 2016, https://www.insidehighered.com/news/2016/12/14/students-penn-remove-portrait-shakespeare.

"Jeopardy Contestants Painfully Avoid Black History Questions as Long as They Can." *Huffington Post*, February 19, 2014, https://www.huffpost.com/entry/jeopardy-black-history-month_n_4815162?guccounter=1.

Jilani, Zaid. "What Happens When You Educate Liberals about White Privilege?" *Greater Good Magazine*, May 20, 2019, https://greatergood.berkeley.edu/article/item/what_happens_when_you_educate_liberals_about_white_privilege.

Jost, John T., Laurie A. Rudman, Irene V. Blair, Dana R. Carney, Nilanjana Dasgupta, Jack Glaser, and Curtis D. Hardin. "The Existence of Implicit Bias Is beyond Reasonable Doubt: A Refutation of Ideological and Methodological Objections and Executive Summary of Ten Studies That No Manager Should Ignore." *Research in Organizational Behavior* 29 (2009): 39–69.

Jussim, Lee. "Mandatory Implicit Bias Training Is a Bad Idea," *Psychology Today*, December 2, 2017, https://www.psychologytoday.com/us/blog/rabble-rouser/201712/mandatory-implicit-bias-training-is-bad-idea.

Jussim, Lee, Akeela Careem, Zach Goldberg, Nathan Honeycutt, and Sean T. Stevens. "IAT Scores, Racial Gaps, and Scientific Gaps." In *The Future of Research on Implicit Bias*, edited by J. A. Krosnick, T. H. Stark, and A. L. Scott. Cambridge, UK: Cambridge University Press, in press.

Kazin, Michael. "Howard Zinn's History Lessons." *Dissent Magazine*, Spring 2004, https://www.dissentmagazine.org/article/howard-zinns-history-lessons.

Kelly, Amita. "Orioles' Adam Jones Receives Ovation at Fenway after Alleged Epithets." *NPR*, May 3, 2017, https://www.npr.org/2017/05/03/526710441/watch-orioles-adam-jones-receives-ovation-at-fenway-after-alleged-epithets.

"Kimberlé Crenshaw on Intersectionality, More than Two Decades Later." Columbia Law School, June 8, 2017, https://www.law.columbia.edu/pt-br/news/2017/06/kimberle-crenshaw-intersectionality.

King, Susan. "The Hard Run to First." *Los Angeles Times*, April 14, 1996, https://www.latimes.com/archives/la-xpm-1996-04-14-tv-58266-story.html.

Koks, Paul. "Six Challenges of Qualitative Data Analysis." *Online Metrics*, July 14, 2015, https://online-metrics.com/qualitative-data/.

Krishnan, Manisha. "Dear White People, Please Stop Pretending Reverse Racism Is Real." *Vice*, October 2, 2016, https://www.vice.com/en_us/article/kwzjvz/dear-white-people-please-stop-pretending-reverse-racism-is-real.

Kronen, Samuel. "#ItsOkayToBeWhite," *Areo*, February 17, 2020, https://areomagazine.com/2020/02/17/itsokaytobewhite.

Krysan, Maria. "Does Race Matter in the Search for Housing? An Exploratory Study of Search Strategies, Experiences, and Locations." *Social Science Research* 37, no. 2 (2008): 581–603.

Krysan, Maria, and Sarah Moberg. "A Portrait of African American and White Racial Attitudes." University of Illinois Institute of Government and Public Affairs, Trends in Racial Attitudes, September 9, 2016, https://igpa.uillinois.edu/programs/racial-attitudes, https://igpa.uillinois.edu/report/portrait-african-american-and-white-racial-attitudes, and https://igpa.uillinois.edu/sites/igpa.uillinois.edu/files/reports/A-Portrait-of-Racial-Attitudes.pdf.

"Labor Force Statistics." US Bureau of Labor Statistics, https://www.bls.gov/webapps/legacy/cpswktab3.htm.

Lardieri, Alexa. "Despite Diverse Demographics, Most Politicians Are Still White Men." *US News and World Report*, October 24, 2017, https://www.usnews.com/news/politics/articles/2017-10-24/despite-diverse-demographics-most-politicians-are-still-white-men.

Leung, Sofia. "Whiteness as Collections." April 15, 2019, https://sleung.wordpress.com/2019/04/15/whiteness-as-collections/.

Levari, David E., Daniel T. Gilbert, Timothy D. Wilson, Beau Sievers, David M. Amodio, and Thalia Wheatley. "Prevalence-Induced Concept Change in Human Judgment." *Science* 360, no. 6396 (June 29, 2018): 1465–67.

Lilienfeld, Scott. "Microaggressions: Strong Claims, Inadequate Evidence." *Perspectives on Psychological Science* 12, no. 1 (2017): 138–69.

Lincoln, Abraham. "Slavery as the Fathers Viewed It." Address at Cooper Union, New York. February 27, 1860. In *The Works of Abraham Lincoln, Vol. III, Speeches and Presidential Addresses, 1859–1865, Anecdotes and Conversations of Lincoln by F. B. Carpenter*, Newton & Cartwright. New York: The Current Literature Publishing Company, 1907. http://www.abrahamlincolnonline.org/lincoln/speeches/cooper.htm.

Lopez, Gustavo, Neil G. Ruiz, and Eileen Patten. "Key Facts about Asian Americans, a Diverse and Growing Population." Pew Research Center, September 8, 2017, https://www.pewresearch.org/fact-tank/2017/09/08/key-facts-about-asian-americans/.

Lopez, Ian Haney. *White by Law*. New York: New York University Press, 2006.

Loury, Glenn. "Social Exclusion and Ethnic Groups: The Challenge to Economics." Paper prepared for the Annual World Bank Conference on Development Economics, Washington, DC, April 28–30, 1999.

———. "Why Does Racial Inequality Persist? Culture, Causation, and Responsibility." *The Manhattan Institute*, May 7, 2019, https://www.manhattan-institute.org/racial-inequality-in-america-post-jim-crow-segregation.

Lukács, György. *History and Class Consciousness*. London: Merlin, 1967.

MacDonald, Heather. "The Cost of America's Cultural Revolution." *City Journal*, December 9, 2019, https://www.city-journal.org/social-justice-ideology.

Machiavelli, Niccolò. *Discourses on the First Ten Books of Titus Livius*, translated by Christian E. Detmold. New York: Random House, 1950.

Mackaman, Tom. "An Interview with Historian James Oakes on the New York Times' 1619 Project." World Socialist Website, November 18, 2019, https://www.wsws.org/en/articles/2019/11/18/oake-n18.html.

McIntosh, Peggy. "White Privilege and Male Privilege: A Personal Account of Coming to See Correspondences through Work in Women's Studies." Working Paper 189, Wellesley Centers for Women, Wellesley, MA, 1988. See National SEED Project on Inclusive Curriculum.

McKibben, Sarah. "Robin DiAngelo on Educators' 'White Fragility.'" *Educational Leadership* 76, no. 7 (April 2019): http://www.ascd.org/publications/educational-leadership/apr19/vol76/num07/Robin-DiAngelo-on-Educators'-£White-Fragility£.aspx.

McManus, Bob. "Fixated on Race." *City Journal*, August 28, 2018, https://www.city-journal.org/html/richard-carranza-16136.html.

McWhorter, John. "Stop Policing the N-Word." *Time*, May 3, 2016, https://time.com/4316322/larry-wilmore-obama-n-word/.

McWhorter, John. *Winning the Race: Beyond the Crisis in Black America*. New York: Penguin, 2006.

Meehan, Adam, and J. L. Bell. "Phillis Wheatley." George Washington's Mount Vernon, https://www.mountvernon.org/library/digitalhistory/digital-encyclopedia/article/phillis-wheatley.

"Mexican–American War 1846–1848." *Encyclopedia Britannica*, https://www.britannica.com/event/Mexican-American-War/Invasion-and-war.

"Michael Ayers on Locke and Berkeley (1987)." YouTube, https://www.youtube.com/watch?v=WJzQF7eknKA.

Mills, Charles W. *The Racial Contract*. Ithaca, NY: Cornell University Press, 1997.

———. "White Ignorance." In *Race and Epistemologies of Ignorance*, edited by Shannon Sullivan and Nancy Tuana. http://shifter-magazine.com/wp-content/uploads/2015/10/mills-white-ignorance.pdf.

Morrison, Toni. *Song of Solomon*. New York: Alfred A. Knopf, 1977.

National Baseball Hall of Fame. "Wesley Branch Rickey." https://baseballhall.org/hall-of-famers/rickey-branch.

"Negro Leagues." U-S-History.com, https://www.u-s-history.com/pages/h2079.html.

Nevins, Allan, and Henry Steele Commager. *A Pocket History of the United States*, 9th ed. New York: Pocket, 1992.

"New Business Item 11." National Education Association, Houston 2019 Representative Assembly, George R. Brown Convention Center, https://ra.nea.org/business-item/2019-nbi-011/.

Nietzsche, Friedrich. *The Birth of Tragedy* and *Genealogy of Morals*. New York: Doubleday, 1956.

———. *Will to Power*, edited by Walter Kaufmann. New York: Vintage, 1967).

"NPR's Jennifer Ludden Talks to Author Robin DiAngelo about Her Latest Book, White Fragility: Why It's So Hard for White People to Talk about Racism." August 18, 2018, https://www.npr.org/2018/08/18/639822895/robin-diangelo-on-white-peoples-fragility.

"The Origins of Slavery in Virginia." Virginia Places, http://www.virginiaplaces.org/population/slaveorigin.html.

Oswald, Frederick L., Gregory Mitchell, Hart Blanton, James Jaccard, and Philip E. Tetlock. "Predicting Ethnic and Racial Discrimination: A Meta-Analysis of IAT Criterion Studies," *Journal of Personality and Social Psychology* 105, no. 2 (June 2013).

Pan, J. C. "Why Diversity Training Isn't Enough." *The New Republic*, January 7, 2020, https://newrepublic.com/article/156032/diversity-training-isnt-enough-pamela-newkirk-robin-diangelo-books-reviews.

Partin, Elliot. "1st Rhode Island Regiment." *Blackpast*, November 17, 2010, https://www.blackpast.org/african-american-history/first-rhode-island-regiment/.

Paslay, Christopher. *White Fragility Explored: Examining the Effects of Whiteness Studies on America's Schools*. Lanham, MD: Rowman & Littlefield, 2020.

Patterson, Orlando. "Race, Gender, and Liberal Fallacies." *New York Times*, October 20, 1991, https://www.nytimes.com/1991/10/20/opinion/op-ed-race-gender-and-liberal-fallacies.html.

Pew Research Center. "On Views of Race and Inequality, Blacks and Whites Are Worlds Apart." June 27, 2016, https://www.pewsocialtrends.org/2016/06/27/1-demographic-trends-and-economic-well-being/.

Pluckrose, Helen, and James Lindsay. *Cynical Theories: How Activist Scholarship Made Everything about Race, Gender, and Identity—and Why This Harms Everybody*. Durham, NC: Pitchstone, 2020.

———. "The Influence of Anti-Racist Scholarship-Activism on Evergreen College." *Areo*, January 20, 2019, https://areomagazine.com/2019/01/20/the-influence-of-anti-racist-scholarship-activism-on-evergreen-college/.

Pluckrose, Helen, James Lindsay, and Peter Boghossian. "Academic Grievance Studies and the Corruption of Scholarship." *Areo*, October 2, 2018, https://areomagazine.com/2018/10/02/academic-grievance-studies-and-the-corruption-of-scholarship/.

Powell, John A. "Post-Racialism or Targeted Universalism?" *Denver University Law Review* 86 (2009).

———. "Whites Will Be Whites: The Failure to Interrogate Racial Privilege." *University of San Francisco Law Review* 34.

Powell, John A., and Jason Reece. "The Future of Fair Housing and Fair Credit: From Crisis to Opportunity, Symposium: New Strategies in Fair Housing." *Cleveland State Law Review*, 2009.

"Publisher Places a Politically Correct Warning Label on Kant's *Critiques*." *Open Culture*, March 20, 2014, http://www.openculture.com/2014/03/publisher-places-a-politically-correct-warning-label-on-kants-critiques.html.

Putterman, Louis. "Why You Should Vote." *Psychology Today*, November 2, 2018, https://www.psychologytoday.com/gb/blog/the-good-the-bad-the-economy/201811/why-you-should-vote.

Quillian, Lincoln. "Why Is Black-White Residential Segregation So Persistent? Evidence on Three Theories from Migration Data." *Social Science Research* 31, no. 2 (June 2002): 197–229, https://www.sciencedirect.com/science/article/abs/pii/S0049089X01907264.

"Race/Ethnicity of College Faculty" (data for fall 2017). *US Department of Education, National Center for Education Statistics*https://nces.ed.gov/fastfacts/display.asp?id=61.

Rampersad, Arnold. *Jackie Robinson: A Biography*. New York: Alfred A. Knopf, 1997.

Rangarajan, Sinduja. "Here's the Clearest Picture of Silicon Valley's Diversity Yet: It's Bad. But Some Companies Are Doing Less Bad." *Reveal News*, June 25, 2018, https://www.revealnews.org/article/heres-the-clearest-picture-of-silicon-valleys-diversity-yet/?utm_source=Reveal&utm_medium=social_media&utm_campaign=twitter.

Riley, Jason. *False Black Power*. West Conshohocken, PA: Templeton, 2017.

Rimer, Sarah. "Why Is It So Hard for White People to Talk about Race?" *BU Today*, February 28, 2019, https://www.bu.edu/articles/2019/white-fragility.

"Robin DiAngelo: White Fragility Book Talk." Urban Grace, 902 Market Street, Tacoma, WA, https://www.brownpapertickets.com/event/3492403?cookie_header=1.

"Robin DiAngelo on 'White Fragility.'" *Amanpour and Co.*, September 21, 2018, http://www.pbs.org/wnet/amanpour-and-company/video/robin-diangelo-on-white-fragility/.

Rock, David. "Is Your Company's Diversity Training Making You More Biased?" *Psychology Today*, June 7, 2017, https://www.psychologytoday.com/gb/blog/your-brain-work/201706/is-your-company-s-diversity-training-making-you-more-biased.

Roediger, David R. "White Looks: Hairy Apes, True Stories, and Limbaugh's Laughs." In *Whiteness: A Critical Reader*, edited by Mike Hill. New York: New York University Press, 1997.

Rosal, Patrick. "To the Lady Who Mistook Me for the Help at the National Book Awards." *Literary Hub*, November 1, 2017, https://lithub.com/to-the-lady-who-mistook-me-for-the-help-at-the-national-book-awards/.

Sanneh, Kelefa. "The Fight to Redefine Racism." *The New Yorker*, August 19, 2019, https://www.newyorker.com/magazine/2019/08/19/the-fight-to-redefine-racism.

"Scottsboro Boys." History.com, February 22, 2018, updated June 10, 2019, https://www.history.com/topics/great-depression/scottsboro-boys.

Serwer, Adam. "The Fight over the 1619 Project Is Not about the Facts." *The Atlantic*, December 23, 2019, https://www.theatlantic.com/ideas/archive/2019/12/historians-clash-1619-project/604093/.

Sharman, Jon. "Sarah Jeong: *New York Times* Journalist Who Tweeted 'Cancel White People' Is Victim of 'Dishonest' Trolls, Claims Former Employer." *The Independent*, August 3, 2018, https://www.independent.co.uk/news/media/ny-times-journalist-sarah-jeong-racist-tweets-white-people-trolls-verge-a8475596.html.

Singal, Jesse. "Psychology's Favorite Tool for Measuring Racism Isn't Up to the Job," *The Cut*, 2017, https://www.thecut.com/2017/01/psychologys-racism-measuring-tool-isnt-up-to-the-job.html.

Stampp, Kenneth M. *The Peculiar Institution.* New York: Alfred A. Knopf, 1956.

Staub, Michael E. The Whitest I: On Reading the Hill-Thomas Transcripts. In *Whiteness: A Critical Reader*, edited by Mike Hill. New York: New York University Press, 1997.

Steven Pinker. "Why Do Progressives Hate Progress?" https://www.youtube.com/watch?v=PnitLNObR7c.

Sue, Derald Wing, Christina M. Capodilupo, Gina C. Torino, Jennifer M. Bucceri, Aisha M. B. Holder, Kevin L. Nadal, and Marta Esquilin. "Racial Microaggressions in Everyday Life." *American Psychologist*, May–June 2007.

Sullivan, Andrew. "When Racism Is Fit to Print." *Intelligencer*, August 3, 2018, http://nymag.com/intelligencer/2018/08/sarah-jeong-new-york-times-anti-white-racism.html.

Sullivan, Shannon. *Good White People.* Albany: State University of New York Press 2014.

Tabarrok, Alex. "Why Sexism and Racism Never Diminish—Even When Everyone Becomes Less Sexist and Racist." *Marginal Revolution*, June 30, 2018, https://marginalrevolution.com/marginalrevolution/2018/06/sexism-racism-never-diminishes-even-everyone-becomes-less-sexist-racist.html.

Teffer, Matt. "White Fragility: Are White People Inherently Racist?" *Australian Financial Review*, January 4, 2019, https://www.afr.com/life-and-luxury/arts-and-culture/white-fragility-are-white-people-inherently-racist-20190102-h19mh9.

Terry, Robert W. "The Negative Impact on White Values." In *Impacts of Racism on White Americans*, edited by Benjamin P. Bowser and Raymond G. Hunt. Beverly Hills, CA: Sage, 1981.

Tetlock, Philip, and Gregory Mitchell. "Calibrating Prejudice in Milliseconds." *Social Psychology Quarterly* 71 (2008): 12–16.

———. "Popularity as a Poor Proxy for Utility: The Case of Implicit Prejudice." In *Psychological Science under Scrutiny: Recent Challenges and Proposed Solutions*, edited by Scott Lilienfeld and Irwin D. Waldman. Hoboken, NJ: John Wiley and Sons, 2017.

"The Peculiar Institution." https://www.ushistory.org/us/27.asp.

The Status of Women in the US Media 2014, Women's Media Center, https://wmc.3cdn.net/6dd3de8ca65852dbd4_fjm6yck9o.pdf.

Thurman, Jerrica. "AACTE Announces Robin DiAngelo as 2020 Opening Keynote Speaker." American Association of Colleges for Teacher Education, October 2, 2019, https://edprepmatters.net/2019/10/aacte-announces-robin-diangelo-as-2020-opening-keynote-speaker/.

US Bureau of Labor Statistics Economic News Release on Employment, https://www.bls.gov/news.release/empsit.t02.htm.

US Census Bureau, American Fact Finder, Selected Population Profile in the United States, 2014 American Community Survey 1-Year Estimates, https://archive.vn/20200213015935/http://factfinder.census.gov/bkmk/table/1.0/en/ACS/14_1YR/S0201//popgroup~-07#.

US Census Bureau, Historical Income Tables: Households, https://www.census.gov/data/tables/time-series/demo/income-poverty/historical-income-households.html.

US Library of Congress. "Today in History—September 17." https://www.loc.gov/item/today-in-history/september-17/.

"Understanding the Intent in Tort Law." LAWS, https://tort.laws.com/intentional-interference/with-a-person/meaning-of-intent.

Van Bavel, Jay. "Social Identity and Morality Lab." New York University Department of Psychology, https://www.psych.nyu.edu/vanbavel/lab/research.html.

Van Der Valk, Adrienne, and Anya Malley. "What's My Complicity? Talking White Fragility With Robin DiAngelo." *Teaching Tolerance* no. 62 (Summer 2019): https://www.tolerance.org/magazine/summer-2019/whats-my-complicity-talking-white-fragility-with-robin-diangelo.

Voegeli, William. "Thomas Sowell's Inconvenient Truths." *Claremont Review of Books* 15, no. 3 (Summer 2018): https://www.claremont.org/crb/article/thomas-sowells-inconvenient-truths/.

Waldman, Katy. "A Sociologist Examines the "White Fragility" That Prevents White Americans from Confronting Racism." *The New Yorker*, July 23, 2018, https://www.newyorker.com/books/page-turner/a-sociologist-examines-the-white-fragility-that-prevents-white-americans-from-confronting-racism.

Warren, John T. "Whiteness and Cultural Theory: Perspectives on Research and Education." *The Urban Review* 31, no. 2 (1999).

"'When I See Racial Disparities, I See Racism.' Discussing Race, Gender and Mobility." *New York Times*, March 27, 2018, https://www.nytimes.com/interactive/2018/03/27/upshot/reader-questions-about-race-gender-and-mobility.html.

"White Fragility in America Tour with Robin DiAngelo and Jack Hill." April 17, 2019, https://www.friends-select.org/school-news/post/~board/all-school-news/post/white-fragility-tour-with-robin-diangelo-and-jack-hill.

"White Fragility: Robin DiAngelo Explored the Challenges in Discussing Race with White Americans." C-SPAN, June 30, 2018, https://www.c-span.org/video/?447421-2/robin-diangelo-white-fragility.

"White Fragility: The New Racism, and More Effective Steps to Undoing Racism." Lecture by University of Michigan School of Social Work graduate and therapist Andy Horning, https://www.youtube.com/watch?v=05hU4QKBhss.

"Who Were the Scottsboro Boys?" *American Experience.* https://www.pbs.org/wgbh/americanexperience/features/scottsboro-boys-who-were-the-boys/.

Wilentz, Sean. *No Property in Man* Cambridge, MA: Harvard University Press, 2018.

Zinn, Howard. *People's History of the United States.* New York: HarperCollins, 1980, 1995, 1998, 1990, 2003, 2015.

INDEX

ABOUT THE AUTHOR

Jonathan D. Church is an economist with two decades of experience working in the private and public sectors. His professional background is in antitrust, intellectual property, valuation, inflation, index number theory, statistics, and finance. In 2016, he began writing a weekly column for The Good Men Project, with a focus on current affairs, social justice, and masculinity. In 2018, he was diagnosed with a low-grade brain tumor, which led not only to brain surgery and radiation, but also a decision to pursue his passion for writing and scholarship without restraint. Outside of his day job and time with his daughter, he spends most of his remaining time as an independent scholar writing on economics, finance, and social justice. He has been published in *Quillette*, *Areo Magazine*, *Arc Digital*, *The Agonist Journal*, *Merion West*, *The Good Men Project*, *Culturico*, *New Discourses*, *The Washington Examiner*, *The Daily Stoic*, and *The Federalist*. He has also published poetry in *Lummox*, *Big Hammer*, and *Street Value*, as well as short stories in *Vending Machine Press* and *The Agonist Journal*. He graduated from the University of Pennsylvania with a B.A. in economics and philosophy, and from Cornell University with an M.A in economics. He is also a CFA charter holder. Any time left over is spent exercising and playing chess.

Made in the USA
Coppell, TX
19 February 2021

50517548R00146